TWAYNE'S
RULERS AND STATESMEN OF THE WORLD
SERIES

Hans L. Trefousse, Brooklyn College
General Editor

HENRY II PLANTAGENET

(TROW 19)

Henry II Plantagenet

By JOHN SCHLIGHT

U.S. Air Force Academy

Twayne Publishers, Inc.   ::   New York

TO
Nora
Julie
John
Gretchen

Contents

Maps

Chronology

1133 5 March. Henry Plantagenet born at Le Mans.
1135 1 December. King Henry I of England dies near Gisors.
      Stephen of Blois seizes the English throne.
1139 Civil War begins in England as Matilda the Empress arrives on the island.
1142–
1144 Henry Plantagenet's first visit to England.
1147 Henry Plantagenet's second visit to England.
1148 Matilda leaves England after failing to gain the throne.
1149 Henry's third visit to England. Knighted at Carlisle by David, king of the Scots.
1150 Henry invested with Normandy.
1151 Geoffrey Plantagenet dies. Henry inherits Normandy, Maine, and Anjou.
1152 18 May. Henry marries Eleanor of Aquitaine in Poitiers.
1153 6 January. Henry invades England.
      17 August. William, Henry's first son, is born.
      November. Treaty of Winchester ends the Civil War.
1154 25 October. King Stephen dies at Canterbury.
      3 December. Pope Adrian IV elevated.
      19 December. Henry and Eleanor crowned at Westminster Abbey.
1155 January. Thomas Becket made chancellor at Bermondsey.
      28 February. Henry, the second son of Henry and Eleanor, born at Bermondsey.
      July. Revolt of marcher barons put down.
1156 Probable year of the infant William's death.
      May. Henry defeats revolt by his brother Geoffrey.
      June. Matilda, Henry's first daughter, born in London.
1157 July. Malcolm, king of the Scots, surrenders the northern counties.

July–August. Henry defeats Owen of Wales.

8 September. Richard, Henry's third son, born at Oxford.

1158 Spring. Becket's embassy to Paris. Young Henry betrothed to Princess Margaret.

Death of Henry's brother Geoffrey. Conan IV made duke of Brittany.

23 September. Geoffrey, Henry's fourth son, is born in England.

1159 June–September. Toulouse Campaign.

30 August. Pope Adrian dies.

1 September. Pope Alexander III elevated.

1160 2 November. Marriage of young Henry and Princess Margaret.

1161 18 April. Theobald, archbishop of Canterbury, dies.

September. Eleanor, Henry's second daughter, born at Domfront.

1162 24 May. Thomas Becket elected archbishop of Canterbury. Consecrated 3 June.

1163 April. Henry forces Rhys of Wales to do homage.

October. Westminster Council.

1164 25 January. Constitutions of Clarendon.

October. Becket flees to Continent from council at Northampton.

1165 May. Philip Augustus born to Louis VII and Queen Adela.

May–August. Henry's expedition to Wales.

October. Joanna, Henry's third daughter, born at Angers.

1166 January–February. Assize of Clarendon.

Cartae Baronum.

June–July. Henry puts down Breton revolt.

Fall. Becket forced to leave Pontigny.

1167 March. Raymond of Toulouse does homage to Henry.

10 September. The Empress Matilda dies.

24 December. John, Henry's fifth son, born at Oxford.

1168 Henry's daughter Matilda marries Henry the Lion, duke of Saxony and Bavaria.

1169 6 January. Conference at Montmirail.

13 April. Becket excommunicates English bishops.

1170 5 April. Council at Windsor. Inquest of Sheriffs.

Eleanor, Henry's daughter, marries Alphonse VIII of Castile.

14 June. Young Henry crowned at Westminster Abbey.

July. Conference at Fréteval.

October. Final accord between Henry and Becket at Amboise.

29 December. Becket is murdered at Canterbury.

1171   21 February. Conan IV dies.

17 October. Henry lands in Ireland.

1172   17 April. Henry returns from Ireland.

21 May. Henry absolved from Becket's murder at Avranches.

1173   21 February. Becket is canonized.

5 March. Beginning of his sons' revolt against Henry.

July. Siege of Verneuil by King Louis.

August. Henry defeats Breton insurgents.

17 October. Earl of Leicester surrenders near Cambridge.

1174   8 April. Richard of Dover becomes archbishop of Canterbury.

8 July–8 August. Henry brings prisoners to England. Defeats eastern rebels.

13 July. William of Scotland captured at Alnwick.

21 August. King Louis lifts the siege of Rouen.

30 September. End of the revolt.

1176   26 January. Council at Northampton. Reorganization of the itinerant justices.

Richard campaigning in Aquitaine.

1177   13 February. Joanna, Henry's daughter, marries King William of Sicily.

8 May. John crowned king of Ireland at Oxford.

1179   Grand Assize.

1 November. Philip Augustus crowned king of France at Reims.

1180   April. Ranulf de Glanville becomes chief justiciar of England.

18 September. King Louis VII dies.

1181   30 August. Pope Alexander dies, succeeded by Lucius III.

1183   11 June. Young Henry dies at Martel.

30 June. Henry and Philip meet at Gisors.

1184   Assize of the Forests.

July. Archbishop of Cologne visits Canterbury.

1185   March–April. Embassy of Heraclius from Jerusalem.

31 March. John knighted at Windsor.

25 April. John arrives at Waterford, Ireland.

19 May. Baldwin, bishop of Worcester, becomes archbishop of Canterbury.

24 November. Pope Lucius dies. Succeeded by Urban III.

December. John returns from Ireland.

1186 19 August. Prince Geoffrey dies in a tournament.

1187 May–June. War between Henry and Philip Augustus.

4 July. Saladin defeats Christians at Hattin.

2 October. Jerusalem falls to Saladin.

11 October. Pope Urban dies. Succeeded by Gregory VIII.

17 December. Pope Gregory VIII dies. Succeeded by Clement III.

1188 13–21 January. Conference at Gisors. Henry and Philip agree to Crusade.

January–February. Richard attacks Toulouse.

February. Saladin Tithe proclaimed in England.

1189 4–9 June. Conference at La Ferté Bernard.

12 June. Le Mans taken by Philip.

6 July. Henry Plantagenet dies.

Prologue

THE SEA WAS CALM AND THE PROSPECT GOOD FOR A SMOOTH CROSS-ing to England. Up and down beside the wooden wharf at the tiny Norman port of Barfleur bobbed the White Ship, the latest and largest addition to the English royal fleet. The smallness of the fishing village, with its single quayside street of taverns and lodging houses, gave little hint of the town's status as the main transportation link between the two halves of the powerful Anglo-Norman state. Even though weather or convenience occasionally forced the use of alternates such as Cherbourg, Wissant, or Dieppe, it was normally through Barfleur on the Cherbourg peninsula that the English kings, their messengers, and often even their armies, passed on their numerous voyages to and from the island.

It had been more than four years since many of those now awaiting passage had left England with their king, Henry I Beauclerc, to set up court on the Continent in support of the monarch's campaign against his mainland enemies. The intervening years had witnessed a frenzy of activity by which Henry, the last of the three sons of William the Conqueror, had successfully consolidated and defended the duchy of Normandy against its neighbors. Since that day fourteen years before when he had imprisoned his brother Robert and taken the duchy from him, the king had been working to weld kingdom and duchy into a unified state secure for its inhabitants and fearsome toward its enemies. Now, in November, 1120, that day had arrived and the flood of royalty, nobility, soldiers, and bureaucrats who had brought it about was eager to return to England.

The bulk of the fleet, along with the king, had already left during the afternoon on the 90-mile voyage to Southampton and only the White Ship remained, scheduled to depart after dark with the younger set aboard. Most prominent of those who waited for the last sailing was the king's son, Prince William, a self-indulgent and somewhat haughty youth of seventeen who had much to justify his pride. As he was the only legitimate son of the king, his succession to the throne of England was assured. In addition, looking ahead to the day when the young prince would rule in his place, Henry had invested his son only the year before with the duchy of Normandy, and the stabilizing effect of the recently concluded campaign greatly enhanced the value of this inheritance. Also, during the previous year William had married Matilda, whose father was the count of Anjou, that pivotal region directly south of Normandy. For over a century the Norman dukes had been at odds with this southern neighbor and when Henry's father seized England in 1066 he transferred Normandy's rivalry with Anjou to the island kingdom. Throughout the succeeding five-and-a-half decades the Angevin count had relied upon his lord, the French king, to support him against the pressure of the Norman dukes turned English kings—William the Conqueror, William II Rufus, and, now, Henry I. Prince William's marriage to Matilda was, as most medieval marriages, a diplomatic gambit designed, in this case, to wean the Angevin count from the side of his lord and, hopefully, to bring about at some future date the absorption of the troublesome county into the growing empire. William, therefore, as heir to the English throne, duke of Normandy, and son-in-law of the count of Anjou, represented the best hope to date for fulfillment of the Anglo-Norman dream, born 54 years before, of hegemony in Western Europe.

Many prominent lords and ladies of the realm made up the prince's retinue. In addition to William's half-brother Richard and half-sister Matilda (two from among the nineteen royal bastards),[1] several of the leading barons were to escort the prince across the channel. Among them were Richard, the powerful earl of the strategic western English county of Chester, upon whom the king depended for defense against the ever-rebellious Welsh; his brother-in-law Geoffrey Ridel, a royal justice and one of that small group of "new men" whom the king had raised from the dust to become his personal advisers;[2] William Bigod, a military power in eastern England; Walter d'Evreux, and many others. These were men who were indispensable to the king in keeping the machinery of the state running and whose names appeared with regularity as witnesses to the great charters through which the monarch's will was translated into action. For unlike its modern counterpart, medieval government was a highly personal arrangement which revolved around the person of the king. In this state, where the king *was* the government, his personal money was used to run the state, his private army was employed to defend it, and his own court (the *curia regis*), composed of family, barons, and servants, helped him to administer it. As long as the monarch lived, there was a government; when he died, there was none until a successor was crowned. In Henry's time the court still operated substantially as an undifferentiated body in which each member dealt with all types of activities, whether of political, military, administrative, or legal consequence. Specialization still lay several generations in the future, although during Henry's reign a few members of the court began to confine their activities to fiscal matters and gain special expertise in the area of finance, thereby creating the tender beginnings of the Exchequer. Later in the century other members of the court would branch out into other specialized departments of state. But for the most part the barons who boarded the White Ship were universal men whose advice was sought by the king across the entire spectrum of matters concerning his governance of the realm. It had taken Henry many years of hard work to win over the loyalty, or at least the cooperation, of these men for, even though his father had imposed on England a system of loyalties by granting land in return for services,[3] the arrangement was never fully effective and it often required a goodly amount of persuasion, threats, and legal and military pressure to make it work. Henry had used all these techniques with great skill and the men who were now about to cross the channel formed a reliable cornerstone of his government.

Also accompanying Prince William was Archdeacon Geoffrey who, as the "executive officer" to the bishop of Hereford, handled the business affairs of that western ecclesiastical see. His inclusion in the royal retinue reflects the close bond that still existed between the secular and spiritual powers of the medieval state. In the course of the eleventh century the Church had become one of the most powerful institutions in Europe thanks to a movement spearheaded by the monks of Cluny and adopted by the mid-century papacy by which the Church, in attempting to set its own house in order, joined hand-in-glove with the secular monarchs to have its principles filter down into the very marrow of medieval life. Ecclesiastical influence was apparent on every side and had been responsible for such activities as the First Crusade, near the end of the century, and the continuing drive to ameliorate the horrors of warfare. The Conqueror, pious and politically shrewd, had embraced this reform while he was still the duke of Normandy and transferred the strong church-state partnership to England when, waving the papal banner,[4] he seized the island in 1066. In what amounted to caesaropapism, he introduced the heretofore ignored papal reform to the church he found in his new domain. The instrument of his new ecclesiastical policy was the Norman clergy which rapidly replaced its Anglo-Saxon predecessor. William's close working relationship with his hand-picked Archbishop of Canterbury, Lanfranc, had resulted in a tight reorganization of ecclesiastical practices and administration throughout the Anglo-Norman lands. In their war against the clerical malpractices of simony and marriage the king and archbishop, who was more lawyer than theologian, struck at the legal system which had sheltered the abuses and ordered that "no cleric cited shall be tried according to the law of the hundred court, but he shall submit to God and his bishop in accordance with the canons and the episcopal law." By pulling clerical cases out of the secular courts William granted the Church its own jurisdiction over matters concerning the "rule of souls," and ecclesiastical courts sprung up throughout England to handle the business lost by the secular tribunals. Each diocese was subdivided into a number of judicial areas, each in the care of an archdeacon. This sudden deluge of legal business resulted in a type of law that was "uncertain and unauthoritative, procedures that were hurried and irregular, and archdeacons that often were worldly, mercenary and unjust."[5] In the machinery of the church courts the role of the bishops, once paramount, gradually receded as this swarm of archdeacons assumed control of ecclesiastical litigation. Indeed, in England the archdeacon came to rank as the most distinguished cleric after the bishop and abbot.[6]

In his zeal to cleanse his new land of clerical abuses, however, the Conqueror had planted the seed of an even greater problem. His system of separate secular and church courts could work well only as long as the king and archbishop were in agreement. But the partnership between these two leading figures in England began to weaken soon after William's death when the Church, inspired by yet another reform (of Pope Gregory VII, 1073–1085), began to place an increasingly liberal interpretation on what it meant by the "rule of souls" and claimed jurisdiction over more and more legal cases which formerly had fallen within the purview of the secular courts. The strain had been the greatest under the Conqueror's successor son, William Rufus, who ignored the need for creating a fine balance between the secular and spiritual spheres and banished Lanfranc's successor, Anselm, from the kingdom. Although the typical medieval nostrum of compromise had been applied to the ailing relationship early in the reign of Rufus's successor, Henry I, nothing essential had been settled and the underlying tension between jurisdictions remained. Prince William's clerical companion aboard the White Ship, therefore, represented the potential for a disastrous collision between Church and State—an encounter that was in fact to come to a climax exactly fifty years later.

Less dramatic, perhaps, than these nobles and churchmen, but of no less importance were those members of the king's household who were to be William's fellow travelers aboard the White Ship. The passenger list included constables, stewards, and chamberlains—men whose jobs carried more official weight and responsibility than their titles implied. The use of the king's personal household servants to carry out royal decisions had been developing gradually since Carolingian times, and men bearing domestic titles had come, in the three centuries since the death of the Great Charles, to assume increasingly larger roles in the management of government. Although these men were to become even more important in succeeding generations, they had come a long way by the time of Henry I and were essential for putting into practice the decisions made by the king and his court. Unlike the great barons of the king's court, however, these householders had well-defined duties and restricted their talents to specified areas. The constable, while still responsible for the royal stables and the horses and hawks used for the king's pleasure, had already added to his functions that of quartermaster general of the monarch's army. The role of the steward had transcended the kitchen and come to include supervision of the entire household —he was, indeed, recognized as the principal lay officer of the household. Likewise, the duties of the chamberlain had over-

leaped the bounds of the king's bedroom and were already beginning to focus on the financial aspects of government. Taken
together, this group of magnates, clerics, and officials represented
a major segment of Henry's court.

Except for its larger size, the galley which was to transport
this impressive group of passengers across the Channel differed
little from those Viking craft which three centuries earlier had
carried Henry's marauding ancestors to the coasts of England
and Francia, or from the ships which had borne his father's army
toward the conquest of England. It would be another century
before sails would replace human muscle as the main source of
power for these craft,[7] and on this voyage the single sail would
relieve the rowers of but a mite of their exertions. The trip would
take anywhere from eighteen hours to two days depending on the
height of the sea-swells and the accuracy of the rudimentary navi-
gation equipment. The absence of a reliable method for determining longitude posed no problem to these sailors who, by heading due north, could keep the ship pointed toward Polaris until
they reached the English shore.

Shortly after sunset the White Ship pushed away from the dock
at Barfleur and headed for the open channel. The sailors, drunk
according to most accounts, announced "with true seamen's
hilarity"[8] that they would race the king's ship to the English
shore. In their haste to overtake the rest of the fleet, however, the
crew missed the narrow opening that led out through the string
of reefs that encircle the peninsula and drove the vessel onto
the dangerous rocks. Working frantically with their oars, the
seamen tried to free the ship from the reef, but the cold water
rushed in through the gaping hole throwing the 300 passengers
into a panic. Prince William managed to climb aboard a small
boat, but as he was rowing toward safety he heard the cries of his
sister Matilda pleading for help. Turning his skiff around he
headed back to rescue her. As he drew near to the sinking galley,
however, too many of the struggling passengers tried to clamber
aboard his boat and, in the darkness and confusion, it foundered.
With the exception of a butcher from Rouen who survived to tell
the tale, all the passengers were lost.[9]

News of the disaster was kept from the king for several days,
but when he was finally told of it he was dumbstruck. Bad enough
was the personal loss of his son who, in the words of a contem-

porary, "instead of wearing embroidered robes, floated naked in the waves; and instead of ascending a lofty throne, found his grave in the bellies of the fishes at the bottom of the sea." [10] But even worse was the realization that the king's work of the past two decades in taming England and molding a successful anti-French policy in Normandy was now in jeopardy through the lack of a bona fide heir. The loss of the White Ship threatened to return England to the uncertainties of 1066 from which the Conqueror had lifted her. The succession was now up for grabs, the tenuous diplomatic balance which Henry had woven among his Continental rivals was in danger of unraveling, and the advances made in England since the time of William I seemed certain to be undone.

CHAPTER I

The Education of a Prince
(1133–1144)

NEAR THE CONFLUENCE OF THE RIVERS SARTHE AND HUISNE IN Le Mans, the capital city of the French fief of Maine, Countess Matilda of Anjou gave birth to a son in March, 1133. It was Matilda's first child after sixteen married years, the last five of which had been to the infant's father Geoffrey, count of Anjou. The geographical site of the nativity was significant, situated as it was midway between Normandy to the north and Anjou to the south. Contemporary observers could make much of the fact that this newborn child symbolized the bridging of the gap between the ambitions and accomplishments of his Norman mother and Angevin father. Like Emperor Charles four centuries later, this infant, named Henry after his grandfather who occupied the English throne, was the fruit of two of the most aggressive and ambitious families in Western Europe.

Through Matilda and into the child flowed the blood of William the Conqueror whose arrival in England in 1066 had set the island kingdom on what was in many ways a new course.[1] Before he went to England William had done a remarkable job of making Normandy the most united and centralized province in western France, not so much by creating new centers of power as by harnessing already existing ones to his cause. Through the technique of identifying his own interests with those of the tough, aggressive Norman aristocracy and the strong, influential Church, he stabilized the duchy in the midst of unstable neighbors and laid the groundwork for his conquest of England. After seizing the island he joined it to Normandy by importing the closely-knit Norman aristocracy, the devout and well-organized Norman monasticism, and Norman political, military, financial, and social practices[2]—in short, the very people and institutions that had raised Normandy itself above the welter of adjoining French states. England and Normandy became a family federation as both regions shared the same ruler, the same aristocracy, and many of the same institutions of government and society.

But for all his sagacity William's work remained unfinished by the time of his death in 1087 and to his sons, William Rufus and Henry, in turn, fell the task of preserving their inheritance and building upon the foundations their father had bequeathed to them. Rufus had little success. Early in his reign a fissure opened in the Anglo-Norman union when Normandy, led by the Conqueror's oldest son, Robert, started to pull out of the federation. Since the Norman and English aristocracies were virtually identical, the disaffection spread to the island where the barons staged a litany of revolts against the Red King. Henry I did considerably better. After ascending the English throne in 1100 he brought Normandy back into the fold by snatching it from his brother and keeping it tightly bound to England. It took the king six years to return his possessions to the condition they had enjoyed nineteen years earlier, but his pacification of Normandy brought in its train the pacification of England and allowed Henry to pick up where his father had left off. It was this reconstruction that had been interrupted by the maritime disaster of 1120.

The infant Henry's mother Matilda was the older[3] sister of the unfortunate Prince William and the only remaining legitimate child of Henry I. Once the king had overcome his grief at the loss of his son he tried to rebuild the edifice but the materials at hand were fragile. Matilda's chances of succeeding him were clouded by several seemingly insurmountable barriers. For one thing, she had been married to the Holy Roman Emperor and was unacceptable to many of the English barons who feared that a union of the kingdom and empire would result in a submergence of the Anglo-Norman state into the larger German realm. For another, as a woman her claim to the throne flew in the face of an unwritten English tradition of male monarchs. Further, she was an obstreperous woman, hardly the type to ingratiate herself with those who could decide her future. Finally, baronial uneasiness with many of Henry's centralizing measures made it less than likely that the nobles would endorse his daughter who could be counted on to continue her father's policies.

The English king tried everything he could to ward off the disintegration which seemed certain to succeed him. In 1121 he married Adela, the daughter of the count of Louvain, in hopes of another son to carry on his work. But none was forthcoming. When Matilda's imperial spouse died in 1125 she returned home where some arm-twisting by her father squeezed from the reluctant English barons an oath to recognize her as his successor. But such promises were always tenuous and their fulfillment hinged more upon the status of forces at the moment of the king's death than upon the binding power of a vow. Therefore Henry backed up his position three years later, in a replay of his dead son's marriage, by arranging the wedding of his widowed daughter to Geoffrey of Anjou in hopes that this union would prove more fruitful than his own. But the political genesis of the marriage, Matilda's headstrong character, and the fact that she was ten years older and more experienced than her spouse, led to a stormy union. The step down from empress to countess was difficult for Matilda and she resolved to rectify it, at least partially, by keeping lit the fire of her claim to the English throne. Even though the barons in 1131 repeated their oath to recognize her, such promises, like gardens, needed constant cultivation, and she spent most of the infant Henry's childhood years away from Anjou building support for herself in England.

The newborn child's ancestors on his father's side were no less ambitious than his Norman forebears.[4] The tale of the supposed origin of this side of Henry's family from a she-devil delighted medieval ears whenever it was recounted in the courts of Western Europe, and the wild exploits of several generations of Angevin counts had lent plausibility to the legend. In the tenth century the Angevin rulers found themselves in a position analogous to that of the Norman dukes—vassals of the French king who, though eager for expansion, often found their expansive designs hampered by domestic rebels and avaricious neighbors. Early in the next century Count Fulk Nerra, an untiring and easily enraged man, struck out at his neighbors to the south, west, and east. Captured towns were quickly adorned by him with thick-walled stone castles which brought a measure of security to the region. While his rivals remained content with their wooden-palisaded motte-and-bailey fortifications Fulk, out of ostentation and possibly in a bid for immortality, designed his castles for greater permanence, a full century before the idea of stone strongholds spread to the adjoining principalities. Although Fulk spent most of his later years besieging the Loire city of

Tours, it was his son Geoffrey Martel who, after his father's death in 1040, led the Angevins into the enemy capital and joined the county of Touraine to that of Anjou. Then the Angevins turned northward and overran Maine, which brought them to the border of Normandy. Thus was ushered in a decade of military and diplomatic interplay between the infant Henry's paternal great-great-grandfather Geoffrey and his maternal great-grandfather, the Norman duke William the Bastard (but not yet the Conqueror). For half a century the contest remained a stalemate with the Angevins halted at the Norman border while continuing to resist Norman attempts at expansion. Henry I's introduction of his two legitimate children into the comital family of Anjou was aimed at breaking down this resistance and, with luck, bringing about a merger of the two French fiefs. Thus the birth of Henry Plantagenet in 1133 raised Norman hopes for the realization of their long-range policy while at the same time it promised the Angevins fulfillment of their cherished dream of an Angevin count ruling from Rouen.[5]

The French king's role in these struggles between his vassals had so far been relatively minor because, although he was legally overlord of the contending fiefs, his authority was effective only in the regions where he could enforce it by diplomacy or war, and he had been able to do neither. In the century and a half since Hugh Capet had been chosen to preside over the wreckage of the Carolingian Empire (largely because he posed the least threat to his fellow counts) his descendants had held their own, but little more, against the rapacious princes of Normandy, Flanders, Blois, and Anjou. The personal resources which the Capetians brought to the struggle were unimpressive—the Ile de France, a fifty-by-twenty-mile liver-shaped region which housed, on the average, one treacherous baron for every hundred square miles, and a genetic inertia which left them without the aggressiveness and imagination needed to expand the kingdom. That the family survived on the throne at all before the twelfth century was a tribute to the moral preeminence it enjoyed as the successors of Charlemagne, to its consistency in producing male heirs, and to the fact that its rivals' domains were as unruly as its own. In the middle of the eleventh century the French monarchy was still struggling to tame its barons at home; a century later it was in a slightly better position but still far behind the rulers of England and Normandy and not much better off than those of Flanders, Blois, and Anjou.[6] The Normans ignored the French king when they could, for their lord was also a king. The Angevins used him when it suited their purposes, especially against Normandy. As a result, the French monarch had remained somewhat of a background figure in the Norman-Angevin struggle, invited to participate only when his presence could further the aspirations of one party or the other. But all of this was in the process of changing when Henry Plantagenet was born, and before his life had run its course he would find among his severest competitors a revived French monarchy dedicated first to the containment and then to the dissolution of his Anglo-Norman state.

This, then, was the situation into which Henry II was born. His formative years were colored by his parents' grandiose ambitions and his upbringing reflected their hopes that one day he would combine their inheritances. He passed the first nine years of his life at the county seat of Angers where, with his two younger brothers Geoffrey and William, he ripened in the religious and physical qualities necessary for salvation and pleasure in twelfth-century Europe. As a normal part of growing up he absorbed, both by example and precept, the practices and teachings of the Church. Religious instruction, reception of the sacraments, and belief in a God who had a hand in human destiny became an accepted part of the youngster's daily existence. In these pre-Reformation days, when it was as yet not on the defensive against external variations, the Church was still able to embrace within its fold every type of human weakness. The day had not yet arrived when the Church would be dissociated from the State and, ultimately, from society. In the early twelfth century bishops were barons and kings were priests. Daily attendance at mass, a practice that Henry was to continue throughout his life, was considered no more unusual, and probably only slightly more religious, than attendance at court or tournament. Since everyone belonged to the Church, all human foibles were in-house matters which were handled with a greater degree of liberality than was true of later ages. The expression of religion was spontaneous and as natural to young Henry and his generation as were fighting and, a bit later, wenching. During these early years Henry learned that the secular and the spiritual were a continuum. For this reason his later disagreements with the Church were never religious wars of persecution but rather the efforts of a divinely appointed ruler to fulfill his obligations toward an integrated secular-spiritual society.

Learning the arts of horseback riding, jousting, falconry, and hunting must have occupied much of young Henry's time, for these formed part of the education of all noble youth and they appear in Henry's manhood as consuming obsessions. Medieval society was feudal and initiation into this society was marked by the knighting ceremony which was performed only after the candidate had trained in the art of war and had proven that he deserved to be numbered among the elite company of knight-warriors. During Henry's adolescence the military art was undergoing, if not the revolutionary changes of later centuries, at least constant modification in technique and equipment. Besides learning to ride and to achieve at least a modicum of comfort and flexibility in the protective armor of the day—the new chain link overcoat with quilted gambeson beneath; the conical helmet which was still the fashion during his youth; and the protective leg padding—the maturing Henry must have spent many hours perfecting the maneuvers which the soldier of his day was called upon to perform. Such, for example, was the recently developed technique of the couched lance by which a charging knight, his feet planted firmly in the stirrups and his spear snuggled closely against his body, transferred the combined power of destrier and rider to his protruding lance, making of it an attack weapon of fearsome force. In addition, brought up in a land where stone castles had long ceased to be a novelty and at a court where the laying of plans for the reduction of these rock fortresses filled the days and seasons of military inertia between sieges, Henry was continually exposed to the methods of castle warfare and perhaps even this early came to see a contradiction between the military training of the day, which stressed the importance of individual valor, and the realities of siege warfare, which depended for success upon the suppression of individualistic urges and patient cooperation between various technicians. Although military manuals were a thing of the future, Henry's father Geoffrey is known to have possessed a copy of the Roman treatise on war by Vegetius. This fourth-century handbook on martial affairs was the military bible of the Middle Ages and the fact that its precepts were written for the massed warfare of the Roman legions in no way deterred medieval fighters from applying what they could of them to the limited skirmishes of the day. Particularly useful were Vegetius's passages describing the techniques of Roman siege warfare. In this age of the renaissance of stone fortifications the principles of Vegetius fit perfectly and were applied with very little modification. It is likely that a study of this authoritative tome formed part of the young Henry's military education.

But the day had passed in medieval Europe when physical dexterity alone sufficed to equip a man for leadership. New intellectual winds were blowing on Anjou from several directions. A scant hundred miles to the east the French king's capital was vibrating with a new excitement which owed nothing to traditional physical prowess—a student revolt against the established intellectual authority. The gadfly of the movement (if it may be so styled) was a Breton maverick, Peter Abelard, who had been run out of Paris a decade earlier for his revolutionary teaching and life. In 1136, when Henry was three years old, Abelard was back in the city on the Seine wooing students from the university with his theory that the human intellect was as much a gift from God as the Bible and should, as much as that venerable book, be used in the quest to discover what life was all about. Although rationalism was as yet in the first years of its revival, the excitement it engendered was drawing to Paris young scholars whose influence was to be paramount in the succeeding generations. What effect, if any, this intellectual ferment had on the young man growing up in Angers is unknown, but in the very year of Abelard's return to Paris it was informing the minds of several students, notably John of Salisbury and Thomas Becket, whose paths were later to cross that of the young Angevin scion.

To the south of Anjou, in the lands and fiefs below the river Loire collectively called Aquitaine, quite another intellectual departure was in progress. There the looser, gayer Mediterranean personality of the inhabitants was producing a liberalism analogous to that which was sweeping Paris, but one which found expression in song and poetry rather than in philosophy and theology. A generation earlier the Aquitainian duke and Poitevin count, William the Troubador, had given birth to this movement through his poetry and songs which extolled the worth of individual aspirations and the love of life for its own sake. Despite the obvious external differences between the troubador and the Parisian rationalist, they agreed in seeing the potential for truth and beauty in the individual human being. This lusty, "sophisticated" spirit of the south was shared by William's granddaughter, the French queen Eleanor, who arrived in the French capital for her coronation only one year after Abelard resumed his teaching there. By 1137, therefore, the city on the Seine sheltered many of the people who were later to have the strongest influence on the four-year-old youth.

Yet we do know of one intellectual influence on the future English king. Geoffrey and Matilda, occupied elsewhere, placed the formal education of their son in more stable hands. In 1138, when Henry was old enough to start his training, they brought to the Angevin court the celebrated Aquitainian scholar and poet Peter of Saintes, who for four years exposed the youth to the rudiments of twelfth-century learning and, probably, to some of the intellectual gales then swirling around the edges of the small county. As with Aristotle and Alexander, it would be interesting to know the effect of tutor on pupil, but since that information is lost forever, it can only be assumed that when he was not with his horses and falcons the young Henry spent his time learning to read, trying to fathom the basics of the trivium and quadrivium, and imbibing the tenets and rituals of Christianity to which he was to remain faithful throughout his life.

At the Angevin court during these years Henry also received a first-hand view of feudal politics. When he was two years old, and barely within the arena of consciousness, his grandfather, King Henry I, died and the regal aspirations of Matilda were dashed by her cousin, Stephen of Blois, who raced to Winchester to seize the treasury and the throne that accompanied it. Stephen's genealogical claim to England was as valid as hers—he too was a grandchild of the Conqueror. But what rankled Matilda was the barons' disregard of their oath and their acceptance as the new king of one of their fellow oath takers. Their acquiescence was inspired by Stephen's presence on the island while Matilda confined her bid for the throne to an ineffectual sally into Normandy by her husband who continued to think and plan only in continental terms. Geoffrey's misreading of the situation helped to lose for his wife her chance for the English throne.

But the Empress (as she preferred to be called) kept alive her hope of gaining the English crown even after Stephen's coronation. Some of the English lords still supported her, either out of respect for her father and their oath, or for what they stood to gain personally from an unsettled England. Pockets of resistance quickly sprung up in the kingdom and, although Matilda could count on supporters in all parts of the realm, the center of her strength lay in the west around Gloucester, whose Earl Robert was another of Henry I's illegitimate children. Backbone was given to the resistance against Stephen by the Empress when she landed in England in 1139 and organized the opposition to the king. Although Henry remained at Angers with his father, who seems to have considered his wife's expedition little of his business, news of Matilda's progress was the subject of steady conversation and conjecture in the Angevin household. Henry, now old enough to understand what was going on, must have followed avidly the political and military intricacies of the campaign which his mother was waging in England on his behalf. In 1141 her battle appeared won when her soldiers captured Stephen at Lincoln and the whole of the island, except for Kent, hailed her as queen. But at this critical moment her personality intervened and she defeated her own purpose. Instead of conciliating the defeated and promising them reforms, she made immediate and unfair demands for money to strengthen her position. The English turned against her and once again gave their support to Stephen. When Earl Robert was captured at Winchester several months later, the two prisoners were exchanged and Matilda was back where she had started.

Soon after his release in the spring of 1142 Earl Robert came to Angers seeking Geoffrey's assistance in the struggle against the king. He brought with him a request from the Empress that Henry, now nine years old, return with his uncle to England where he could familiarize himself with the country and boost the morale of the men who were helping him to acquire it. When Robert left for the island later that year with 300 mounted knights young Henry was with him.[7]

During the next two years, which he spent at his uncle's court at Bristol, the pace of Henry's indoctrination quickened. To his formal studies, now directed by Matthew, the archdeacon of Gloucester,[8] was added daily exposure to the people and machinery of a ducal court at war. In Robert's household the future king experienced the never-ending comings and goings of a coterie of rich and powerful lords dedicated to the unseating of a king. Most of the important men of the west country, and some from the north and east, came to Bristol at one time or another to discuss their strategy against Stephen. A frequent visitor was Earl Robert's son-in-law Ranulf, the respected earl of Chester and recent convert to Matilda's side, whose military pressure against the king from the northwest formed an important pillar of the Empress's policy. It was Ranulf who had masterminded the siege of Lincoln castle the year before which was climaxed by the capture of Stephen. Another of Robert's allies was Miles, who controlled the county of Hereford directly north of Gloucester, thereby guarding the approaches into central and southern Wales. To the south Matilda relied on the fidelity of Reginald, the earl of Cornwall, another of her father's bastards, and Baldwin of Redvers, the earl of Devon, who had been a favorite of Henry I. Baldwin had earlier been driven from the country by Stephen but had since returned and joined the Empress's party. Many independent lords with strategic castles also backed the imperial cause: Humphrey of Bohun with his castle at Trowbridge; Brian fitz Count whose stronghold at Wallingford, between Oxford and London, provided a strategic salient into royal territory to the east; Alan, earl of Richmond, who kept things stirred up in the north;[9] and David, the king of the Scots, who was Matilda's uncle.

In addition to brushing shoulders with these warriors, young Henry also came to know many of the English prelates who had originally agreed to Stephen's accession but who, after the king scandalized the country in 1139 by seizing church property and imprisoning several of their number, turned against the monarch and were driven into Matilda's camp. The archbishop of Canterbury, Theobald, was sympathetic to the Empress and had even appeared in her army during an unsuccessful siege of Winchester in 1141. As the unofficial primate of England, Theobald worked hard to settle the differences which separated the two factions and, trusted by Matilda and Robert, often came to Bristol to plead his cause. Perhaps even more influential than Theobald was the king's brother, Henry, bishop of Winchester—the man who played a greater part than any other in putting Stephen on the throne and in directing his reign. The prelate had become disillusioned with his brother's actions and was not above dealing with the Angevin party when it appeared that the future might

lie with the Empress. Although it is not recorded that Bishop
Henry ever came to Bristol while his young namesake was there,
his name was a household word in Robert's court and young
Henry could not have helped but absorb a valuable lesson from
his example in how (or how not) to deal with churchmen. Henry
II's visit many years later to the deathbed of this venerable
prelate suggests that in these early years he had developed an
attachment to the person, as well as to the reputation, of his
enemy's chief adviser. Bishop Nigel of Ely, one of the three prelates whom Stephen had jailed in 1139, had sought asylum at Bristol the following year and from him the budding monarch must
have heard some pithy words about church-state relationships.
For the future king, Robert's court was a laboratory where he
met many of the people and learned many of the techniques
which would flavor his coming reign. To such academic subjects
as Latin, logic, and poetry were now added the practical arts of
military organization, war finance, and diplomacy.

While at Bristol Henry had the opportunity to judge the effectiveness of the traditional medieval military organization and see
for himself both the limitations of the system and an experiment
in the search for alternatives. One of the most important innovations which the Conqueror had imported from Normandy to
England had been the practice of raising an army by granting
land in return for a stipulated amount of military service each
year.[10] This scheme of knight service insured an organized, if not
always equal, distribution of the land and a strengthening of
those personal bonds between individuals which were so important to medieval society, while at the same time it guaranteed to
the lord who distributed the land an armed force when he needed
it. The practice had sunken into the marrow of medieval society
both in England and on the Continent. The key to its success lay
in the two-way loyalty, both up and down, between lord and vassals. During ordinary times it worked satisfactorily and a call
from king or lord for armed support was answered by a flock of
vassals eager to uphold their honor and justify the possession of
their fiefs. But in the event of a civil war, such as Matilda and
Robert were waging against Stephen, the king did not enjoy this
loyalty and as a result lost the support of many of his fighters.
Both sides then had to rely on hired soldiers to fill their ranks.
Although some of the earlier English kings had used mercenaries

when they found their feudal resources inadequate, Stephen pushed the practice farther than had any of his predecessors. To command the royal army he hired the Flemish nobleman William of Ypres who, after an unsuccessful bid for the countship of Flanders in 1127, turned to a life of soldiery and sold his talents. With Stephen's money he brought to England an army of paid Flemings to supplement the king's uncertain feudal array. As inconceivable as it might have been to those who were brought up to value loyalty above all else, it often happened that these mercenaries, despite their cruelty and blatant disregard of the unspoken rules of feudalism, proved more faithful than their knightly counterparts. William of Ypres, for example, was one of the few who remained loyal to the king after Stephen fell into the Empress's hands in 1141 and it was he who captured Henry's uncle at Stockbridge later in the year, leading to the king's release and reinstatement. But the king was not alone in hiring mercenaries. Many of Matilda's supporters also relied on paid fighters. The earl of Hereford, Miles, was always surrounded by paid footsoldiers and archers whom he hired from neighboring Wales. And the decisive battle at Lincoln had been largely a contest between Stephen's Flemings and the earl of Chester's hired Welshmen.[11] Another mercenary, William of Dover, built and garrisoned with hired soldiers the castle at Cricklade, east of Gloucester, from which he harassed the king's castles on both sides of the Thames as far east as Oxford.[12]

There existed as yet no formal way of raising money to pay for these soldiers and in their scramble to collect funds each side had, at one time or another, done harm to its own cause. At the outset of his reign Stephen had had an ample supply of money from the royal treasury and from his own large and rich manors. But this was soon spent on soldiers and he seized ecclesiastical revenues, a move that cost him much support. While Henry was at the Bristol court Miles of Hereford tried the same thing by demanding large sums of money from his bishop so he could hire soldiers. The bishop stoutly refused and Miles's accidental death soon after was widely interpreted as divine retribution for his ungodly act.[13] It is unlikely that Henry's tutor, Matthew, failed to take advantage of the incident to impress upon the lad the potential danger of seizing church money to buy mercenaries. Perhaps from this and other instances Henry learned early in life the need to place warfare on a regular, nondiscriminatory financial footing. During these years his uncle showed him one way in which this could be done. After the rapid events of 1141–42 the war settled down to a more even pace with Robert firmly established in the western part of the country. To maintain there a "shadow of peace" he constructed a string of castles and strengthened already existing ones in a north-south line from Bristol to the English Channel. Robert paid for this construction by excusing his vassals from further military service, which was no longer required on the previous scale, in return for the payment of a fee, called a scutage.[14] This example was not lost on Henry in whose hands such commutations would be raised to the level of standard practice.

At his uncle's court Henry also discovered the complexities of the English power structure and the diplomatic links that held it together. He learned, for example, that success against the king depended on more than simple direct military pressure. The real power in Stephen's England lay at the level once removed from the king, among the shifting, kaleidoscopic group of barons who by default had fallen heir to much of the royal power. With one or two exceptions these barons were sincere and dedicated men who were convinced that feudalism, with its personal bonds and legal basis, held out the best hope for maintaining order in England. Far from wanting anarchy, most of them were eager to respect the rights of any king who would respect theirs and who would provide sufficient stability for them to exercise them. Depending upon whether these lords thought Stephen could or could not keep feudalism healthy, they proffered or withheld their support from him. Many of the barons changed sides with the ebb and flow of circumstances, judging at one time that the chances for attaining equilibrium in the kingdom were greater at the king's side, and at another that security could best be produced by siding with his enemies. Such, for example, was Ranulf of Chester who, with his brother William of Roumare, had supported Stephen as late as 1140. The king had heaped honors on the brothers, granting Ranulf many concessions in the north and bestowing on William the earlship of Lincoln and the justiciarship of Normandy.[15] Yet after 1140 the brothers joined the Empress's party and it was Ranulf who was responsible for many of her victories. Henry could see that within Stephen's England there existed a realm within a realm. This was illustrated by the diplomatic agreement between two of the barons, Robert of Leicester and Ranulf of Chester, which bore all the trademarks of those international alliances so dear to early twentieth-century Europe. In return for the granting of a castle, each lord agreed that he would not attack the other or let a third party use his castles to launch an attack on the other. If either earl were forced, by feudal rules, to join his liege lord (the king) in an attack on the other, he was to limit his contribution to the king to twenty knights, and everything that he captured in the attack he was to return to his ally. The conditions of this offensive-defensive alliance could be set aside, and one earl permitted to attack the other, only if a fifteen-day advance notice was given.[16] A similar agreement was in effect, while Henry was at Bristol, between his uncle Robert and Miles of Gloucester whereby the two leaders of Matilda's party promised to look after each other's interests.[17] Miles, like Ranulf, had been one of the king's men and had enjoyed the trusted position as Stephen's constable[18] until the start of the civil war when he switched to the Empress and gained for himself the earlship of Hereford. These baronial agreements reflect the close adherence, bordering on worship, of the powerful barons to the rules of feudalism while at the same time they illustrate the lords' conviction that the king was ill-equipped to enforce these rules and that they had better make their own provisions to insure the peace. Even though the barons were rewarded handsomely for their change of allegiance, it is too simple and cynical an explanation of their actions to attribute them solely to the desire for personal gain. They wanted above all a well-ordered England without which their possessions would be tenuous, at best, and they decided that Stephen could not provide it.

Not all the earls, of course, were so altruistically motivated. One man who evoked alternating encouragement and consternation at Robert's court was Geoffrey of Mandeville,[19] an opportunistic baron who controlled the eastern counties of England. Although Geoffrey had possessed some hereditary lands and offices, his real power came from milking concessions from both parties in the struggle. His personal aspirations had been given a decided boost by the Empress during her brief stint as queen-elect in 1141 when she made him earl of Essex and confirmed his constableship of the Tower of London—positions he retained and added to when he joined Stephen's party later that year. But Matilda needed Geoffrey's support to close a ring around the king. The western counties under Robert, Miles, and Ranulf were solidly behind her, as was much of the north where she could rely on Earl Alan of Richmond and the Scots' king, David. All that was needed to complete Stephen's encirclement was Geoffrey in the east. While he was at Bristol Henry had a ringside seat on negotiations between Matilda and Geoffrey of Mandeville in which the eastern baron promised to fight against the monarch at the other end of England. For the two years of Henry's stay on the island Geoffrey waged a guerrilla campaign in and around the fens near Ely which forced the king to concentrate his attention in the east.[20] Finally, in 1144, the rebel was tracked down and killed.

Henry could not have failed to see in all of this the importance of diplomatic agreements among the English baronage and also to have come to realize what grief could befall a king who allowed power to slip so far from his grasp as to permit the growth of a political structure over which he exercised no control. Upon these observations the young Henry would be called to act within a few years, and his later success as king in dealing with the barons shows that he learned his lesson well during these years in his uncle's household.

CHAPTER II

"Fair England's Royal Diadem Is Thine"
(1144–1154)

HENRY PLANTAGENET'S FIRST STAY IN ENGLAND WAS CUT SHORT in 1144[1] when his father recalled him to the Continent to share in his victory over Normandy. Since 1135, when Stephen had become the Norman duke as well as the English king, Geoffrey had been nibbling away at his northern rival and the English monarch's preoccupation with Matilda on the island had permitted the Angevin count to extend his influence piecemeal over the duchy. Between 1137 and 1141 the important towns of Caen, Bayeux, Lisieux, and Falaise were brought into the Angevin camp. Avranches yielded in 1143 and a year later the citizens of Rouen, disenchanted with Stephen and convinced that Geoffrey Plantagenet was acting as the agent for his eldest son, welcomed the Angevin count into the capital. Although a few regions of Normandy continued to maintain the union with England, the fall of Rouen effectively placed the duchy in Geoffrey's hands. Henry's presence on the Continent was helpful to his father in legitimizing these conquests.

For the next two years the young Plantagenet remained on the mainland helping his father to stabilize the newly won duchy and learning the intricacies of ducal administration. In England during these years his mother was preparing for another assault on Stephen and by the opening months of 1147 her plans were complete. It was Matilda's hope that the union of Stephen's enemies would place her on the throne. Instead, it ended with the Empress's cause in shambles, largely as the result of Earl Robert's death in October. Henry had made a quick second visit to the island earlier in the year and although he accomplished nothing on the battlefield, he did display a glimmer of that diplomatic ability which was later to be one of his most important assets. Shortly before he arrived in England the bishop of Hereford had died and Archbishop Theobald had selected Gilbert Foliot, the

[38]

abbot of Gloucester, to fill the vacancy. Since the episcopal see lay within the lands controlled by the Angevin party, the Empress's approval of the nomination was essential. Henry, quick to realize that nothing could be gained by opposing the archbishop, agreed to the appointment but on condition that Gilbert swear an oath of allegiance to himself and not to Stephen.[2] This move paid off at the time by keeping Theobald sympathetic to the Angevins, and a decade later when Gilbert was to persuade the rebellious earl of Hereford to stop his opposition to the newly crowned Henry. The fourteen-year-old prince had served notice that he had learned the rules of the game and that from then on he intended to play a leading role in his own cause.

In 1149 Henry traveled for a third time to England. He landed at Bristol early in the year and, in the company of Roger, the new earl of Hereford, journeyed north to Carlisle where the two young warriors were knighted by Henry's great-uncle, David, king of the Scots.[3] Henry's novitiate was over as he was accepted into the profession of arms. The knighting ceremony was probably very simple and consisted of little more than Henry kneeling before David who tapped him with a sword. The later accretions to the rite, which were to turn it into a colorful pageant and a semi-religious ritual, were as yet unknown in the early twelfth century. As with many institutions the outward ceremony remained unpretentious as long as the institution was living and meaningful, and only after it lost much of its importance was external pomp substituted for inner meaning.

At Carlisle the anti-Stephen confederates, joined there by Ranulf of Chester, hatched a plot to attack the city of York.[4] But the king, warned in advance of their intentions, rode north with an impressive army and the rebels abandoned their plans. Henry fled south along western back roads and reached Hereford safely. But on the final leg of his flight to Bristol he barely escaped capture by a detachment of royal forces commanded by Eustace, the king's son. Later in the year, during September and October, the new knight led his first serious military expedition into Devon and Cornwall. At the head of an army which included the earls of Gloucester and Hereford, he cleared the two shires of the king's supporters and, by capturing the strategic castle of Bridport, strengthened the right flank of the Angevin line.[5]

By January, 1150, Henry was back in Normandy, encouraged

by the relative success of his first major military venture and by the promises of support he had received while in England. Having been knighted and having proved to his father that he could act on his own, he was invested by Geoffrey with the duchy of Normandy.[6] It had been traditional for the Angevin counts, in imitation of the French kings, to introduce their heirs and successors to the responsibilities of government before their own deaths,[7] and Geoffrey was following the custom. This practice was unknown in England at the time and Henry would later be the first to attempt it. From this time on he styled himself "Duke of Normandy" although he had not yet done homage for the fief to its lord, King Louis VII. This feudal snub was Henry's way of informing the French king that he had come of age and intended to treat the duchy as an independent entity. He hoped to postpone as long as possible the assumption of another feudal bond that would further complicate his imperial plans.

But recognition of the French king's overlordship of Normandy could not be permanently put off. Feudal ties were the cement of society and only the strongest could get by with ignoring them. Louis, ready to enforce his rights by arms, if necessary, allied himself with Eustace and invaded the duchy from the east.[8] Henry realized that in order to pacify Normandy, he would have to mollify the monarch. In August, 1151, he went with his father to Paris where he formally swore allegiance to Louis in return for the king's recognition of him as the Norman duke. Two centuries of bickering between Anjou and Normandy came to an end as the two counties, with Maine in between, were united in the hands of one family. But although Henry bought time by recognizing the French king's rights, he and his father had to pay dearly for the king's neutrality. As part of the agreement at Paris they were forced to hand over to the Capetian monarch the city of Gisors and relinquish their claim to the French Vexin, that borderland district which had been a source of friction between Normandy and France for generations. Little did Henry realize at the time how much diplomatic and military energy he would be called on to expend in the next three decades to recover this buffer area.

On the return journey from Paris to Anjou Geoffrey Plantagenet fell ill and, sensing his approaching death, made out a will in which he left to Henry all of Normandy, Maine, and Anjou with

the exception of three important castles which he bequeathed to
his second son, Geoffrey. William, the youngest son, received
nothing directly but was to be provided for by his brothers. The
will stipulated, however, that if Henry were to become king of
England, Maine and Anjou would then revert to Geoffrey since
Henry would then have his mother's possessions of England and
Normandy. The dying count then made the lords who were present swear that they would not bury him until Henry, who was
away hunting, had taken an oath to abide by the conditions of
the will. Geoffrey understood fully the depth of his oldest son's
ambitions and the callousness with which he was wont to pursue
them. Henry arrived late at his father's deathbed and at first
balked at the lords' insistence that he take the oath. Finally, after
much discussion and pleading by the bishops and nobles, he
swore to honor his father's last wishes, but he did so with bad
grace and with mental reservations.[9]

Hard upon Henry's promotion to the countships of Maine and
Anjou came another stroke of luck which was to treble his territory and guarantee the continuation of the dynasty he was creating. Mutual dissatisfaction between the French king Louis and
his queen, Eleanor, rose to the surface early in 1152. The queen, a
medieval feminist with a strong streak of independence, had
found Paris and the king too confining after her return from a
crusade to the East in 1147. Louis had also had enough of the
marriage which had failed to produce a male heir—the first such
failure for the Capets in almost two centuries. These factors had
been troubling the marriage for some time and it was only the
mollifying hand of Louis's adviser, Abbot Suger, that had kept
the union intact. The abbot was a practical man who had viewed
the marriage of Louis and Eleanor as more than a "remedium
concupiscentiae"—Eleanor had brought to it as a dowry the entire southwestern Mediterranean part of France. But Suger's restraining influence disappeared with his death in 1151 and in
March of the following year a church council at Beaugency, after
arriving at the startling conclusion that the royal pair were too
closely related to have been married in the first place, annulled
the union. Upon receiving news of her freedom, Eleanor hurried
home to Poitou, but her journey was not without incident. Two
unsuccessful attempts were made, first by Count Theobald of
Blois and then by Henry's younger brother Geoffrey, to abduct

the duchess as she traveled south. The ex-queen, with her free-floating duchy of Aquitaine, became for the moment the most sought-after woman in Europe.

Eleanor's availability was not lost on Henry. At the age of nineteen the duke was climbing rapidly up the feudal ladder and had much to gain from a marriage with the duchess. Within the space of little over two years he had been knighted, assumed forthright command of the struggle against the English king, been created duke of Normandy, and succeeded to the counties of Maine and Anjou. With the heart of his envisioned empire now secure between the Channel and the Loire, the time had come to tack on the appendages—Aquitaine to the south and England to the north—and Henry saw in Eleanor the opportunity to acquire both with one act. A marriage to the Aquitainian duchess would seal Louis's loss of the southern arm of his pincer in which he had hoped to squeeze the upstart Norman duke, while at the same time it would weaken the French king sufficiently to free Henry for his English plans. In addition, it would provide Henry with a valuable increase in men and money for the expedition to the island. Finally, the union held out the possibility, always uppermost in medieval political minds, of a male issue to carry on his work. Far down on the list of Henry's motives, if even present, was what would later be called "romance" which barely, if ever, figured in noble marriages. To Henry, up till then dominated by his mother, the prospect of marriage to the duchess of Aquitaine must have appeared as a replay of his own parents' conjugal union. Like Matilda, Eleanor had but recently descended from royal rank but retained a patrimony which would be important to Angevin expansion. The duchess was older by a decade than Henry, the same difference in age that had separated Matilda from Geoffrey. And Eleanor, like her future mother-in-law, was casting about for a new niche in the political wall of Europe to replace the one she had just vacated.

A scant two months after the former queen reached Poitiers, in May, 1152, she and Henry Plantagenet were married in the Poitevin capital.[10] In the absence of evidence that Henry and Eleanor knew each other or had ever met before the Plantagenet trip to Paris, it seems likely that during the duke's visit to the French city with his father agreement was reached between him and the queen, and that the ambushes of Theobald and Geoffrey were aimed at preventing the annexation of Aquitaine to Henry's territory in the north. The wedding ceremony was unheralded, almost surreptitious. There were good reasons for dispensing with outward display. The blood ties that connected the bride and groom were no less binding than those which had so recently provided the legal basis for Eleanor's separation from her first husband. In addition, both partners were technically Louis's vassals and should, in accordance with feudal law, have obtained their lord's permission to marry. A well-advertised wedding, replete with ecclesiastical pomp and pageantry, would have added insult to the serious injury already inflicted on the French king by both partners.

News of the marriage infuriated Louis who belatedly came to realize the implications of Eleanor's departure. But aside from throwing together a hasty and ineffectual alliance between the trio of Eleanor's castoffs (Theobald, young Geoffrey, and himself), there was little the king could do but watch from Paris as the spreading Angevin behemoth grew before his eyes. The allies invaded Normandy in July, but instead of weakening Henry the attack actually strengthened him by giving him an excuse to strip his brother of the three castles which his father had left him. The threat to Henry was over by August and he spent the early winter months traveling with his new wife through Aquitaine sizing up his new vassals, who were as rebellion-prone as any in Europe, and trying, with little success, to persuade them that he had replaced Louis as their duke. In the course of his progress messengers arrived from his fellow knight Roger of Hereford, who was in England, informing Henry that his military position on the island was deteriorating rapidly. Stephen had reinforced his siege of the castle at Wallingford, which had been going on for over a year, by building two counter-castles opposite the city's main fortification and had captured the bridge which held the key to the town. The siege was too firmly entrenched to break, reported the envoys, and even though Roger had drawn the king with many of his troops away from Wallingford by feigning an alliance with Stephen against the city of Worcester, he could not keep up the pretense much longer. Unless Henry came quickly with an army, he pleaded, the Angevin cause in England had no future.

After borrowing some money, Henry contracted for infantry soldiers from his new fief of Gascony and arranged for ships to carry them to England. On the 6th of January the invasion force, consisting of 36 transports and 3000 men, crossed from Barfleur to western England. The young duke's arrival on the English shore was hailed by his adherents as an event only slightly less momentous than the Savior's appearance eleven centuries earlier. Sang Henry of Huntingdon, later, with perceptive hindsight:

> Heir to thy grandfather's name and high renown
> Thy England calls thee, Henry, to her throne:
> Now, fallen from her once imperial state,
> Exhausted, helpless, ruined, desolate,
> She sighs her griefs, and fainting, scarcely lives:
> One solitary hope survives.
> She turns to thee her dim and feeble eye,
> But scarce can raise the suppliant's plaintive cry;
> "Save me, oh save me, Henry, or I die:
> Come, saviour, to thy own; by right divine
> Fair England's royal diadem is thine." [11]

Such praise bore little relation to reality. Henry was met in England by an anxious William of Gloucester and a nervous Reginald of Cornwall, his kin and new leaders of the Angevin forces since the death of Robert. Once he was filled in on the details of the situation around Wallingford Henry and his advisers decided against marching directly to the relief of the castle, which lay deep within royal territory, and settled instead on a strategy of gradual approach to the beleaguered fortress from the west and the north. The first step was to seize the castle of Malmesbury which had been driven, like a wedge, between Henry's two main centers at Bristol and Gloucester. Malmesbury was attacked in February by what was, in effect, a family army led by the descendants, legitimate and otherwise, of Henry I. Henry Plantagenet's chief lieutenants were his uncle Reginald, a bastard of the former king, and William of Gloucester, son of the dead Robert who had also been an illegitimate offspring of the prodigious Henry Beauclerc. The campaign almost aborted at the outset when Henry's Gascon mercenaries, assigned the mission of scaling the outer walls of the town, flowed over the parapets, burst into the church and monastery, and ruthlessly massacred the clergy and civilians who had taken shelter there. Henry's allies were horrified and strongly urged him to send the "profane

THE BRITISH ISLES IN
HENRY II'S TIME

SCOTLAND

Carlisle Newcastle
Tyne River

IRELAND

Dublin

York

Anglesey Lincoln

Rhuddlan Chester

Nottingham

Shrewsbury Leicester
Wexford
Waterford WALES Ely

Cardigan

Pembroke Hereford Gloucester

Oxford London
Thames River
Bristol Canterbury
Salisbury Dover
Southampton

scoundrels" back to the Continent. The duke knew that the success of this campaign depended on his wooing of the powerful English lords who were at the moment wavering undecidedly between the king and himself and that the image he created of himself was the key to winning them over. During his earlier visits to the island he had seen the revulsion that could be generated by the actions of mercenaries who, cynical of feudal restraints, fought their battles to win without regard for those tacit gentlemanly understandings which normally kept medieval warfare limited and relatively bloodless. For over a decade the island had been subjected to this "savage crowd of barbarians who had swarmed to England in a body to serve as mercenaries," and who, "affected neither by bowels of compassion nor by feelings of human pity, were unceasingly occupied in pillaging the goods of the poor and murdering men in every quarter." [12] These hired soldiers were hated by all Englishmen except those who paid them and Henry had to weigh the undeniable military benefits of keeping them in his pay against the harm that their actions were likely to bring to his cause. He yielded to allied pressure (especially since the city was already in his hands) and packed the offending hirelings off to their homeland.[13]

Although the city had fallen to Henry, the castle at Malmesbury continued to hold out against the duke. King Stephen rushed more forces to relieve the fortress but found the besiegers too powerful. The two opponents met and agreed to destroy the castle, but before the sentence could be carried out the castellan, Jordan, defected from the king and handed the stronghold over to Henry. The Angevins had completed their first step in driving back the king. Henry's drive then began to pick up momentum. As a result of Malmesbury's fall Robert Beaumont, the earl of Leicester, who had been waiting to see which way the contest would go, decided to support the young duke and placed his thirty midland castles at Henry's disposal. This was the break that Henry had been waiting for, since he now had the royal territory surrounded on two of its three sides. Leaving Malmesbury, he marched north to Leicester to consolidate his new castles, and then headed for Wallingford with the cream of the Angevin army —Ranulf of Chester, Roger of Hereford, William of Gloucester, and Reginald of Cornwall. Stephen, visibly shaken by the recent defections and realizing that his power was quickly slipping from his hands, also went to Wallingford for a showdown with his nephew. While Henry's troops stood off from the town, and Stephen's besiegers steeled themselves for the expected attack, a furious debate raged inside the royal pavilion between the king and his advisers, whose spokesmen included his brother Henry of Winchester and Archbishop Theobald. The clerics finally convinced the monarch that he could not win against the combined might of Henry which was growing stronger each day and that, for the sake of England, the best course of action was to try to reach an accommodation with the Norman duke. Stephen rode out to meet Henry, and the two leaders agreed to a cease-fire and to general guidelines for a more permanent accord. They concluded that the war should end and that Stephen should remain as king for the rest of his life unmolested by Henry or his allies. For his part, Henry was recognized as Stephen's heir and apparently was to have some immediate share in the government.[14] The two adversaries further promised to rid England of the mercenaries and the unauthorized castles that dotted the country—the two military items which had plagued the island during the struggle and presented the strongest threat to future peace.

It is doubtful that Henry, or probably even Stephen, expected this agreement to be any more permanent than any other truce with which medieval campaigns usually ended. Although the king was 58 years old he was in good health and there was no reason to doubt that, with Henry's opposition removed, he had several good years ahead of him on the throne. The young duke, on the other hand, rapidly catapulted into a central position in European politics, had matured into an impatient pragmatist who could hardly have relished the prospect of a long wait for his inheritance. Too much could happen to change the situation before the king died. For one thing there was Eustace, the king's son, whom Stephen had earlier tried to associate with him on the throne, and who took his disinheritance badly. For another, the longer England and Normandy remained separated the harder it would be to reunite them. Although the agreement reached at Wallingford took this separation into account by stipulating that the barons of each party would swear allegiance to the leader of the other faction, it also legalized the breach between the two countries which, if it continued too long, would produce discontents which could only be settled when England and Normandy were, once and for all, either joined or separated. Impetuous by nature, and distrustful of agreements relating to the future, Henry left the Wallingford parley undoubtedly formulating ways he could circumvent his promises as soon as the time was ripe.

But he need not have bothered, for his dilemma was solved most unexpectedly by an unseen hand. Eustace, enraged by his father's capitulation and disregard for his own claims, began to work off his anger by plundering the eastern counties of England. In the course of this campaign he was taken ill and died. This final blow was too much for the king who, in November, sent representatives to Winchester to meet with Henry. The terms of the settlement which had been tentatively agreed on at Wallingford were officially sealed.[15] A weary England was relieved at the settlement and the return to peace which it promised. Together the king and duke made a ceremonial progress through southern England, from Winchester to London, Oxford, Canterbury, and Dover. Henry's partisans did homage to Stephen, and the king's backers recognized the Norman duke as the king's partner and successor.

But Henry dared not tarry too long in England. The French king had been taking advantage of his absence from Normandy to inspire revolts against him. Just before Easter of 1154 Henry returned to the Continent, drawn there by uprisings in Normandy and Aquitaine. While he was putting down one of these revolts at Torigny in October news arrived of Stephen's death— news which meant that Henry Plantagenet's struggle for England was over and that now his writ ran from Scotland to the Pyrenees. He did not have to hurry to England, as had his predecessors, to claim his prize for the succession had been carefully worked out and agreed upon by all concerned, and Archbishop Theobald could be relied upon to see that the agreements were honored. It was not until early December, therefore, that Henry recrossed the Channel and the week before Christmas that the archbishop placed the crown on his head.

Henry Plantagenet was now the most imposing figure in Western Europe. The aggregation of his possessions outshone any Europe had seen since the days of Charlemagne, and his rise had been among the most rapid in the Continent's history. But to what did he owe his good fortune? How large was his personal role in his own success? It is too late to be able to separate with any certainty his own contribution from that of his advisers or from that of factors beyond his control. Some points, however, are clear. From his parents he inherited a tenacity and energy which enabled him to outlast even his most stubborn rivals. Matilda had for two decades stuck to her goal of winning her inheritance in the face of setbacks and disappointments that would have melted the resolve of less hardy souls. That she passed on this fortitude to her eldest son became apparent when he joined the struggle for England and was to become even more obvious later on. The Empress had left England in 1148 shortly after the death of her commander, Robert, and the mantle fell on young Henry. Although she probably continued to pull the strings from across the Channel, Henry displayed in his campaigns of 1149 and 1153 an obstinacy and determination of his own which he could have acquired only through the genes or example of his mother. Geoffrey Plantagenet, on the other hand, lived on in his son through the continental perspective which Henry possessed and was to carry with him throughout his life, even after he became the English king. To the young duke the expeditions to England were sideshows and his acquisition of the crown seemed important to him mainly because it would bring peace to Normandy by calming the fears of the Norman baronage that they would one day have to make a choice between their possessions on one side of the Channel or the other. Henry also saw, and was to continue to see, England as a treasury by which he could support an empire whose heart lay in his continental lands. As satisfied as he was with his success in England, he must have been even more proud of the fact that Normandy and Anjou were united in the same hand—a merger that even his illustrious great-grandfather had not brought about.

To what degree did Henry's baronial partisans in England make the decisions that put him on the throne? It is unlikely that before 1149 Henry was much more than a figurehead and rallying point for the Angevin cause. Until her departure from the island in 1148 his mother retained personal command of the Angevin forces which were led by those old, grizzled barons who had fought alongside Henry I before following his daughter. Surely the teen-aged Henry, knighted only in 1149 and still to take part in his first respectable military campaign, cannot have exercised much more than a legal authority over these experienced warriors, and most likely sat quietly in the midst of their councils. But by 1149 most of the old guard among Matilda's followers were gone and had been replaced by their sons, men of Henry's own age and generation. When Robert of Gloucester died in 1147 his son William took his place. In 1149 Roger succeeded Miles in Hereford. With the death of each member of the old guard, Henry's moral and personal authority increased. By the end of 1153 young Malcolm had replaced his father David on the Scottish throne and the earldom of Chester, one of the most important for the Angevins, had passed from the old to the young Ranulf. Henry became more of a leader of this young and eager group than he could ever have been of the old timers. Yet he remained careful to heed the advice and counsel of others. It was at the behest of the young earl of Hereford that he led his army to England early in 1153 and he dismissed his mercenaries at Malmesbury shortly afterwards at the urging of his allies. Archbishop Theobald, too, played a major role in Henry's success by modifying the duke's propensity toward rashness. It was he, for example, who persuaded Henry to agree to a cease-fire when he had the king on the run.

Yet as masterful and opportunistic as Henry was, contingencies, especially timely deaths, greatly aided his cause. Prince William's drowning in the White Ship brought the inheritance of England to his side of the family; his own father's death at the critical moment gave him the basis for creating an empire; Abbot Suger's demise paved the way for his advantageous marriage and the annexation of Aquitaine; the fortuitous disappearance of Eustace removed his only serious rival in England; and Stephen's convenient death so soon after the Winchester accord avoided further contention for England and ushered Henry peacefully onto the throne.

CHAPTER III

A New Broom
(1154–1156)

THE WIDESPREAD WAR-WEARINESS OF THE ENGLISH WHICH FORMED
the backdrop of Henry Plantagenet's arrival on the throne, coupled with their willingness, if it meant more order in their lives,
to countenance a swing of the political pendulum in the direction
of autocracy, provided the new king with a blank check with
which to construct his policies. These external factors jibed well
with the personality of the young monarch who, at 21, had matured into a young man of fierce determination and a dominating
temperament and who had already learned that success in his
new role hinged upon his ability to rid the land of those centrifugal, democratic proclivities which had done in his predecessor.
Henry revealed the outline of his policy at his coronation and
then spent the first years of his reign bringing his plan to life
throughout his extensive state. Behind the multifarious military
and diplomatic activities of these first years lay his determination
to cleanse the Angevin possessions, and England in particular, of
the remnants of anarchy which for two decades had settled upon
them like a blight.

Archbishop Theobald anointed Henry and Eleanor on the
19th of December in the abbey church at Westminster, then still
the original low, dark, Romanesque structure several miles up the
Thames from London that Edward the Confessor had completed
ninety years earlier shortly before his death. It was a relatively
simple building, as yet uncluttered with the memorabilia which
during the next eight centuries would transform it into a mu-
seum. As was the custom, the newly crowned king issued a coronation charter, a sort of printed "inaugural address" in which he
made a unilateral promise to his subjects:

I am granting and giving by this charter, confirmed to God and the
Holy Church and to all my counts, barons and subjects, all the conces-

sions and grants, liberties and free customs which king Henry my grandfather gave and granted them. Likewise I outlaw and abolish for myself
and my heirs all the evil customs which he abolished and outlawed.[1]

Few of those assembled at Westminster that December morning
could have found much with which to disagree in this statement
since it was general enough to please almost everyone and it
struck a sufficiently conservative note to inspire a sense of security. Henry said what his subjects wanted to hear, namely that he
was going to bring back the good old days of his grandfather by
reviving the rights and freedoms which Englishmen had enjoyed
during the first three-and-a-half decades of the century. No refer-
ence was made to the intervening twenty years since the death of
Henry I, blotted out of history, as it were, by silence.

But while it is easy (and quite common) to judge the actions of
medieval men in terms of an innate conservatism which led them
to oppose novelty and change, such an interpretation of Henry
Plantagenet's coronation charter would be a mistake. For the new
king was using this appeal to the past as a springboard for the
introduction of some startling innovations. The return to his
grandfather's days, as will be seen, was to entail a major re-
shuffling of the baronial arrangements which had sprouted under
Stephen. At the same time, under the guise of restoration, Henry
would be able to nip in the bud any revolts that might be
abuilding against him within his own party, since a return to the
earlier status meant the destruction of illegal castles and the exile
of mercenaries, both of which had strengthened his own adherents as well as those of his erstwhile rival. The new king realized
that he could use this seemingly conservative approach as a two-
edged sword which he could wield to make him the sole authority
in the realm. He thus indicated on the first day of his reign that
he had the ability to make what was new sound old and to clothe
his personal aspirations in garments pleasing even to those who
disagreed with him.

What Henry had in mind became more apparent two weeks
later, after the Christmas vacation, when he met with his advisers
at Bermondsey, across the Thames from Westminster. There he
translated the platitudes of the coronation charter into a specific
plan of action aimed at restoring peace to the kingdom and pro-
tecting the rights of the crown.[2] From the monastery at Bermond-

sey he issued instructions for the expulsion of the mercenaries, the destruction of the offending castles, and the reinstatement of all fiefs in the kingdom to their 1135 posture. The first two items had been agreed upon two years earlier by Henry and Stephen, but as long as Stephen lived little had been done to put them into effect. During the twelve months when there had been, in effect, two kings, the decision as to which mercenaries and castles were to go had been postponed. Now that Henry ruled alone he began to act, and within three months of the Bermondsey meeting the mercenaries were either gone from the country or disarmed and following peaceful pursuits, and the razing of baronial castles was well under way. The third decree, which called for the redistribution of the land, presented a tougher problem for in many cases it was going to bite deeply into the possessions of his former allies. But this did not stop the king who was announcing, in effect, that a new day was dawning in England and that former alliances would not be allowed to stand in the way of his pacification and reorganization of the realm.

Henry II's impartiality and desire to treat fairly both former friends and foes was reflected by the men he chose at Bermondsey to help him run the kingdom. He divided the duties of the justiciar between two very capable barons: Robert, earl of Leicester who, until Henry's final campaign in 1153, had supported Stephen; and Richard of Luci, a partisan of Stephen until the king's death. In these appointments Henry's need for expert advice and professional assistance overrode the narrow divisions of the past. Although it is unlikely that any specific division of functions between the two men was made at this time, Richard during the next 24 years would concentrate on administrative and military aspects of the kingdom, while Robert, "a prudent man, learned in letters and well versed in matters of law," was to improve greatly the judicial and financial workings of the Exchequer. Within this latter body, which was to have an important history during Henry's reign, Robert rose to the presidency before his death in 1167.[3] Henry's choice of these two men was a signal that the criteria for deciding who was a friend and who a foe had changed with the coronation and that from that moment on those who worked loyally for his program of centralization were to be his friends, while those who opposed the increase of monarchical power were his enemies, regardless of former affiliations.

As Treasurer of the Exchequer the king chose Nigel, the bishop of Ely, whose uncle, Roger of Salisbury, had virtually created that institution during the reign of Henry I. Nigel was one of the prelates whom Stephen had imprisoned sixteen years earlier when he needed the church money to refill his treasury. In this appointment the king satisfied his grandfather's party by forging a link with Henry I's financial institutions while at the same time bringing into his household one of the most experienced financial administrators of the kingdom.

For the post of chancellor Henry picked a member of Archbishop Theobald's household, Thomas Becket, the archdeacon of Canterbury. The archbishop and Henry of Winchester had pushed for Thomas's selection as a means of preserving the Church's influence at the royal court.[4] Henry appointed Becket not only to please the prelates, but also because Thomas's character, as Henry saw it, fit in well with his plans to create a "cabinet" led by his own type of man: learned, aggressive, and loyal. Thomas was not, strictly speaking, a member of the feudal class. His father had been a London merchant and Thomas grew up among the burgesses of the city who were beginning to carve out their own niche in medieval society unbound by feudal oaths and responsibilities. It is probably reading too much into the situation to see in the king's choice an attempt to gain favor with the bourgeoisie, since Thomas had long since moved out of that society. Yet ideas formed in his early life remained with the new chancellor and were to color some of his later decisions.

The court which Henry constructed early in 1155 was to expand throughout his reign and gain a reputation as a literary and cultural center and the hub of active diplomatic and political interchanges with France, Germany, Scandinavia, Rome, and Sicily. Historians, lawyers, economists, and poets were in constant attendance on the monarch and all of the great figures that comprise the twelfth-century renaissance in England appeared at one time or another in the king's entourage. Among the more famous members of this early court was the new chancellor's secretary, John of Salisbury, who had returned from his studies on the Continent two years earlier to serve in Archbishop Theobald's household. John was to remain as Becket's assistant until Thomas's death and was to convert his experiences and observations of the politics of Henry's court into a renowned treatise on the corrupting influence of political power. By elevating this brilliant group of men Henry, in spite of his autocratic temperament, surrounded himself with a body of advisers more learned than himself and upon whom he thought he could depend for the success of his program.

Much has been written, but little settled, concerning Henry's own intellectual capabilities. Some of his contemporaries praised his erudition and one of his advisers, Walter Map, went so far as to attribute to him "a knowledge of all tongues spoken from the coasts of France to the river Jordan." [5] Another eyewitness described the king as a good scholar who used what spare time he had left over from fighting and hunting to pore over his books and hold discussions with the learned men of his court.[6] But in light of the more voluminous evidence of quite a different nature, such praise should probably be relegated to the realm of courtly flattery. Those who knew him best agreed, to a man, that Henry was extremely impatient and lacked the mental serenity which characterizes the serious scholar. It is likely that even as a youth Henry's pragmatism overrode the offerings of his excellent teachers and tutors. Modern judgment in general agrees with the implication of William Stubbs who builds a strong case for the brilliance of the king's court but remains significantly silent as to Henry's own aptitude.[7] It seems that Henry, although himself scarcely a deep thinker, appreciated—up to a point—what the intellectual efforts of others could do for him and tried at Bermondsey to create a brain trust which he could harness to his own ends. It was the conflict between these two sides of Henry's personality—his need to dominate and his equally strong dependence on learned counsel—that was to give the king some of his most anxious moments in the years ahead.

Having laid the groundwork at Bermondsey for the reorganization of the realm, Henry turned with his customary alacrity to the question of providing permanence to his dynasty. Although kingship in England was theoretically elective, the choice of anyone other than the ruling monarch's designee would lead to feudal entanglements which could, as in the case of Matilda, plunge the kingdom into civil war. For it was the land, with the title as adjunct, which was handed down from father to son, and nothing was more conducive to anarchy than a landless title or a titleless land. Normally it was the eldest son who inherited his father's land, and the title went with it. This general rule, however, was often modified by extenuating circumstances. As with most matters within the Anglo-Norman state, complicating factors were introduced by the existence of different customs in the two parts of the amalgam. Before his death, for example, William the Conqueror had willed Normandy (his own land) to his eldest son, and England (his land by conquest) to his second son. The result had been the threat of an almost permanent separation between the two lands. Henry I only prevented the split by military action when he took Normandy from his brother and tried to prevent a recurrence by having the Anglo-Norman barons swear to recognize his daughter as his successor. Stephen had tried the same thing with his son Eustace but the English lords, led by Archbishop Theobald, saw that it would result in the election of the king's undesirable son, and refused to take the oath.[8]

Henry, therefore, was determined that the question of succession be settled at the outset of his reign. Eleanor had more than fulfilled her part of the marriage bargain by producing two sons during the first three years of their marriage. The first boy, William, had been born on the Continent in August, 1153, while his father was in England storming the castle of Malmesbury and closing the ring around Stephen. In February, 1155, while the new king was campaigning to recover lands in eastern England, a second son, Henry, was born. Henry Plantagenet wasted no time in making sure that the English lords, who had sworn allegiance to himself only three months earlier, now took an oath to his sons. On the 10th of April, 1155, he called them together at Wallingford where they agreed to recognize the two-year-old William as Henry's heir and, in the event of William's death before he became of age, to consider the infant Henry as next in line.[9] By designating his oldest son as heir to England Henry reversed his great-grandfather's policy and showed that he considered England his by hereditary right. William was indeed to die before coming of age[10] and the oath which the barons took on this occasion to Henry was to cause unforeseen difficulties between the king and his yet unborn sons. But all of this was still in the distant future and by April, 1155, the king had every reason to be happy with the direction in which his plans were going.

In the meantime steps had been taken for the recovery of the crown lands. Several of Henry's former allies balked at the execu-

tion of the Bermondsey decrees by refusing to part with their possessions. The most stubborn resistance came, as was to be expected, from the frontier barons of the Welsh marches. Since the
days of the Conqueror these western English earls of the buffer
shires had been granted a freer hand in ruling their honors than
had the other English lords, mainly because of the constant threat
of the warlike Welsh. Conditions on the western fringes of the
kingdom were analogous to those which prevailed in the American West during the nineteenth century where an army tried,
often with little success, to maintain peace amidst a racially
different society. Due to their greater distance from the seat of
government the English marcher barons had developed the habit
of acting with more independence than those closer to the eastern
haunts of the king, with the result that, as in America, legal, political, military, and judicial practices grew up with their own
local flavor little influenced by the rest of the country. The western barons were extremely jealous of their freedom and it could
not have come as a complete surprise to Henry when one of them,
his fellow knight and former comrade-in-arms, Roger of Hereford, defied his order and refused to give up his castles in
Gloucester and Hereford. Although Roger, at the urging of Gilbert Foliot, quickly relented and was allowed to keep his title of
earl, Henry protected himself against a recurrence of the revolt
by retiring the title when Roger died later that year. More persistent was the revolt of another marcher lord, Hugh Mortemer, whose castles to the north of Hereford at Wigmore, Cleo-
bury, and Bridgnorth sat astride the gateway into England from
Wales. It required a prolonged siege which lasted well into July of
1155 to force Hugh to part with his border posts. By seizing these
fortifications Henry showed that he meant what he said while, at
the same time, he assumed direct responsibility for the continuing
Anglo-Norman campaign to subdue these unruly western neighbors.

Henry Plantagenet, as much as any and probably more than
most medieval lords, was addicted to hunting and it was to this
pastime that he turned for relaxation after the strenuous activity
of his first seven months on the throne. In the company of his
strong adventuresome comrades, including his new chancellor,
Becket, the king whiled away the late summer months of 1155
chasing fox and red deer in the New Forest and the other large

tracts of southern England which had been set aside for the king's
pleasure. With a good horse beneath him and probably a falcon
on his arm the young king, always at home in the outdoors, must
have felt a great sense of well-being while hunting in the dark,
beautiful woods of his new kingdom. A royal hunt in Anglo-
Norman times was a well-organized affair and not the haphazard,
wanton slaughter it is often pictured as being. At the royal hunting lodge within the forest a large retinue of the king's officials,
including the Chief Hunter, knight-huntsmen, and the hunt
servants, would spend the night before the hunt making preparations. Weather forecasts and the location of the herds would be
obtained from the Keeper of the Walk and decisions made as to
the areas to be used and clothing to be worn. Setting out from the
lodge early in the morning, the party of sportsmen, escorted by a
retinue of foresters, would ride quietly through the forest until it
arrived at the hunting ground where the herds of deer were
known to graze. Here the hunters would dismount and each
would take up his post, at a spot suggested by the Chief Hunter,
behind a sheltering clump of bushes or small trees which bor-
dered on an open field. At a signal from the Chief Hunter a company of beaters would approach the grazing herd and, by clap-
ping their hands and shouting, chase them out into the field past
the waiting sportsmen who, with bows and arrows, would have an
open shot at their quarry. Animals that were bagged in this way
were taken immediately by a forester to the lodge where they
were made ready for the coming feast, while the hunting party
moved on to another hunting ground where the ritual was repeated.[11]

Many hours in the saddle and at the hunting lodge in close
proximity to many of the leading men of the realm gave Henry a
chance to discuss informally the conditions of the kingdom and
the steps that might be taken to improve it. One item that came
up during this summer of 1155, and which the king must have
spent many hours mulling over and debating with his hunting
companions, was the question of Ireland. The incumbent pope,
Adrian IV, who had been elected only a fortnight before Henry's
coronation, was an Englishman (the only one ever to occupy the
chair of St. Peter) and sensitive to affairs of his native land. During the summer he issued a bull,[12] based on the honored Donation
of Constantine,[13] in which he confirmed the English king's legal

authority over Ireland and proclaimed his right to conquer it. To the impatient Henry the opportunity was too good to let slip by and in September at a full meeting of his household in Winchester he proposed an expedition to the island. Matilda was present at the meeting and, with wisdom born of experience, she opposed the plan, sensing that there were as yet too many loose ends within the Anglo-Norman state requiring the king's attention before he could take on a new military venture outside it. Her opposition was the deciding factor in Henry's decision to postpone the project.

Matilda's farsightedness became apparent at Christmastime when news arrived at the royal court, still at Winchester, that the king's brother Geoffrey had run out of patience on the Continent waiting for Henry to hand over Maine and Anjou which, by the terms of their father's will, should have become his when his brother succeeded in England. Henry had no intention of letting slip from his grasp these two counties which formed the strategic bridge between his northern and southern Continental possessions and told Geoffrey that the will was invalid since he had been pressured into agreeing to it over the putrescent body of his father.[14] But the younger brother was not to be denied and took the only legal means left to him—he appealed to the overlord of the counties, King Louis VII, to help him gain what was rightfully his. The French king, playing the balance-of-power game and only too eager to discomfit the powerful Henry, seconded Geoffrey's claim and encouraged his resistance.

This was the first serious challenge to Henry from the Continent since he became king and the nature of his response shows that he lacked none of the skill in the "sugar plum and whip" tactics of which his grandfather and great-grandfather had been masters. His first step was to collect enough money to provide him with the option of either buying off his brother or, failing that, hiring an army to subdue him. The king's preparations for his first overseas campaign are instructive in that he did not insist that his new English subjects cross the Channel to fight an Angevin war, although he had every right in feudal law to do so. Three sources of military manpower were theoretically available to Henry to fight his wars and defend his possessions: the English militia, the feudal knights, and mercenaries. The first of these, the direct successor of the Anglo-Saxon fyrd, was an untrained mob of citizens called out to defend the kingdom in times of danger. Although it had been used during the previous reign it was not at all suited for overseas campaigning and had always been limited to skirmishes against invaders or home-grown rebels. Henry obviously could not use the fyrd against his brother. The traditional warriors used by English kings away from home were from the second group, the knights of the feudal army who owed their lords two months' service each year during times of war. But for this campaign Henry decided against using his English knights and excused them from service. The job could be done, he felt, with his feudal troops from Normandy supplemented by the third military force, hired soldiers.

But the treasury, still bearing scars from the years of Stephen's mismanagement, was dangerously low. The recorded revenue that Henry received from the kingdom that year amounted to barely one third of the £66,000 that Henry I had been enjoying annually towards the end of his reign.[15] So to pay for the expedition Henry Plantagenet laid an extraordinary levy on the kingdom. He required each of the vassals of his clerical tenants-in-chief who were excused from the campaign to pay a fee based on the amount of military service they owed. He then used the money to hire mercenaries. Here again Henry relied on a technique which his grandfather had used [16] and which he had seen employed on occasion by his uncle Robert several years before. When this measure brought the king only about £500 he supplemented it by demanding "gifts" from the barons and burgesses, bringing the total to about £2700. The tax was bitterly opposed by Archbishop Theobald. Of Chancellor Thomas's reaction we have no indication, but he probably agreed with it and might even have suggested it.[17] Had Becket joined the archbishop in denouncing the tax the chroniclers would certainly have included the fact in the list of his grievances against the king which they were later to record in minute detail.

In January, 1156, Henry took his money with him to Normandy, glad no doubt to be back on the Continent, at the center of his possessions. His reaction to this first serious rebellion was typical of the approach he was to take to similar disturbances later in his reign. To Henry war was a last resort, to be applied only after diplomacy had failed. "He always dreaded the fierce arbitrament of war, and with supreme wisdom he tried every method before resorting to arms." [18] This attitude set him apart from many of his less sophisticated contemporaries whose instinctive reaction to a challenge was to reach for hauberk and sword. Soon after his arrival in Normandy the king hastened to the Vexin, that sometimes neutral ground between Normandy and France, to talk with the French king. Unable to convince Louis of the rightness of his cause, even by waving before the Capetian a papal dispensation from his oath, Henry returned to Rouen where he conferred with the Flemish Count Thierry to whom he was related by marriage. The two rulers made a deal in which Thierry promised to supply soldiers to the English king for use in England, Normandy, or Anjou in return for an annual stipend which Henry was to pay him. This was a long-standing arrangement between the English rulers and the Flemish counts, called a money-fief, which represented a half-way position between feudal and mercenary military service. The tradition of this financial alliance went back to Henry I, and possibly farther, and had been maintained by Matilda during her war with Stephen.[19]

Thus armed with soldiers and money, the king turned next to deal directly with his brother. He summoned him to Rouen and offered him a cash settlement for the disputed counties. Geoffrey scornfully refused the bribe and returned to Anjou where he placed on alert his three castles which Henry had recently returned to him. Two of these strongholds were in Touraine, the county directly east of Anjou, which the Angevins had annexed a century before and which was the geographical kingpin of the Angevin empire, situated between the Ile de France and the duchies on the Atlantic coast. From its capital, Tours, roads radiated in all directions granting access from France into Normandy, Anjou, Poitou, and Aquitaine.[20] As long as the Angevins held Touraine they could cut the French king off from his western fiefs. Henry sent his mercenaries and Norman knights down the eastern border of Anjou and laid siege to his brother's castles at Chinon in Touraine and Mirabeau in Poitou, thereby effectively cutting Geoffrey off from French assistance. The two castles surrendered in May and Geoffrey was forced to hand over the third, at Loudun. Not only had he failed to gain his inheritance, but he lost what he already held. Defeated, Geoffrey accepted his brother's earlier offer of an annuity which amounted to £1000 sterling and £2000 in Angevin money.[21]

Geoffrey's rage at the loss of Maine and Anjou was partially offset several months later when the Breton town of Nantes fell into his hands. Brittany, on the Atlantic coast, was a rich and populous duchy due to the happy location of the city of Nantes at the spot where the river Loire empties into the ocean. Although the Normans had for several generations claimed authority over the duchy, it had remained independent under the strong guidance of its dukes. But Duke Conan III's death in 1148 had ushered in a period of anarchy as his son, grandson, and viscount fought with each other for control. Shortly after Geoffrey submitted to his brother in Touraine, the citizens of Nantes drove Hoel, Conan's disavowed son, from the city and, according to some accounts, asked Geoffrey to rule them.[22] Since Henry was in the vicinity, however, the possibility of his connivance in the affair cannot be discounted. Geoffrey accepted the offer and became the count of Nantes and, in effect, duke of southern Brittany.

Henry II's adroitness during the summer of 1156 had permitted him to retain Maine and Anjou, compensate his dispossessed brother, and bring Brittany closer to his empire. Only one loose end remained to be tied before he could feel confident of his possessions: the duchy of Aquitaine. When he had visited the "Poitevin Empire" shortly after his marriage Henry had been given a cool reception by many of the turbulent southern barons who followed the example of their suzerain, Louis, in refusing to acknowledge Henry's marriage and his claim to their loyalty. Although Louis had since given up his claim to direct possession of the duchy, the barons still refused to recognize Henry as more than the husband of the duchess. Once again the French monarch's immense prestige challenged the English king. Henry saw that the only way he could incorporate this land rich in revenue, soldiers, and wine into his empire was to swear allegiance for it to Louis who was still its overlord. Louis, deeming it better to have all of Aquitaine in the hands of one vassal, even his rival, and perhaps secretly hoping that the barons would become as big a thorn in Henry's side as they had been in his, accepted the Angevin's homage for the duchy. In October, after settling with his brother, Henry took Eleanor and two of his children—Henry, now the oldest since William's death earlier that year,[23] and the four-month-old Matilda—south to receive the homage of the Aquitainians.

In Aquitaine, as elsewhere in the feudal Europe of the twelfth century, preservation of social order depended upon the strength of the personal bonds which were born of the act of fealty and homage. But also in Aquitaine, as elsewhere, local conditions determined the degree to which these bonds were effective. Whereas in Normandy the barons were tied closely to the duke by clearly delineated obligations, the chief barons of Aquitaine enjoyed more independence because of the imprecision of their obligations and the larger geographical area of the duchy. Each of the nine counties that made up the fief presented a different face to the new ruler, who had acquired a fief rich in the tradition of baronial discontent. The procession of barons which trooped north to Poitiers in the autumn of 1156 to place their hands between Henry's was a potpourri of medieval characters. From Poitou, the capital of the duchy since the tenth century and the important commercial and transportation bridge between the northern and southern civilizations of France, came the powerful viscounts of Thouars and Châtellerault, along with the formidable Lusignan family, as much to size up their new duke as to be looked over by him. From farther south, in Angoumois, the geographical link between Poitou and Bordeaux and the hothouse of rebellion against ducal authority, traveled the representatives of the house of Taillefer. From the city of Saintes, isolated from its county on the ocean west of Angoumois, came the count of Saintonge whose control was limited to his city and few neighboring castles. The remainder of the county was in the hands of an independent baron, Geoffrey, the lord of Rancogne, ensconced in his fortress of Taillebourg north of the comital city. From east of Poitou, out of the rich and strategic county of Berry, journeyed the strong lords of Issoudun, Deols, and Châteauroux—princes to whom the duke's authority was little more than a distant shadow. The count and viscount from Marche and Auvergne, if they came at all, did so as if to a pro forma ritual whose restraining influence on their authority was negligible. It must have been with some sense of relief that Henry saw the approach of the lords of the Limousin and of Gascony, for he knew that they, of all the Aquitainian barons, took the ties of vassalage most seriously.

These counties of southern France were not entirely unknown to Henry. A century earlier his ancestors Fulk Nerra and Geoffrey Martel, at the height of their imperial splurge, had gained a foothold in many of these fiefs. Angevin influence had waned in the area after 1060 and Henry was now restoring it to what was, in his mind, its rightful place.

Over the semi-sacred ceremony of homage hung the shadow of the absentees—that group of lords both within Aquitaine and on its fringes who continued to recognize only the French king. Among these was Raymond, the count of Toulouse, whose influence stretched from the eastern edge of Gascony to the borders of the Holy Roman Empire. As Henry sat in Poitiers receiving the submission of the Aquitainian barons he was already relishing the prospect of pushing his empire to the Mediterranean by reviving an ancient Aquitainian claim to Toulouse. But much remained to be done before such a grandiose scheme could be seriously entertained. Although the program of returning the English castles to the crown was well under way there were still areas on the island which required the king's presence and in April, 1157, he recrossed the Channel to attend to these problems.

CHAPTER IV

On the Fringes of the Realm:
Wales and Toulouse (1157–1159)

THREE REGIONS OF BRITAIN WERE STILL GIVING HENRY II TROUBLE in 1157, and soon after his arrival in England early in the year he set about to stabilize them. In the east, where Stephen had enjoyed his greatest strength, Hugh Bigod and Stephen's son, William of Mortain, clung stubbornly to their garrisons. Within weeks of his landing the king was in Essex where he forced Hugh to relinquish his castles, including the powerful fortress at Framlingham, and persuaded William to surrender "Pevensey and Norwich and everything he held of the crown as well as his own castles in Normandy and England." [1] Henry and Stephen had agreed at Winchester four years earlier that William would be allowed to retain those possessions which had belonged to Stephen before he became king and Henry now returned these lands, but kept for himself the most strategic castles. These he garrisoned with hired troops as insurance against attempts of the barons to reoccupy them. [2]

The second area of concern was the north, which was next to experience the unifying hand of the king. During his climb to the throne Henry had won the Scots over to his side by promising them that they could keep the northern marches of England which they had taken from the distracted Stephen. Now that he was king, however, he saw things in a different light and treated the new Scots ruler, Malcolm, just as he had treated the English barons, by demanding the return of the counties of Northumberland, Westmorland, and Cumberland. Malcolm came to Chester where he met Henry and turned over to him the frontier lands with its important castles at Bamborough, Carlisle, and Newcastle-on-Tyne. [3] But the English king, not wishing to create an enemy in the north, gave Malcolm the earldom of Huntingdon for which the Scots king swore allegiance. Throughout his campaign to repossess his grandfather's lands Henry combined, with great finesse, the reoccupation of lost territory with the creation of powerful vassals who could serve his purpose, and often was able to turn real or potential enemies into allies.

Henry II then turned his attention to the west. In July he summoned his council to Northampton to discuss the details of a military campaign against these unsettled western neighbors. This council marked the opening of a two-year period during which Henry was to move like a whirlwind, mating military campaigns with diplomatic pressure to forge a strong feudal band around the perimeter of his realm. The first step was in Wales. Like the Scots, the Welsh had taken advantage of England's disturbed conditions under Stephen to recover many parts of their country which the Normans had taken from them earlier. Henry's decision at Northampton to move against the Welsh was motivated not only by his desire to reduce this military threat to the English marcher shires, but equally by his wish to keep his own border vassals from becoming too powerful. As long as the Welsh continued to attack from the west the king had no choice but to delegate more power and responsibility to his marcher barons than was healthy for his policy of strengthening the central government. Fresh in his mind were the recent revolts of the earl of Hereford and Hugh Mortemer which would probably never have taken place had these barons not been allowed so much independence.

Although the mountainous physiognomy of Wales and the mobility of its people had frustrated the attempts of Henry's predecessors to reduce the Welsh princes to vassalage, one factor favored the English kings. Wales, like Aquitaine, was not a political monolith and the Welsh princes fought as much against each other as they did against the English. For almost a century the northern Welsh principality of Gwynned had been expanding southward until by Henry's time its king, Owen the Great, ruled the upper two thirds of the country, as far south as Cardigan. But the price Owen had had to pay for his success was a debilitating conflict with the other Welsh rulers: Rhys, the prince of South Wales (Dehuebarth); Madog, the ruler of the central area of Powys; and his own brother Cadwaldr, whom he had expelled from Wales in 1152. Henry encouraged these petty rivalries and used them to his own advantage. Cadwaldr's desire for revenge against his brother was part of the reason for Henry's decision to undertake the campaign in 1157.

The expedition was planned as a full invasion into the north of the country to put an end to Welsh anarchy and harassment of the border districts.[4] A month before the Northampton meeting a summons had gone out calling to arms one third of the English knights for the Welsh campaign. The service of the remaining two thirds was commuted to a cash payment for the support of those who did serve and to enable Henry to hire mercenaries whose brand of warfare was better suited to Welsh conditions than that of the feudal knight. The English strategy called for a combined land and sea offensive against Owen in the north. While the ground forces were moving along the northern shore of the country, a fleet from Pembroke in the south was to sail up the west coast bringing supplies and intercepting any aid that might come from Ireland for the Welsh. His plan to hug the coastline and to supply his army by sea shows that Henry appreciated that the absence of usable roads in the country would have made it foolhardy for an invading army to rely heavily on overland logistical support. The army assembled in July at Chester, the jumping-off point for the invasion of Gwynned. Alongside the English knights were the lighter, more mobile Welsh mercenary archers who were provided by the enemies of Owen. In this mixed composition of the army is seen a recognition by Henry that the traditional feudal warfare to which he was accustomed in England and on the Continent would be of little value in Wales. Welsh strategy invariably was that of guerrilla warfare—to fade in the face of an invading army into the mountain retreats and wait until hunger or the dependably poor weather of the country forced the enemy to retreat.

The first English objective was the stronghold of Rhuddlan on the northern shore, in the estuary of the Clwyde River. The only route to Rhuddlan ran along the narrow coastal plain which rimmed northern Wales. Owen concentrated his forces at Basingwerk, a castle along Henry's route of march, fifteen miles to the west of Chester. Suspecting that the English king might try to bypass this roadblock, the Welsh prince placed some of his troops in ambush along the only possible bypass road, just south of Basingwerk. Henry marched the main body of his army against Basingwerk while he personally led a contingent south of the castle and fell into the trap. Although English casualties in the ensuing battle were high, the Welsh were routed from the forest and Owen retreated to the mountains west of Rhuddlan. The English army pursued him and took Rhuddlan without a fight. Despite his losses Henry had achieved a tactical victory. But the expedition moved no farther. The fleet, which was supposed to resupply the English at Rhuddlan, had stopped off at the island of Anglesey where it was attacked by the irate islanders and lost most of its soldiers and supplies. Although this disaster forced Henry's military machine to grind to a halt, the king's diplomacy turned what could have been defeat into victory. Owen, for unknown reasons, responded favorably to Henry's call for an end to hostilities and did homage to the English monarch for his principality. After leaving garrisons at Rhuddlan and Basingwerk, Henry returned to England with at least part of the Welsh problem seemingly solved. There remained only Rhys, in the south, to contend with, and the English king decided to deal with him at a later date.

By August Henry was back in Chester, from where he launched a one-year royal progress which brought him into every corner of his kingdom. Even a cursory examination of his movements during the next twelve months is sufficient to justify his reputation as a nervous workhorse who felt compelled to take a personal role in all the affairs of his realm. After leaving Chester he moved south through Warwickshire to Malmesbury, Windsor, Woodstock, and Oxford. By December he was back in the north with his court at Stamford and Lincoln where he spent Christmas. The new year began with the king in the far northern reaches of the country inspecting the garrisons of the castles which he had recently taken from the Scots. The return trip southward, which began in mid-January, brought the royal party down the center of the island through Yorkshire, where it paused at the fortresses of Doncaster, Peak, and York; then into Nottinghamshire and the residences at Blythe and Nottingham; and finally into Oxfordshire, Hampshire, and Wiltshire. By Easter (April 20) Henry was back in the west at Worcester, from where he began a four-month tour through Shropshire, Gloucestershire, Somerset, Carlisle again, Winchester, and, finally, in August, to Southampton where he embarked for Normandy.[5]

The journeys were characterized by continuous and varied activity as the king garrisoned the reverted castles in the north and west, heard pleas in his court, issued charters, inspected the sheriffs and judges, took stock of the financial conditions of the counties, hunted, fought, and wenched. He was accompanied, as always, by his court, which included Chancellor Thomas, the justiciars Robert and Richard, the military constable of England, Richard Humet, chaplains, chamberlains, dapifers, and the crowd of minor officials needed to run a court on the move. Eleanor, pregnant again, missed the first part of the tour but after her fourth child, Richard, was born at Oxford in September[6] (1157) she joined her husband and the royal pair celebrated Easter at Worcester by wearing the crown. Only one significant military event marked the year. In July, 1158, Rhys struck against Gloucester, and Henry, alert to any opportunity to strengthen his borders, counterattacked and, in a brief battle, defeated the Welsh prince and forced him to take an oath of allegiance to him.

Even though not all the king's movements during the year are recorded, the distances he traveled on trips known from royal charters and other evidence add up, by even the most conservative estimate, to about 3500 miles. The addition of numerous side trips and hunting expeditions of which we have no details, would multiply this figure many times over. This was an impressive amount of travel in the England of the Middle Ages, where road conditions were very poor and the weather harsher than it is today. Henry was a physical fitness addict who was able to maintain this pace by keeping himself in top physical condition. His prodigious energy was the subject of conversation throughout the kingdom and is discussed by a contemporary who knew him well:

He fights the obesity which threatens by sobriety and exercise and, thanks to walking and horsemanship, he preserves his youthful vigor and tires out his strongest companions. From morning to night he is engaged unceasingly on affairs of state. He never sits down except when he mounts his horse or takes a meal and he frequently rides in one day a journey four or fives times the length of a normal day's ride. It is very difficult to find out where he is or what he will do during the day for he frequently changes his plans. The fidelity of his followers is subjected to severe tests for they are frequently forced to wander through unknown forests for three or four miles after nightfall before they find lodging in sordid hovels. Nevertheless, in this way, while other kings are resting in their palaces, he is able to take his enemies by surprise and off their guard and he inspects everything, taking particular care to judge those whom he had made judges of others.[7]

From this description, and many others like it, we get an insight into Henry's character and his gimmicks of leadership. The key to his personality was a metabolism that allowed him to pursue his objective with untiring energy, undeterred by the effect of his actions on those around him. The chronicler is probably being polite, in typical medieval fashion, when he writes that the loyalty of the king's followers was severely tested. We can only imagine the grumbling and complaining among his followers when, after a grueling day's ride, they were roused unexpectedly in the cold dark hours of the early morning and ordered to pack up camp and start on another day which would see them in the saddle for sixteen hours. There is no way of knowing with certainty whether Henry's practice of changing plans without notice was a studied one or the natural expression of an impatient personality. The memoirs of many later military writers set it down as virtuous to keep their subordinates in the dark about future plans, and of Henry's success with this technique there can be little doubt since it created around him a band of followers who, if not always in positive agreement with his decisions, found the rewards of cooperating sufficient to keep them from open opposition. Several centuries later Machiavelli was to put into words what Henry II practiced instinctively, namely that fear creates firmer bonds of loyalty than does love. This principle worked well for Henry Plantagenet during the early years of his reign, but it required his ubiquitous presence to insure its continuation. Only twice during his life was he to depart from this method of dealing with people and allow personal considerations to overrule the impersonal; the result was the two most conspicuous failures of his reign.

Henry's trip to the Continent in August, 1158, which was to last over four years, began as a continuation of the border-strengthening campaign that he had initiated in England. Two of Normandy's borders spelled trouble for Henry and he was anxious to pacify them. Since in both areas he could come into conflict with the French king, Henry went immediately to meet with Louis. The first important matter they discussed was the question of the Vexin, that eastern portion of Normandy which Henry's father had turned over to Louis in 1151. In Louis's eyes the Vexin was a buffer zone between the two kings' domains which shielded him, as long as he controlled it, against a surprise attack on his kingdom from the west. Henry, on the other hand, saw it as a dagger pointing at the heart of his duchy and giving Louis a decided advantage should be decide to try to strip him of his possessions. Earlier that year Henry had set in motion a plan whereby he hoped to gain control of the county not by military force but by diplomacy. In the spring he had sent an embassy to Paris, headed by his chancellor, Becket, to negotiate a marriage between his son Henry and Louis's daughter Margaret. The French king, persuaded by the charismatic Thomas that the Vexin was a small price to pay to see his daughter on the English throne, agreed to the plan and entrusted the county with its three powerful castles at Gisors, Neaufle, and Neufchâtel, to the Knights Templars. They were to hand over the Vexin to Henry when the prince and princess were wed. In September Henry came to discuss the details of the arrangement and to take Margaret, as was the custom, back with him to Normandy to be brought up in his household. After the meeting Henry went to Paris, collected his future daughter-in-law, and entrusted her to his Norman seneschal, Robert of Newburgh.

The second matter discussed by the two kings concerned the duchy of Brittany which had been seized by Conan IV the previous month upon the death of Henry's brother, Geoffrey. The English king was preparing to lead an expedition against Conan but first wanted Louis's assurance, as suzerain of the disputed area, that he would remain out of the fray. Once again the French king, cut off physically from his fief by Henry's possessions, had little choice but to accede to the Angevin's request. The meeting ended on a friendly note and it appeared that an era of cooperation was about to open between England and France. As soon as he arrived in Normandy Henry instructed his barons to assemble at Avranches at Michaelmas (September 29) for the campaign against Conan. The army gathered as ordered, but before it could set out for Brittany Conan came to Avranches and submitted to the English king. Henry accepted Conan's oath of fealty and made him duke of Brittany.[8]

Never one to sit still for long, the migratory monarch then set out on an inspection tour of the religious houses and castles of Normandy and his northern possessions. His first stop was the nearby Abbey of Mont St. Michel perched atop a rock island off the coast near the Norman-Breton border. Its Norman abbot, Robert, who was one of the chief chroniclers of the twelfth century, had invited the king and his barons to visit the abbey for the celebration of their patron saint's feast day and nothing was spared to make the visit a success. The king was lodged in the abbot's newly constructed chamber and a special mass of thanksgiving was celebrated in Henry's presence. After the service the royal retinue retired to the refectory where, the abbot tells us, he had a hard time persuading the king and his followers to eat.[9] This is not surprising. Medieval meals among the secular nobility were rather wild affairs, where food was washed down with generous quantities of mead and wine and often accompanied by loud and crude horseplay. Gerald of Wales, for instance, who was Henry's chaplain, wrote of the excellence of the "sixteen costly dishes" offered him by the lord of Canterbury on one of his visits there. Henry's own table had gained a notoriety of sorts for the quantity, if not the quality, of its fare. So disagreeable were the food and drink that the crowds of scholars and poets who were in constant attendance there dreaded the ordeal. The wine was so sour and muddy that "one had to close his eyes, clench his teeth, wry-mouthed and shuddering, and filter the stuff rather than drink it." Meat and fish, often long past its prime, was served ill prepared, prompting one diner to note that "we who sit at meat need fill our bellies with carrion and become graves for sundry corpses." [10]

By contrast monastic repasts, while lacking some of the austerity prescribed for them by Saint Benedict, were relatively subdued affairs at which the monks ate in silence. Hand signals were used to have the food passed. The thumb and middle finger, curved to form an O, for example, brought the water (eau) in French refectories. The food was adequate but plain, and although the rules were relaxed during royal visits one can imagine with what discomfort and forced pleasantries these tough warriors partook of the abbot's generosity. But the abbot and monks were well rewarded for their trouble. Before he left the king granted them the rights to the revenues from the nearby churches in Pontorson.

Leaving the abbey behind, the royal party traveled south to Nantes, where Henry inspected his new fief. It then headed for Henry's birthplace at Le Mans, stopping on the way to besiege the castle of Thouars, which fell in three days. The viscount, who had raised the flag of rebellion against Henry, was banished, the walls of his castle were torn down, and the keep garrisoned with the king's soldiers.[11] At Le Mans Henry met with his new ally, Louis, who was on a pilgrimage to Mont St. Michel. Together the monarchs traveled back to the abbey and from there to Avranches, Bayeux, Caen, and finally to Rouen where the French king looked in on his infant daughter. Among the ideas traded by the new allies was a plan that had been germinating in the back of Henry's mind since his earlier visit to Aquitaine: he proposed to send an expedition south into Toulouse to add the large southeastern fief to his realm by forcing the submission of its count, Raymond, as he had forced Malcolm, Owen, Rhys, and Conan. The addition of Toulouse would round out his borders and give him access to the Mediterranean. A feudal excuse with which to coat the attack on Raymond with a veneer of legality was ready to hand. Two generations earlier, when Eleanor's grandfather ruled Aquitaine from Poitiers, Toulouse was part of his duchy. But the Toulousian count had broken the feudal bond over an unpaid debt and the county had gone its own way ever since. Louis himself, while still married to Eleanor, had briefly entertained the idea of a military campaign against the southern count but had abandoned the idea in favor of diplomacy. Henry now saw an opportunity to extend his realm to the Mediterranean by reviving the Poitevin claim, but realized that Louis's neutrality was important to the scheme. The English king had every reason to believe, in view of the good relations that presently existed between him and Louis, that the French king would promise his support and close his eyes to the seizure. But such was not the case. Raymond of Toulouse was Louis's brother-in-law, having married the king's widowed sister five years before. During this autumnal circuit the French monarch informed Henry that he was not about to throw away the fruits of this diplomacy to strengthen Henry's hand.

Louis's refusal to cooperate, however, did not deter Henry from going ahead with the campaign. At the Christmas court in Cherbourg he and his advisers made detailed plans for the expedition and during the first six months of 1159 the energies of Henry's

English and Continental courts were devoted to seeing that all was in readiness for the march to the south. Henry decided, for a number of reasons, to build his army mainly of mercenaries. For one thing, Toulouse was over 500 miles from London and the time that would be used in mustering the English feudal army, transporting it to the Continent, and marching to and from Toulouse would alone eat up most of the sixty days of service owed him by his knights. Henry felt that it would be more efficient and create fewer problems if he once again excused most of his English knights and collected a scutage instead.

Another reason for the king's decision is suggested by a chronicler who remarks that Henry, "considering the length and hardships of the campaign, did not want to inconvenience either the feudal troops which his barons owed him, or the multitude of townsmen or rustics." [12] A generation had passed since an English king had called upon the English feudal array to cross the water to fight on the mainland; indeed, by the middle of the twelfth century most English knights had completely fallen out of the habit of serving their lords overseas. The absence of Continental campaigns during Stephen's time, coupled with the stability which Henry had provided for England, had diluted much of the martial spirit of the island's knights who, for the most part, were not interested in leaving their homes and fields to fight on far-flung borders. This was reflected in the difficulties that many lords were experiencing in making their vassals answer a summons to war. Typical was the complaint of the abbot of Evesham who lamented the half-hearted service which his knights performed for the king.[13] And since Henry was in the process of strengthening his own court at the expense of the barons' feudal courts, the barons were finding it difficult to punish their knights who did not show up for military service. The solution that was becoming increasingly acceptable at all levels was to permit the undertenants to buy off their military commitment by paying a scutage. This arrangement satisfied the knights, who could then remain at home; the barons, who avoided lengthy and costly litigation in their courts; and, probably most of all, the king who was pleased to see the baronial courts lose some of their business and, with it, some of their power.

There was also a purely military reason why Henry preferred mercenaries against Toulouse. The campaign was going to re-

quire many sieges in which the expertise of hired military special-
ists counted for more than that of the heavily armored feudal
cavalry. Knights were trained, much like their successors in late
nineteenth-century France, in the school of *élan* which taught
that personal bravery and the rightness of one's cause would overcome any obstacle on the field of battle. But this military theory
was of dubious value in siege warfare which required patient,
tedious cooperation between several arms of military technicians;
moreover, the assault on and breaking down of city walls often
succeeded only by treachery and deceit against the defenders.
Group effort and the use of dishonorable tricks were the stock in
trade of mercenaries, not of feudal knights. Although hired soldiers were looked upon with scorn in England, mercenary warfare
was a way of life on the Continent, and the king was prepared to
buy as many soldiers as he needed to capture Toulouse.

During the spring of 1159 diplomatic preparation kept pace
with military planning as Henry's agents fanned out into all corners of the empire gathering allies and making deals against the
count of Toulouse. In order to outflank the county, Henry came
to an agreement with Raymond Berengar, the count of Barcelona
and regent of Aragon, who was a sworn enemy of his namesake to
the north. The count promised soldiers for the assault on Toulouse in return for the betrothal of his daughter to Henry's son,
Richard, who was then just over one year old. Having provided
for the encirclement of Toulouse to the south, the English king
tried once more to talk Louis into changing his mind and remaining out of the fray. But when in March the French king declined,
Henry sent out a notice to his chief tenants both in England and
on the Continent ordering them to appear at Poitiers in June
accompanied not by their vassals but by mercenaries hired for the
occasion with the money collected from scutage. Unlike the scutage of three years before, however, this one was collected from
the lay barons as well as the churchmen and probably represented
an extension of the levy to a wider spectrum of the feudality. So
great were the sums of money that flowed into the Treasury
(close to £11,000) that eyewitnesses were prompted to comment
that "it could support the whole immense army in a siege of Toulouse until November." [14]

The army that was assembled at Poitiers by the 24th of June
was immense indeed and provides one of the few examples be-

tween Hastings and the Hundred Years' War of a concentrated medieval military force. The king's tenants-in-chief and mercenaries converged on the Poitevin capital from England, Normandy, Maine, Anjou, Aquitaine, Gascony, Brittany, and Barcelona. Malcolm, the Scots king, was there with a force that had required 45 ships to transport from his realm, and Becket commanded a contingent which alone numbered 700 men. Nothing was lacking in the way of supplies and equipment. The stockpiles of arrows, bows, swords, lances, axes, and wood, leather, and metal for building siege equipment were so great as to render the chroniclers speechless.

This vast military machine moved out of Poitiers on the 24th and headed toward Toulouse 250 miles away. It passed through the Limousin and into Guienne where it regrouped at Agen, on the banks of the Garonne, before plunging into Raymond's territory. After crossing the Garonne, Henry's army seized the castle of Cahors and then marched on to Toulouse where it arrived on July 6. The city was strongly defended and the attacking forces were required to prepare for a full-scale siege of the capital. Machines were built to be used against the formidable city walls by going under, over, and through them. Miners and sappers set to work digging tunnels under the strongest points of the walls; their intention was to set fire to the wooden tunnel supports in hopes that the collapsing tunnel would bring down the section of wall above it. Ladders and large protective towers were built and moved into place along the walls so that the attackers could overrun the forces defending the parapets. Portable protected cabins, mounted on wheels and with large pointed log rams protruding from their fronts, were rolled up to knock holes in the stone walls. At the same time mangonels and trebuchets, employing the principle of counterpoise, kept up a steady barrage of huge stones and dead animals, the intent being to terrify the inhabitants by destroying their buildings and spreading disease. But the defenders held firm against all these stratagems and the siege dragged on through July and August.

Early in September King Louis came south and, in a meeting with the English king, tried to persuade him to abandon the siege. When Henry proved adamant the French monarch called for reinforcements from the north and entered the city as a token of his support for his brother-in-law. Then things began to go wrong in the English camp. Unsanitary conditions, unavoidable in an army encamped so long in alien territory, led to an epidemic which taxed even further the already overextended supply lines from the north. The loyalty of many of Henry's barons began to waver when they saw their lord besieging his suzerain within the city. Becket advised an immediate attack on the city before the French reinforcements arrived, as it would be impossible to do so afterwards. Henry dismissed this suggestion and ordered that the siege be lifted. He would not, he said, break the feudal rules and take part in an attack on his overlord. Such a statement was not in keeping with Henry's character and it was likely that it was the deterioration of his army which prompted his decision. The bulk of the army retreated northward, strengthening the castles which it had seized on the southward trek. Becket, furious at the king's decision, kept his army in the south and led it on plundering raids throughout the county.

Although Becket's plea to attack the city was militarily sound, Henry's decision to give up the siege was more farsighted. The king was determined to adhere at all costs to his policy of tight control over his vassals and, as bitter as it must have been for him to call off the siege, the example he would have set for his own vassals had he disregarded his feudal oath and taken the city and king would have been far more disastrous than his military failure. It is doubtful that Henry considered his failure final, since he had already shown on several occasions that military defeat could be redressed by diplomatic victory.

Following the retreat from Toulouse the two monarchs spent several autumnal months skirmishing around the eastern borders of Normandy and Anjou. In November they agreed to a winter cease-fire and before it ran out in May Henry and Louis settled on the terms of peace which confirmed the results of the past two years of warfare. The Vexin borders were set once again, largely to Louis's advantage, while Henry was allowed to keep the castles and strongholds which he had captured in the county of Toulouse.[15]

By Christmas 1159, on the fifth anniversary of his coronation, Henry could take pride in the fact that he had achieved the first step toward his goal of restoring stability and order to the Anglo-Norman-Angevin state. The last vestiges of democratic anarchy had been removed from England and ubiquitous royal castles dotted the land as a guarantee against its return. The firm control that he had acquired over the normally troublesome border princes had been illustrated in the support he had received at Toulouse from Malcolm and several of the Welsh leaders. The presence at his side during that campaign of the barons from Normandy, Anjou, Brittany, and Aquitaine was a clear sign that these lords also recognized his rule. In many ways the conglomerate army that marched against Raymond late in the summer of 1159 bore witness to the long way that Henry had come toward realizing his dream of ruling a loyal and obedient empire.

Yet despite the good face that Henry tried to put on the events of 1159, his first major "foreign" war had ended in defeat and revealed some ominous cracks in his empire—fissures which he was to spend the rest of his reign trying to keep from spreading. Nowhere were the harmful effects of the Toulouse venture more pronounced than in the economic state of the realm. Henry had, in effect, pawned his lands by channeling a large part of their revenues into the expedition. Had Toulouse been taken, the expense would probably have been offset by the opening of new and rich resources and additional revenues from the Mediterranean. As it was, the failure to take the southern county only exacerbated the economic problem and showed the king that a lot of hard work would be required before he had his financial house in order. Nor was Henry's clash with his chancellor beneath the walls of Toulouse an inconsiderable matter. It became evident, for the first time as far as we know, that Becket had a mind of his own and a will equal to that of the monarch. Although their disagreement did not lead at the time to a rift between king and chancellor, it is easy to see, in the light of later developments, how Henry might have begun at this time to look somewhat differently on his friend. Finally, Henry's failure to take Toulouse put a dent in the image of invincibility which up till then had been a major asset in his military and diplomatic success.

CHAPTER V

The Quiet Enjoyment of Their Lands
(1159–1162)

IN THE MIDDLE AGES POLITICAL POWER WAS VIEWED, BOTH BY THE few who theorized about it and the many who maneuvered to acquire it, as a limited quantity whose total could not be increased but only redistributed. In the middle of the twelfth century this game of redistribution was still a three-sided affair between the monarchy, the nobility, and the church, although a fourth player, the urban bourgeoisie, was preparing to enter the lists. Henry II had set about at the beginning of his reign to reshuffle this power in his favor and had completed most of the more dramatic, outward steps which made him undisputed feudal ruler of nobles and churchmen. The barons had submitted to him and had been made to realize that open opposition on their part would be met by an immediate, often personal, response from the gregarious king. By 1159 his vassals from Scotland to the Pyrenees gave every appearance of satisfaction with the mantle of feudalism with which Henry had surrounded them. Royal relations with the church, too, had on the whole been peaceful, due in no small measure to the accommodating nature of Archbishop Theobald.

But more than this veneer of feudal subservience was needed before the state could be considered truly secure. Even the most autocratic ruler could not long survive by repression alone, but rather had to achieve, as a minimum, his subjects' acquiescence by providing them with security in their day-to-day existence. In short, "the protection of his subjects in the quiet enjoyment of their lands and goods was a main problem of a medieval king," [1] and after his failure at Toulouse Henry Plantagenet channeled the bulk of his energy toward the creation of a stable, well-oiled administrative machine which would insure such protection.

Not that Henry had done nothing before 1159 toward restoring administrative order. His appointment on the morrow of his coronation of a chancellor[2] for England was to some degree a revival of an institution which had flourished under his grandfather but of which little was heard during the time of Stephen. The chancellorship had grown by 1135 to the point where the incumbent was in some ways the king's vicar who, during royal absences, was entrusted with running the kingdom. But as far as we know there was no official chancellor between 1135 and 1155, probably because Stephen so rarely left the island. Henry II's appointment of Becket was one of his first steps in bringing order back to the realm. His selection of Robert and Richard as justiciars pointed in the same direction. The office of justiciar had blossomed during the first decades of the century into one involving superintendence of the many activities of the royal court—judicial, fiscal, military, and political—but the thread of its development, too, is lost under Stephen. Surely the labors of government were performed during his time, but to all appearance in a less organized and more laissez-faire manner than before.[3] Henry II's obsession with details made him intolerant of disorder and he began his reign by tightening up the relaxed atmosphere he found at the royal court.

In the arena of royal finances Henry had also made some changes before 1159. Of all the activities of the kingdom handled by the royal household, only those dealing with finance had started down the path of specialization by the time of Henry I.[4] The Treasury, which had been the cornerstone of the fisc for earlier kings, had begun to lose its preeminence by the time of Beauclerc and had become overshadowed by the Exchequer whose members began to separate themselves from the household and think of themselves as financial experts. By the time of Henry's death they had developed a relatively sophisticated method for accounting and recording (on Pipe Rolls) the credits and debits accumulated in the counties for the king by his agents, the sheriffs. It is clear from its language and entries that the single surviving Pipe Roll from Henry I's reign was no experiment and that others had preceded it. But again, from Stephen's years we hear very little of an organized fiscal institution—few references to the Exchequer and no sign of its accounts. Although silence is hardly a conclusive argument for the absence of these institutions, it does suggest at least a breakdown in the procedures for preserving their records. Probably more is true. It is more likely that Ste-

phen's hectic hustling about the island resulted in a general administrative decadence than that the records were kept but lost in
the destruction that accompanied his reign. At any rate, concur-
rent with Henry II's appointment in 1155 of Nigel as Treasurer
and Robert of Leicester as head of the Exchequer came a reap-
pearance of the Pipe Rolls, which from that year on continue in
unbroken sequence. Several other of the Angevin's financial decisions before 1159 helped to pump new life into his grandfather's
institutions. His selection of Richard fitz Nigel to replace his father at the Treasury in 1158 strengthened this link with the past.
The scutages of 1156 and 1159 were also resurrections from the
earlier part of the century.

Yet these steps were largely a prelude to what lay ahead. Starting in 1159 Henry Plantagenet began to depart from his ancestor's practices and to go beyond what had been done earlier. But
he did so under the banner of returning to past customs. The law
now became the focus of Henry's domestic reform; from the law,
in his eyes, all else flowed. The king and his advisers could see
that the greatest advance for their policy could be made by shifting the balance of power in the legal tribunals of the realm.
Henry himself had always taken a personal interest in things
legal, although the origin of his interest and knowledge is difficult
to ascertain. The twelfth century was a legal century in which the
study and practice of the law, like economics in the early twentieth century, pushed all else aside. Many of the bright, young clergymen of Henry's England had studied law at Bologna and
brought their interest back with them when they returned to the
island. In addition, it was during these years that England was
being introduced, from the Continent, to the alien Roman legal
system of Justinian which brought in its train its cousin, Canon
Law. The chief exponent in England of this un-English system of
laws was Theobald, who in 1149 had imported to Oxford a
Lombard Roman legist, Vacarius. Although English conservatism
and suspicion of foreigners had successfully blunted the impact of
this alien legal culture, it could not stifle discussion of its nature
and precepts. It is even possible, in view of Archbishop Theobald's connections with the Plantagenets and Henry's later legal
awareness, that the king had studied under Vacarius[5] and that,
while he rejected his brand of law, he retained the conviction
that everything else he wished to accomplish in his lands must

have a legal foundation. He began, therefore, in 1159 gradually to introduce measures which would attract to his court many of the cases which formerly were the private preserve of baronial or ecclesiastical tribunals.

The division of judicial labor was, in 1159, essentially unchanged from what it had been at the time of the Conqueror: barons brought their cases to the king's court, clerics to the church court, and others to the feudal court of their lord or to the local court of the sheriff. In Henry's eyes there were too many courts with too many and varied sets of rules; this situation allowed much of what went on in his own kingdom to escape his notice and even possibly to threaten the peace of the land. He was determined to do something about it and to redress the balance. As regards baronial courts he had already made a good start before 1159, since every time he seized the lands of a lord he took into his own hands, even if only temporarily, the legal rights which were attached to the fief. Also, as a strong king, he possessed a large reserve of power in his own court and royal justice remained the type most sought after by the laity. Henry had kept a tight rein on the distribution of royal justice. Anyone who wanted to have his case heard in any but the king's court had first to obtain the king's permission to do so through a writ authorizing the procedure. Since Henry was always on the move this often presented the plaintiff with the problem of tracking down the monarch to obtain the writ. In 1159, for example, a lesser lord of England, Richard of Anesty, sought judgment on a claim to some land that required decisions from both the ecclesiastical and royal courts. Since Henry was on the Continent at the time prosecuting his war against Toulouse, Richard was forced to make several trips in pursuit of the royal court, following it in turn to Normandy, Toulouse, Gascony, and then back north again to get the writs necessary to have his case heard first by the archbishop, then by the pope, and finally by Henry himself. Each step of the procedure involved months of delay and postponement, and the case stretched out over four years before Richard's perseverance was rewarded by a favorable judgment.[6] The fact that this man, and many others like him, was willing to chase the king from one end of the realm to the other for permission to have a relatively minor matter brought to justice shows the prestige that the king's court enjoyed in legal matters. Henry held in his hands a potential judicial power which, if properly manipulated, could gain for him ascendancy over the other courts of the land.

But if the king had made some progress against the baronial courts during his early years, the same could not be said of the ecclesiastical tribunals. Since the time of the Conqueror church courts had played a major role in dispensing justice in England, as they had already been doing in Normandy before 1066. But the existence of these two courts, secular and ecclesiastical, side by side, required that the boundaries of jurisdiction be clearly drawn to avoid conflict. For the most part they had been drawn before Henry arrived on the scene. To the church courts were reserved cases concerning either a cleric or a "spiritual matter." There was little disagreement as to who was a cleric. A person in any of the holy orders, whether the four minor or the three major ones, fell into this category and came under the cloak of the spiritual courts. What constituted a spiritual matter, however, was often less clear, and before Henry's time most altercations between the monarch and the Church arose from this lack of definition. On some points both sides agreed. Church courts could decide, without royal interference, cases involving internal church matters, spiritual functions, the regulation of church corporations, matters concerning land given to the Church as alms, sexual laws, morality, simony, perjury, and, finally, questions relating to marriage, annulment, and legitimacy. One of the writs that Henry gave to Richard of Anesty, for example, authorized him to go to the archbishop's court for a judgment on the legitimacy of Richard's adversary, even though neither of the parties to the suit was a cleric. But other areas of jurisdiction were less well defined and on these issues the kings proved less accommodating, especially when they sensed an unwarranted extension of church power or an opportunity to extend their own. Areas in which English kings and their advisers generally felt that church jurisdiction bit too deeply into their feudal rights, thereby preempting the royal prerogative, included the questions of last wills and testaments, contracts and oaths, and decisions as to who should receive the profits from church property.

Despite the general agreement between the secular and spiritual powers, the boundaries between the two jurisdictions vacillated from reign to reign depending on the relative strength of the kings and archbishops. Henry I had swung the balance in favor of his royal court, but Stephen had permitted many of the gray areas between the two jurisdictions to be decided in the Church's favor. Henry II now set about, slowly at first and under the guise of returning to his grandfather's practices, to curb what he considered the excessive power of the spiritual forums. His meddlesome personality could not abide the continued presence of an institution which escaped his direct control and over which he did not have the final say.

In his campaign to weaken these two rival legal institutions Henry was groping in a germinal way toward the modern concept of sovereignty, which views political power as absolute within the confines of a state and is intolerant of any interference from without. In its complete form this idea was still many centuries in the future and would require a basic shift away from feudal values before its victory would be total. Yet many of Henry's actions against the baronial and church courts indicate that he had a glimpse of the idea of sovereignty and knew what steps he had to take to obtain it.

During the winter cease-fire of 1159 Henry Plantagenet held his Christmas court at Falaise and also reviewed the condition of justice in his continental lands. There had been frequent complaints, he discovered, over the arbitrary manner in which suspects were haled before judges in both secular and ecclesiastical courts. Knights and priests were often arraigned solely on the basis of charges brought against them by their superiors, the barons and bishops. In view of the oath of obedience that existed between the accused and the accuser, the degree of objectivity in the courtroom was left to the honor and fair-mindedness of the accuser. In his travels Henry had witnessed just such a case two years before when he sat in on the court of the archbishop of York. A case was being heard there against a dean who had blackmailed his vassal by threatening to accuse his wife of adultery.[7] The poor man had no recourse against the dean since if he refused to pay the blackmail he would be haled into court and forced to take the ordeal simply on the dean's accusation. Although this case was exceptional, and many if not most of the lords and spiritual superiors acted conscientiously since their oaths obliged them to be fair towards their vassals, it was still too much to ask of any judicial system that the same man act as prosecutor and, in effect, judge.

Possibly with this case in mind Henry issued at Falaise a decree stating that in the future throughout Normandy accusations could be brought into court only by a group of neighbors whose familiarity with the details of the case would lessen the degree of arbitrariness. Judges were prohibited from hearing cases that were not initiated by such juries of accusation.[8] But Henry Plantagenet did not invent the jury of accusation. Four centuries earlier the Frankish counts had employed such juries in their courts and, although the practice of using them died out when the curtain of darkness descended on Europe in the ninth century, it was revived and used sporadically in the tenth and eleventh centuries. The Norman kings had, on occasion, relied on juries to discover the extent of their rights, and the facts about England compiled in the Domesday Book of Henry's great-grandfather owed their existence to just such inquests.[9] Henry's father had also admitted the testimony of witnesses to the courts of Anjou. What Henry was now doing was to make of the accusing jury a regular, mandatory feature of the courts. Even though the jury played as yet no part in the final decision of these courts—guilt or innocence continued to be determined by the ordeal or compurgation—Henry, by regularizing the jury, set in motion a train of events that would culminate shortly after his death with the jury taking on the responsibility of deciding guilt or innocence.[10]

This edict of 1159 applied only to Normandy and there is no indication that the requirement for the jury of accusation spread to England before the monarch's return there four years later. In the meantime, Henry had many pressing matters to settle on the Continent. The interplay of continental politics had been complicated earlier in the year by the death of Pope Adrian. Emperor Frederick Barbarossa, pressing as always his claim to Italy, had opposed as Adrian's successor the canonically elected Alexander III, an enemy of the imperial cause, and had set up his own pope. A new dimension was added to European politics as each ruler had to decide which of the pontiffs he would recognize. In the past common opposition to Louis had placed Henry and the emperor on good terms with each other and Henry had to be careful of rejecting Frederick's pope lest it upset this delicate relationship. The English king, however, gambled on Frederick's preoccupation in Italy and on his own ability to handle Louis without imperial assistance, and raised no objection when the English bishops in June, and the Norman prelates the following month, recognized Alexander. The French hierarchy did likewise and in July, 1160, the two kings met at Beauvais and agreed to support their bishops' decision.

In spite of their agreement on the pope, however, the ever tenuous relations between Henry and Louis were soon strained again. The two monarchs had settled their latest spat the previous May by a peace treaty whose terms were not such as to hold out too great a hope for a permanent settlement. Except for the castles which Henry had captured during the Toulouse campaign and which he was allowed to keep, the geographical situation had reverted to what it had been before the outbreak of hostilities. By the same treaty the two kings had renewed their earlier pledge that young Henry would marry Margaret and that she would bring the Vexin as her dowry. It is doubtful that Louis ever expected the marriage to take place since the principals were still infants and it would be a long time before the ceremony could legally be performed. Impatient Henry, however, was not willing to let nature take its course and Louis provided him with the opportunity in the fall of 1160 to regain the strategic buffer zone. Shortly after the kings departed from their meeting at Beauvais the French queen died and Louis quickly remarried, this time to Adela, the sister of the count of Blois. The marriage changed, once again, the equation of continental politics by raising the possibility of a male heir to the Capetian throne and a consequent collapse of Henry's scheme to recover the Vexin. The English king moved swiftly. Shortly after Louis's marriage he rushed to Normandy where he conferred with the papal legates who were still there after attending the council. By brandishing before them a not-so-veiled threat to withdraw his support from Alexander he wrung from the cowed prelates a dispensation waiving the canonical age for marriage. In November the five-year-old prince was wed to the three-year-old princess. Henry sped to the Vexin and took the disputed castles from the Templars.

Louis reacted predictably by strengthening his alliance with his new brother-in-law, Theobald of Blois, and together they attacked Henry. The English monarch, having had plenty of time to prepare, was ready and counterattacked by seizing Theobald's fortress at Chaumont on the river Loire. With the onset of bad weather both sides broke off hostilities until the following spring by which time Henry's winter preparations, which included the collection of another scutage and the hiring of mercenaries, made him too strong for his adversary. In the summer of 1161 a truce was arranged between the monarchs and in October, at Fréteval, Louis agreed to Henry's occupation of the Vexin. The ten-year struggle, which had begun when Henry's father ceded the Vexin to Louis, was over and Henry set about garrisoning the existing castles and building new ones against the day when the contest would be resumed.

While Plantagenet and Capetian were waging their war of maneuver in the no-man's-land between France and Normandy, news reached Henry that Archbishop Theobald had died. Of the three major deaths that had occurred within nineteen months, namely those of pope, queen and archbishop, it was the latter that was to have the greatest impact on the king's program for his realm. At every major turning point in Henry's fight for the English crown and his later struggle to strengthen it, Theobald had played a major supporting role. It was he who had persuaded the pope to oppose the coronation of Eustace and who had arranged the terms of the Treaty of Winchester by which Henry was assured of the kingdom. Theobald had remained steadfastly on Henry's side during the king's early struggles with the barons and had aided the royal cause immeasurably by recommending his own archdeacon, Becket, as chancellor. Henry owed the primate a great debt. The king would now have to find a replacement with whom he could work with the same, or even greater, facility. But this was a decision not to be taken lightly and Henry, impressed as much by the healthy revenue which came to him from the vacant see as by the gravity of the decision he had to make, was in no hurry to fill the unoccupied chair.

With the Vexin settled, at least for the time being, the king was able to turn to the plethora of other matters which had gone unattended during his war with Louis. The twelve months following the Peace of Fréteval were filled with halcyon days for the king and were to form, as it turned out, one of the few prolonged periods in his reign when he could concentrate, uninterrupted by major crises, on the pleasant internal tasks of kingship. He spent much of this time consolidating his continental possessions which he hoped to turn into a strong, viable state. Abbot Robert informs us:

He strengthened and repaired nearly all of his castles which were situated on the borders of Normandy, and he made a royal park and a royal residence near Rouen. Near Caen he built a house for lepers, an astonishing structure. In addition, he repaired the hall and the chambers on the outskirts of Rouen; and not only in Normandy, but also in England, in the duchy of Aquitaine, in the earldoms of Anjou, Maine and Touraine he either repaired the old castles and royal residences or built new ones.[11]

Henry was caught up in a building craze that was transforming the architectural physiognomy of Europe. In continental and English towns master masons, using the newly rediscovered principles of geometry, oversaw the construction of numerous churches and secular architectural structures. In some villages, older churches and castles were rebuilt or added to along the more modern Romanesque lines; in others, completely new edifices were started which, by the time they were finished years later, would result in the modified Romanesque buildings called Gothic. The French king took the lead in this architectural explosion, but Henry was not far behind. Whereas the emphasis in the Ile de France, however, was on houses of worship, the English king's money was spent on refurbishing castles by the addition of stonework and the construction of more comfortable quarters for the occupants. Throughout his continental lands, especially where they abutted the French kingdom, Henry's fortresses were rebuilt with stone. In Normandy, besides the peaceful and humanitarian structures mentioned by the chronicler, the king rebuilt during this period the Vexin castles of Gisors, Neaufle, and Neufchâtel, which he had acquired through his son's marriage, and the castles at Mortain and Moulins, which he had taken over the previous year. In eastern and southern Anjou Henry had the military posts at Fréteval, Chinon, and Mirabeau reconstructed. The work went on apace in England during the king's absence. In the early years of his reign, when he was relieving his barons of their strongholds with regularity, he had lavished money on the preparation of the castles which he did not destroy. Now during this period a second wave of military construction swept the island as large amounts of the royal revenue were diverted to the improvement of the castle at Scarborough against the Scots[12] and of the forts and residences at Windsor, Arundel, Oxford, Conisborough, and many others.

In September, 1161, while Henry was with Eleanor at Domfront, the queen bore her sixth child, a daughter who was given her name. This was the third successive royal Plantagenet child to be born in the month of September—testimony to the fact that matters of state were not the sole activities pursued by the king at his annual Christmas courts. The baptism of the infant Eleanor was a glittering affair presided over by Henry, cardinal of Pisa, the same papal legate who had performed the marriage ceremony for the baby's brother a year earlier. The cardinal was assisted by the bishop of Avranches and Henry's friend Robert, the abbot of Mont St. Michel.[13] Following the ceremony the king returned to Normandy where he passed Christmas with his family at Bayeux. Early in the new year Henry had the remains of two tenth-century Norman dukes, Richard I and Richard II, translated to the church at Fécamp. He also had his falcons and falconers sent over from England[14] and spent a good bit of his time at his favorite pastime of hunting.

Henry took time out from these pleasant duties to settle one important matter of state which he felt could no longer be postponed, namely the choice of a successor to Archbishop Theobald. Several considerations prompted him to change his mind and not wait until he returned to England to fill the see. Rumors were circulating that he was purposely postponing the decision as a way of recouping some of the financial losses he had suffered at Toulouse. This cast him in the same light as his royal great-uncle William II who, at the end of the preceding century, had kept the see of Canterbury vacant for four years in order to collect its revenues. Henry wanted no comparisons made between himself and that son of the Conqueror who had so embittered his subjects. There was the even more important consideration that as long as the archbishopric was vacant many of the ecclesiastical functions of the kingdom had to be suspended. To Henry the most critical of these was the coronation of a new king. The Angevin monarch, eager to have his eldest son crowned while he himself was still alive, felt that the time had come to choose a primate.

The right to elect the archbishop lay, according to Canon Law, with the monks of Christ Church, Canterbury, but no English king was about to sit by idly while others chose the man who was almost his equal and with whom he would have to work most intimately. So intertwined had become the spiritual and secular responsibilities of bishops, and especially of this leading bishop of the realm, that the king's role in his selection seemed only natural and right. This entire matter of the monarch's right to choose his right-hand men had been argued at great and bitter length in all the principalities of Europe during the preceding century when the papacy had sought to reform the church by separating it from the lay feudality and eliminating secular interference with the process of selecting its prelates. The conflict had been settled in England during Henry I's time by a compromise, of sorts, whereby the king's desires continued to be a major ingredient in the final decision.

And Henry's final decision in this case was his friend and chancellor, Thomas Becket. The reasons for his choice were obvious. Thomas had served him exceedingly well as chancellor and had always been of one mind with the king as to how the State should be run. Henry had of late been experiencing some opposition from the Church, particularly over the question of his scutages, and he anticipated more in the future when he intensified his campaign to bring the ecclesiastical courts into line. In what better way could he return the Church to its "proper" relationship with the State and settle the problem of double allegiance than by installing his alter ego at the head of the institution? For Thomas would combine in his person, as had no previous archbishop of Canterbury, the chancellorship and the primacy of the English church. A similar arrangement was working well in the Holy Roman Empire where the archbishop of Cologne served as chancellor to the emperor and, were the experiment to succeed in England, Henry could remain on the Continent, where he preferred to be, secure in the knowledge that in the hands of his son Henry and the chancellor-archbishop the affairs of the island would prosper. The king was also moved in his decision by personal feelings. He was truly fond of Thomas and felt that the prestige and riches of the office of archbishop were well deserved rewards for this friend who had masterminded most of his diplomatic victories in the past seven years. Finally, Becket's elevation had been Theobald's dying wish and in fulfilling it Henry would appear to be heeding the desires of the Church.

But there were obstacles to Thomas's election. He was neither priest, nor monk, nor reputed for holiness and, as chancellor, had accumulated his share of enemies. None of these objections were insuperable, however. Prelates were chosen primarily for their administrative ability and with this Becket was well supplied. Further, the English clergy were as interested in maintaining good relations with the king as Henry was with them and no one had easier access to the king than did Thomas. Henry had no doubt that the proper amount of pressure, supported by Theobald's recommendation, could melt any opposition that might arise to Thomas's selection.

To make sure that the electors knew his desires and heard the arguments in favor of his candidate, the king sent Richard of Luci, along with Becket, from the Continent to England in May, 1162. The pair went first to London where the tenants-in-chief took an oath to recognize young Henry as co-king, although he could not formally be crowned until a new archbishop had been installed. The entourage, including the young king, then moved to Canterbury where, in a speech to the assembled prelates and monks, which was seconded by the papal legate and the venerable Henry of Winchester, the justiciar announced the wishes of the king. "Lest the church be in any way oppressed," he told his audience, "or thrown into disorder by remaining long bereft of a shepherd, be it known to you that the king accords you full freedom of election provided, however, that you choose a man worthy of so great an office and equal to the burdens thereof." Fair enough. So far Richard's admonition adhered to the spirit of the church-state compromise of 1107. But then came the pressure. "It is incumbent on you," he continued, "to elect one under whose protection you may rejoice before God and man. For if the king and archbishop be joined together in the bond of affection and cherish each other in all friendship, there is no doubt that times will be happy and the church will preserve her estate in joy and tranquillity." [15] The justiciar left no doubt in the minds of the clergymen that Henry was demanding the election of Thomas Becket, the only candidate who fit the description of the speech. Overcoming their scruples that Thomas did not wear the habit of a religious order the monks chose him as their next archbishop. There was some opposition both from those who resented the king's interference and from those who opposed Thomas on personal grounds, but this quickly melted away. On the 2nd of June Thomas was ordained to the priesthood and within 24 hours consecrated bishop.

Things were falling nicely into place for Henry II, both abroad and in England. He had cleverly managed the "legal" occupation of the Vexin and placed Louis in a position where he had no choice but to accede. On the island he had eased his son and his most loyal friend into the two top positions in the realm, from which they could superintend the unfolding of his program to unite State and Church into a monolithic organization under his direction. The horizon appeared bright and sunny to Henry Plantagenet, with no cloud in view that could limit his perception of the possibilities of consolidating and expanding the lands that recognized him as their lord.

CHAPTER VI

The Challenge from Canterbury
(1162–1164)

NO SOONER HAD HENRY PLANTAGENET COMPLETED THE CONSTRUC-
tion of this political edifice than cracks began to appear in its
foundation. The first fissure was created by Thomas Becket.
Hardly waiting for the unction of episcopal consecration to dry,
the new archbishop took the first of many remarkable steps—he
resigned the chancellorship. Having assumed a new position with
a new set of responsibilities, he was determined to carry these out
the way he saw fit. The archbishop was smart enough to see, and
unyielding enough to act on the vision, that in order to fulfill his
new obligations, which several days of elaborate religious ritual
had brought home to him, he would have to make a choice between the two jobs. To his mind a fundamental change had occurred in church-state relations since the time of the Conqueror
and therefore a new type of archbishop was needed. His three
predecessors in the see of Canterbury had been brought to the
post from the abbey of Bec in Normandy to assist the Anglo-
Norman kings in introducing and consolidating Norman caesaro-
papist ecclesiastical practices on the island. But now the trans-
plantation was complete and a strong branch of the Catholic
Church had taken root in England, one no longer the dependent
of Normandy. Becket knew that Lanfranc, Anselm, and Theobald had maintained peace with their respective kings by com-
promising and, although he never criticized the accommodations
of these great archbishops, he felt that the day had passed when
concessions to the monarchy would be of benefit to either party.
In his view the settlements that had been made in the past were
not compromises at all but thinly disguised triumphs of the secular authority over the spiritual. It was precisely against such com-
mingling of the secular and spiritual kingdoms that the reform-
ing popes had fought since the time of Hildebrand, and Becket
had now come to agree with them.

In addition, Thomas found himself in a position which the earlier prelates of Canterbury had not known. None of them had been raised from the chancellorship or had been called upon to combine the often incompatible requirements of both positions. Whatever success they had had in maintaining the Church's identity in the face of royal pressure had stemmed from their status as members of the loyal opposition, a stance that Thomas could never assume as long as he remained chancellor. Also, seven years as the king's alter ego had given Thomas a clear insight into what the king was really after and he was aware of Henry's plans to debilitate the church courts and of the degradation that would be visited on anyone who stood in his way. In his eyes retention of both the chancellorship and the archbishopric would result in satisfaction of the requirements of neither position. When Henry had informed him before the election of his intention to raise him to the archbishopric Thomas warned the king that "he could not cleave to God and obey the royal will, or give precedence to the lives of the saints without making an enemy of the king." [1] His abjuration of the chancellorship was a reaffirmation of this conviction.

Of Thomas's sincere conversion to the demands of his new position there can be little doubt. Henry, sensing this, flew into one of his famous Angevin rages when he heard of the resignation. How could his right-hand-man, who had argued so forcefully in the past for his own royal prerogatives vis-à-vis the Church and upon whom he depended so strongly for guidance, now perform such a *volte face?* To a mind such as Henry's Thomas's preference for principle, even to the point of personal disloyalty, was incomprehensible. Within the black and white cavities of the king's mind the idea was forming that Becket must have been carrying on a false front all these years in hopes of greater preferment, and that his present rejection of the secular office was an act of disloyalty and even treason. Determined to handle the matter personally, Henry finished his business on the Continent and by the end of 1162 was ready to return to England. After a weather delay which kept him at Cherbourg over Christmas, the king finally reached the island in January after having been more than four years abroad.

But Becket's resignation was not the only English matter with which the king had to grapple. Much court business had piled up

while he was away, matters which he could not or would not en-
trust to his justiciars. The first order of business was to tackle the
weaknesses of the financial system which had been exposed by the
Toulouse fiasco. Henry felt certain that he was not getting all
the money that was due to him from his feudal rights and, with an
eye toward tightening up his fiscal procedures and squeezing
more money from his rights, he called his council together in
London during May. Although the Toulouse expedition had
ended in military failure it did show the king the fiscal potential
of converting feudal military service into cash. Henry and his advisers saw this as one area which, if properly organized, could
lighten their financial burden by adding to the revenues coming
in from the kingdom. It was common knowledge that many of the
king's undertenants were receiving service from more knights
than they owed to the king by reason of their feudal oath. There
was nothing illegal about this; as long as a baron fulfilled his
obligation to the king by supplying him with the required number of knights he was, in effect, free to do whatever he wished
with the land that was left over. Over the years since the Conqueror had first parceled out the land to his tenants, the tendency
had gained momentum among many of the barons to satisfy the
king with knights from only part of their fiefs while retaining the
rest as their own armies. Since the barons' quotas for knight-
service had not changed since the time of William a sort of
"knight inflation" had taken place from which the monarchy was
not benefiting.

To Henry's orderly mind this centrifugal tendency was in need
of curbing, for not only did it strengthen the barons politically
and militarily, but it deprived the crown of a source of revenue.
The king saw an opportunity here to strengthen his own hand by
tying all the English knights closer to himself while at the same
time increasing the amount of service (and ultimately money)
which he would receive from his tenants-in-chief. From London
he sent out writs[2] to each of the sheriffs ordering them to have
every baron living in his county report how many knights he had
had in 1135, at the time of his grandfather's death, how many
new ones he had enfeoffed since then, and how many additional
knights he had to supply from the land that was left over. By
phrasing the questions in this way Henry could tell from a glance
at the replies which barons had more knights than they were pass-

ing on to him. Armed with these facts Henry could (and subsequently did) raise the quotas of many barons by making them correspond to the number of knights they actually had. Since knight-service was rapidly being replaced by scutage the king was in effect increasing the amount of money he could expect to receive from his barons.

It seems unlikely that the lords realized the exact purpose of the survey, the reason being that their returns, which took three years to collect and compile, are remarkably free of the complaints one would expect to find had they known what Henry had in mind.[3] There were a few exceptions. Roger, the sophisticated archbishop of York, ended his list with a plea that "my return may not be allowed to do harm to me or to my successors by preventing the church from recovering or preserving its legal rights." [4] But on the whole Henry seems to have outwitted his rivals. Many of the barons used an inquest of neighbors to gather their information, a further indication that this practice was fast becoming accepted in all legal facets of feudal society. The completed returns, called the *Cartae Baronum,* provide the first kingdom-wide survey since the Domesday Book of eighty years earlier. Henry's change in English knight-service was in one sense a repudiation of his coronation promise in that it altered, rather than reinstated, the feudal status of forces as it existed on the day his grandfather was both alive and dead.

At the same council Henry and his advisers searched for other ways to increase their income. While the *Cartae Baronum* took care of the aristocratic source of cash, there still remained the less exalted but more regular revenues that the king received from the English counties. This money came to the king from the various transactions in the counties: pleas, fines, writs, escheats, etc. Each sheriff was responsible for the activities of his county and for a semi-annual report of the fiscal action that took place there. For this privilege he paid the king an annual sum, called a "farm," after which he was free to collect the revenues of the county for himself. But the pacifying effect on England which Henry's governance had had during the first decade, had brought prosperity to the island, if not to the king, with the result that the sheriffs paid a fixed annual sum while they received an income more in line with the creeping inflation. In this sense they were analogous to the barons in that they received more than they were passing

on to the king. Here too Henry saw a chance to bolster his revenue and ordered a sweeping inquest into the condition of the
farms to determine in which counties the sheriffs' annual payment could be raised to bring it closer to fiscal reality. Since a
sheriff's farm could only be changed when he was replaced, the
fruits of this reform were not realized overnight. Yet the increase
was already noticeable within two years. By 1165 six counties had
new sheriffs, and the total annual sheriffs' fees to the king from
these counties had risen from £1473 to £2408—a hefty increase
of about forty percent.[5]

But Henry was not content to stop there. Encouraged by these
financial successes he moved on to look for yet other ways to make
the country pay for itself. At a council meeting at Woodstock in
July he found another potential source of revenue in the customary gifts which the sheriffs received from their counties. In order
to encourage the sheriffs to make an honest accounting of their
areas the crown had traditionally allowed them to keep from the
county returns an annual bonus based on the size of the county
and the number of fiefs it contained. Henry eyed this "sheriffs'
aid" as money that should come into the Exchequer rather than
go to his paid agents, and at the Woodstock meeting he proposed
that the sheriffs' aid be paid to the crown.[6] During the ensuing
debate opposition to the king's suggestion came from a most unexpected quarter—Thomas Becket, now sitting on the council as
archbishop of Canterbury and no longer as chancellor. Becket
based his argument not on the financial merits of the case but on
its political implications. To him the king was exceeding his traditional authority by trying to convert a voluntary gift into a tax.
If he succeeded in this test case the gates would be opened for
similar conversions throughout the realm. By a strange reversal of
positions, the archbishop saw himself as a defender of the liberties
and "ancient customs" of the realm while Henry, working des-
perately to straighten out the kingdom's financial problems, saw
Thomas as an obstructionist and probably interpreted his action
as a personal attack on himself. The king's fury increased when
Thomas's arguments carried the day and the lords of the council
refused to approve of the scheme. The opposition of his erstwhile
friend took the king by surprise. Becket, who as chancellor had
always taken the lead in asserting and defending the royal prerogatives, was now arguing, sometimes with little substance,

against them. The cruelest cut of all, in Henry's view, was Thomas's use against him of Henry's own argument of citing tradition. To get himself firmly established the king had used appeals to the past but was now ready to discard them when necessary in favor of more radical innovation. Becket, however, by constantly reminding the council of Henry's own conservative statements, was making it difficult for him to do so.

Henry's suspicion that his ex-chancellor was charting a course which could end only in collision with his own was given added fuel during the summer of 1163. After the Woodstock meeting the archbishop returned to Canterbury where he ran afoul of several of the king's barons in his diocese, thereby placing Henry in the embarrassing position of having to choose between Becket and his secular lieutenants. Thomas demanded the return of the castles of Tonbridge, Rochester, Hythe, and Saltwood which had been taken from his see and given to Earl Roger of Clare.[7] Henry, apprehensive over the archbishop's new stance, sided with his vassal and refused to allow the fiefs to be returned to Canterbury. At the same time Becket became involved in a tiff with another of Henry's tenants-in-chief, William of Eynesford. Thomas had appointed a priest to the parish church at Eynesford but William, the lord of the manor, threw Becket's man out and replaced him with his own candidate. This controversy touched on one of the gray areas between secular and ecclesiastical jurisdiction. The right to appoint a priest to a parish (called an advowson) had always belonged to the "owner" of the parish. Before the Norman Conquest bishops normally owned the churches in their sees. But since the time of the Conqueror many churches had been built by laymen who claimed the right of advowson. Becket's accommodating predecessors at Canterbury allowed this claim and it had become customary for lay lords to pick the cleric who was to minister to the spiritual needs of their manor just as they chose their own knights, household advisers, and agricultural overseers. Thomas, inspired by the Hildebrandine vision of separating Church and State, was now refusing to sanction this arrangement. Things might have been covered over had he stopped there and submitted the case to the king's arbitration. Instead, the archbishop excommunicated William bringing down upon his head the wrath of the king. For excommunication, besides its spiritual penalties which were vivid enough, carried with it grave political

implications by cutting the offender off from the society of his
fellow men. For William this meant the release of all his vassals
from their oath of fidelity, and for Henry it meant a severing of
relations with one of his barons. The king was extremely jealous
of his rights over his tenants-in-chief and ordered Becket to remove the ban. The archbishop refused on the grounds that excommunication was an ecclesiastical censure whose secular implications would have to fall where they may. In only one year as
archbishop, Becket had gotten to the heart of the matter and
forced the issue in a case which was symptomatic of the much
larger area of disagreement between the secular and spiritual
claims in medieval Europe.

In the face of Henry's animated insistence on the traditional
practice that tenants-in-chief not be excommunicated without the
king's consent, Becket backed down and reinstated the lord of
Eynesford.[8] But the archbishop's precipitate action, only the latest in a series of antimonarchical moves by which Thomas challenged the king, convinced Henry that immediate steps had to be
taken to return the recalcitrant churchman to the fold. In October he convened at Westminster his full council, both secular
and spiritual, to get the entire broad question of the Church's
role in English society out into the open and settled once and for
all. For two days the assemblage of barons and bishops argued the
pros and cons of the question. The king was particularly disturbed
by the disparity between the punishments meted out in his own
courts and those pronounced by the church tribunals. Sentences
handed down by ecclesiastical courts were uniformly less stringent than those of the royal courts since Canon Law forbade the
shedding of blood while Germanic law clung to the theory of the
deterrent value of mutilation and capital punishment. In his obsession with making legal sanctions uniform throughout the kingdom Henry demanded at this meeting that judicial sentencing
always be done by his secular courts, although church courts
could continue to decide the guilt or innocence of clerics in all
matters and of laymen in spiritual matters. To get around Canon
Law's prohibition against a cleric being sentenced by a secular
court, the king proposed that clerics who were found guilty by a
church court be stripped of holy orders and handed over, as laymen, to the secular tribunal for punishment. Becket's answer to
this was immediate and firm. To do what the king suggested, he

argued, would be to subject a defendant to two punishments, namely degradation and a secular penalty, for the same crime.[9] The archbishop's appeal to Canon Law against double punishment won over the prelates who once again blocked Henry's scheme for reform.

But the debate did not remain long on a rational plane. Seeing that he could not persuade the archbishop and the other prelates by legal arguments, Henry fell back on proclaiming the dignity of his office and demanded, with amazing inconsistency, that the spiritual lords swear to uphold the customs of his grandfather. The king's appeal to tradition in this case was lost on Becket who had set as his goal the destruction of these customs which contradicted divine law. Urged on by him, the church leaders told the king that they would recognize only those customs which did not conflict with their obligations as ecclesiastical shepherds—as they put it, they would obey the royal customs "saving their order." This distinction meant nothing to Henry who was now more determined than ever to force the bishops' total acquiescence. Brushing aside the prelates' qualifying phrase as mere sophistry, he turned his wrath on Becket and ordered him stripped of the castle of Berkhamsted and the honor of Eye, both of which Thomas had held as chancellor.[10] The council broke up in confusion, overcast by the king's glowering rage at the opposition he had encountered.

The most ominous result of the Westminster debate, in Henry's view, was Becket's success in unifying the English clergy against him. What had begun as a small personal feud between king and archbishop had now blossomed, as Thomas possibly intended, into a contest between the universalist clergy faithful to its "international" church and law, and a particularist monarch whose scheme to achieve sovereignty within his country required the isolation of the church in England from "foreign" influences.[11] At a private meeting between Henry and Becket later in the month the two came no closer on the central issue. The king continued to insist on Thomas's unconditional recognition of the unspecified royal customs, while the archbishop persisted in his refusal to allow the bishops to obey secular edicts which contravened divine laws and therefore made their positions untenable. Realizing the failure of his direct approach, Henry backed off and began to apply pressure on Thomas through the archbishop's supporters.

By combining threats and promises he won over two of the English prelates who had never been happy with Becket, Archbishop Roger of York and Gilbert Foliot, the newly consecrated bishop of London and confessor to the king. Most of the Norman prelates also deserted Becket and agreed to observe the king's customs. Even Pope Alexander III, in exile at Sens, advised the archbishop to go along with Henry. Alexander's motive, like those of most of the churchmen, was an alloy of politics and spirituality. He needed Henry's continued support and recognition of his claim to the papacy against Victor IV, the emperor's candidate, and his open espousal of Becket could well lose for him his most powerful patron.

The new approach worked. Aware of the erosion among his supporters, Becket went early in December to Woodstock where he told Henry that he would observe the customs. Although this must indeed have been a most difficult step for the proud archbishop to take, it was less of a capitulation than it has often been pictured. The vagueness of the customs, which had been a stumbling block to Becket's earlier acceptance, now worked in his favor. They were unwritten and indefinite enough to convince Thomas that he could agree to them and that each incident which arose under them would have to be argued on its own merits, in which case he stood a good chance of preserving the workings of divine law. Henry was pleased with Thomas's decision but informed him that since his earlier refusal had been made publicly, so would his recantation have to be made formally at a council. The next council was scheduled for the following month at Clarendon, and the archbishop agreed to repeat there his promise to abide by the royal customs.

At Clarendon, near Salisbury, the great council opened on the 25th of January, 1164, in an atmosphere which was most auspicious for the king. Becket's private agreement to accept the customs, which would soon be made public, allowed the king to rest easy on the church question and concentrate on other pressing matters of state. The first few days of the meeting were taken up with arguments and discussion concerning the recent resumption of Welsh attacks in the west, the coronation of young Henry, and the fiscal and judicial reforms which Henry had begun. During these days Becket, still wrestling with his conscience, delayed the moment when he had to give his assent. Finally he agreed to obey the king "in all that was right," and the prelates followed his example. No sooner had Thomas made his public declaration, however, than Henry, acting contrary to traditional practice, ordered his justiciar to prepare a written list of the customs so that the archbishop could formally affix his seal to it. Once again Henry showed a lack of subtlety which remained his own worst enemy throughout his life. His obsession with order and precise definition smashed the interplay of fragile and tacit forces which is required for successful diplomacy. He disregarded the first law of negotiation, namely, always to give your opponent the opportunity to save face, especially when he is yielding the substance of his position. Instead Henry, the rough-hewn perfectionist, tried to back his clerical opposition into a corner where it could preserve none of its dignity.

When the written customs appeared they were even more detailed and comprehensive, and less conciliatory toward the church party, than Becket had expected.[12] The wide range of matters which they covered shows that much thought went into their preparation and suggests that the list was probably made up even before the council got under way. Not all of the sixteen "Constitutions," as they were called, were concerned with the king's argument with the archbishop. Several provisions required, for the first time by written statute, the use of a jury of twelve men as witnesses in both criminal and civil cases. In an instance where no one could be found to prefer charges against a layman accused of a crime, the sheriff was ordered to round up twelve lawful men of the region who were familiar with the details of the event and have them make the accusation. Although this procedure was common enough in England before Clarendon, its inclusion among the Constitutions marks the formal importation of the jury from Normandy to the island.

The use of a jury to witness the facts of a civil case was prescribed by another clause, later called the Assize Utrum, which concerned disputes over the type of service a vassal owed to his lord. Although all enfeoffed land carried with it the responsibility of some kind of service to the grantor, the nature of this service varied with the nature of the grant. Military service was the most common type in this military society, but it often happened that a layman would give land to a church in return for prayers or religious service instead. Such tenure was called religious tenure or free alms. Often after several generations the original terms of the grant were forgotten and a dispute arose as to the nature of the required service. Whether the land was held by religious or lay tenure was important for it decided in which court, secular or church, pleas concerning the land would be heard. It also had implications for the military (and with scutage, for the financial) organization of the realm. The ninth article of the Constitutions of Clarendon decreed that the decision as to whether (*utrum*, in Latin) a piece of land was held by lay or religious tenure was to be made in a royal court by the judgment of twelve men who knew the circumstances and could testify as to the past history of the fief. Permission to have the controversy brought to the royal court could be obtained by purchasing a writ which instructed the king's justices to hear and decide the case. By this decree Henry took the first of several steps in making his heretofore restricted justice available to a larger segment of the feudal class.

But most of the articles were directed at the disputed area between secular and ecclesiastical courts. Two of them spoke directly to Thomas's recent altercation with William of Eynesford: in the future, any disagreement between a bishop and a layman over the appointment of a parish priest was to be settled in the king's, rather than in the archbishop's, court; and bishops were not to excommunicate tenants-in-chief without the king's prior permission. Henry's growing sense of sovereignty and his desire to amputate the English arm of the Church from the Roman body were reflected throughout the Constitutions, but most strongly in two other provisions: one requiring clerics to obtain the king's permission before leaving the kingdom, and another setting up a chain of command for ecclesiastical judicial appeals running upward from archdeacon to bishop to archbishop to king. Both clauses aimed at excising papal influence from the English ecclesiastical scene by controlling visits to Rome and by placing the king, rather than the pope, atop the spiritual pyramid.

Henry also had included in the Constitutions a clause aimed at standardizing punishments throughout the realm—the very subject that had set him and the archbishop apart at Westminster the preceding autumn. According to this provision

Clerks cited and accused of any matter shall, when summoned by the king's justice, come before the king's court to answer there concerning matters which shall seem to the king's court to be answerable there, and before the ecclesiastical court for what shall seem to be answerable there, but in such a way that the justice of the king shall send to the court of holy Church to see how the case is tried there. And if the clerk shall be convicted, or shall confess, the Church ought no longer to protect him.

In this clause Henry was pushing his demands an important step further than he had at Westminster. The king now decreed that there were some types of cases where a cleric was answerable in a lay court. The argument had progressed from one in which the church court judged and the lay court sentenced clerics, to one in which the lay court, in certain circumstances (decided by the lay court itself) both judged and sentenced a church member.

Did these constitutions actually represent, as Henry claimed, the practices of his grandfather, or were they the "pernicious innovations" that Becket labeled them after hearing them read at Clarendon? It is impossible to separate, with any degree of exactitude, the new from the old among these provisions due largely to the lack of written precedents and the often ambiguous wording of the articles. Many of the procedures upon which the king now insisted existed before, but whether or not with sufficient regularity to constitute a "custom" is debatable. Henry's prohibition against excommunication of his barons without his consent, for example, had been enforced on occasion, as had recourse to a jury for criminal accusations and civil recognitions. There also seem to have been previous attempts by Anglo-Norman kings to limit appeals and visits to Rome and one or two precedents existed for making criminous clerks accountable to secular courts. But even if it could have been shown that Henry's proposals were deeply rooted in the past, Becket's response would probably have been no different. What separated the king and archbishop was more than the personality of the two antagonists. Each had become by the time of Clarendon a fierce and unyielding representative of opposing views regarding the nature and purpose of law. Germanic law, which only in the Angevin lands was maintaining its purity against the spread of the Roman concept of justice, operated pragmatically to settle disputes by appealing to earlier practices. Custom and precedent, rather than an abstract concept of "justice," determined what was just in a given case. This explains Henry's conservatism and obsessive search for the practices of his ancestors. By Roman (and Canon) lawyers, on the other hand, a law was deemed just not because it was aligned to the past, but because it borrowed its justness from an *a priori,* rational, transcendental concept of justice. Thus with perfect sincerity could one member of Becket's party answer the king's demand for obedience to the customs with the reply: "But Christ said 'I am the Truth,' not 'I am the custom.'" [13]

Both Henry's appeal to custom and Thomas's to reason had their weakness. Henry could, and did, choose from among several possibilities the set of precedents that best served his quest for power. For example, he conveniently ignored the conventions of his predecessor, Stephen, although these were customs just as much as the practices of Henry I. But of course Henry II ignored these since they would have strengthened his rivals. The Roman position suffered from the weakness inherent in any rationalism (although to a lesser degree than in the eighteenth-century variety), namely, the lack of universal agreement as to what was rational and whose set of basic principles would be used to construct the edifice of reason. Henry, reared in a rough-and-tumble atmosphere, had little patience with, and probably less understanding of, the abstraction called "justice." What he saw in Becket's position was a threat to his royal dignity and plans. Becket, on the other hand, measured the Constitutions by their rationality rather than their ancestry. For him to have used Henry's argument from custom (in this case ecclesiastical custom) would have left him defenseless since his predecessors' actions strengthened rather than weakened the king's cause.

Aside from its immediate effect on church-state relationships, the Constitutions of Clarendon represented a new departure in English law. At Clarendon an English king, for the first time, attempted to legislate in writing on a realm-wide scale. Until then law consisted of general customs or tribal practices passed orally from one generation to the next. Henry's attempt to reduce these customs to writing explains the depth of the opposition he aroused. Despite his later withdrawal under pressure of the Constitutions, their revival in a future age has led to their inclusion in a small select group of early written laws which form the nucleus of the present-day English Constitution. Probably the most enduring of the Constitutions was one that did not deal directly with the ecclesiastical problem at all, namely, the one requiring a jury of accusation. But the encomiums which were to surround this royal legislation in later centuries were of little assistance to Henry at the time, for the Constitutions represented the end of the possibility of compromise with Becket and a sizable portion of the English Church.

Becket's reaction to the written Constitutions was one of horror, but there was little he could do at the moment aside from refusing to seal them, since he had already agreed at Woodstock to observe them and his agreement had been written into the document. The king had what he wanted and could afford to ignore the archbishop who twice during the summer tried to see him. Realizing that Henry was using him and that his own life might be in jeopardy if he remained in England, Thomas twice tried to reach the friendlier shores of France but was turned back both times, once by uncooperative weather and once by a timorous crew of sailors.

The archbishop's attempts to flee decided Henry to have done with the annoying cleric once and for all. In October he summoned Becket to yet another council, this time at Northampton, where he treated him in a way that can indicate only that he was trying to force the archbishop to resign. In the course of the week-long meeting, whose opening was purposely delayed by the king's hunting, Henry demanded the return by Thomas of monies amounting to almost $850,000 which had been entrusted to him while he was chancellor. Although Thomas had spent this money for the kingdom, he did not argue the point but, not wishing to let money stand in the way of the weightier matters that were involved, agreed to repay it. But Henry's fury was not assuaged. Brushing aside arguments from clergy and laymen alike, he personally decided the fate of the archbishop. But Becket, who from the outset had refused to acknowledge the court's right to try him, dramatically silenced justiciar Robert in mid-sentence as the earl was about to pronounce the king's verdict and ceremoniously marched out of the palace leaving the astonished council buzzing with excited amazement. That night he slipped out of Northampton and fled first to Lincoln and then to Sandwich from where, under the very noses of the king's guards, he crossed to the safety of the Continent.

Henry's controversy with the Church would not have taken the form it did were it not for the temperaments of the two antago-

nists. Earlier in the century his grandfather had disagreed with
Archbishop Anselm on essentially the same theme but the two
had managed to keep the dialogue on a rational plane. Henry
Plantagenet undoubtedly believed that he was following his
grandfather's example in dealing with Canterbury, as he was in
other areas of governing the country. And in some superficial
ways he was. But the telling difference between his problem with
Becket, and that of Beauclerc with Anselm, lay in the upbringing
and temperaments of the rivals. In handling Becket, Henry, for
the first time in his reign, allowed his personal feelings to direct
his course of action. He had dealt with the barons, the prelates,
and even Eleanor and Louis, with an objectivity which permitted
him to settle matters dispassionately and to the advantage of the
crown. But the archbishop he treated differently. Even making
allowance for Thomas's eminent position and the natural hesitancy that any monarch would show in setting out to destroy an
archbishop of Canterbury, Henry let the situation go much farther than he would in regard to any other challenge to his ideas.
No other rival would have gotten half as far as did Becket in
opposing the king. Thomas had given Henry ample opportunity
to move against him. His disagreement over strategy at Toulouse,
his opposition to the sheriffs' aid, his excommunication of William of Eynesford, his unification of the prelates against the king,
his refusal to accept the Constitutions of Clarendon, and his attempts to flee the kingdom—any one of these acts of defiance by a
lesser man would have brought the full weight of Henry's authority down upon the author's head. But in the case of Becket the
king hesitated, for several reasons. For one, he had come to depend very heavily on Thomas's advice and counsel and still considered it worth the effort to seek his rehabilitation. Also, Becket
had strong support among the English people, as was illustrated
when he left the fateful meeting at Northampton and was
cheered by throngs of Englishmen who crowded around the palace gate awaiting news of the outcome of the conference. Henry
also had to consider the effect a strong move against the archbishop would have on his relations with the French king and the
Roman pope. But behind all these considerations lay a trait of
Henry's character of which probably even he himself was not
fully aware but which outside observers noticed and reported.
"Whom he once hated he scarcely ever loved," wrote Gerald,

"but whom he had once loved he scarcely ever called to mind with hatred." [14] During the years that Henry and Thomas had worked and planned together the king had developed an affection for the older chancellor, and "found in Thomas an obedient servant of immense ability and mental agility, who could give him a richer life than his leading barons and industrious minister could do." [15] A strong bond had developed between the two men, one which the king found it difficult to break, even after repeated provocation. Therefore it was only after a drawn-out series of challenges that Henry, at Northampton, was finally persuaded that a hard line must be taken with the archbishop. In only one other case, that of his sons, would this side of Henry's personality make him delay in taking forthright steps to quell opposition and, as in the case of Becket, this too would cause him grief.

Of the two protagonists, Thomas has presented the greater enigma for historians and his motives have undergone greater scrutiny and aroused the greater disagreements. This is understandable since Henry's bureaucratic cravings make sense to the modern observer while Becket's brand of "fanaticism" arouses little sympathy in a society that prides itself on living according to the dictates of reason. But there is further basis for uncertainty. Becket's was far from being a clear-cut personality. Despite his external verve and love of display, his thoughts always remained his own, inaccessible to his contemporaries and to us alike, thereby providing the platform for much conjecture. That Becket was ambitious is agreed to by all. It is also clear that he was no Anselm or Theobald. He lacked monastic training and the tradition of self-discipline that had characterized his predecessors. For all his knowledge of Henry his success was uneven. Yet he was sincere in his defense of the Church and it was this unyielding temperament which brought him into conflict with the king.

While the personalities of king and archbishop determined the form of the conflict, they did not cause it. The struggle between what can only be considered irreconcilable positions had preceded Henry and Thomas by many centuries and was to continue after they were gone. The real difference lay in what each represented, for behind the personalities stretched the deeper problem of how to reconcile the claims of God and man. The question was to be solved, or rather sidetracked, in later centuries by the separation of the two claims into individual compartments. Such a solution was impossible for Henry who, through sacramental coronation, felt as responsible for the divine as for the human claims.

CHAPTER VII

Storm Clouds over the Continent
(1165–1169)

THOMAS BECKET'S DISAPPEARANCE FROM ENGLAND COMPLICATED, but by no means paralyzed, Henry's programs both overseas and at home by injecting another bothersome element into his plans to pacify his mainland possessions and to have his oldest son crowned in England. The king's hope of handling the disagreement with Becket quietly within his own official family vanished with Thomas's flight, for by his voluntary exile the archbishop unleashed forces which the king had been trying to keep below the surface. In the new situation Henry had now to treat more directly with Louis, who provided Thomas with a sanctuary, and with Pope Alexander, whose concurrence was necessary before the young Henry could be crowned.

But the archbishop was out of his grasp and Henry, probably relieved at the disappearance of his antagonist, picked up the thread of state affairs which had gone unattended for almost two years. While his envoys did their best at continental courts to persuade both Louis and Alexander of the rightness of Henry's cause against Becket, the English king turned his attention once again to Wales. The aftereffects of the 1157 campaign against Owen had long since worn off and the Welsh had taken advantage of Henry's absence from England between 1158 and 1163 to resume their attacks against both the Normans in their own country and the western English shires. During the first few of these years Henry had succeeded, by allying himself with Madog, the prince of central Wales, in keeping Owen in the north from uniting with Rhys in the south. But Madog's death in 1160 created a vacuum into which Owen had begun to move. Rhys, too, had continued to be restless. In 1159 he defeated a powerful English army and in 1163 began a full-scale campaign to expel the Normans from Welsh soil. Shortly after his return from the Continent in 1163 Henry had led an expedition into South Wales and had captured the Welsh prince whom he brought back to England as a prisoner. Rhys was permitted to return to his principality after he did homage to Henry, recognizing English suzerainty over southern Wales. But in 1164 he repudiated his oath and seized the main English stronghold at Cardigan. In a surprise move Owen allied himself with his fellow Welshman to form the first unification of Welsh rulers that might be termed "national."

At the Northampton council in October, 1164 (from which Becket fled to the Continent), Henry and his advisers planned an expedition to Wales[1] on a scale only slightly smaller than the Toulouse adventure of five years earlier. In order to come to grips with the highly mobile Welsh he needed light-armed soldiers to supplement his feudal knights, and his tenants-in-chief promised to grant him enough money to support these infantrymen for six months at the going rate of a penny a day per soldier.[2] In addition, the king collected another scutage, the fifth of his reign, which he used to purchase equipment[3] and hire soldiers from the Continent.[4] He also arranged for a Danish fleet from Ireland to assist in the campaign by invading Wales from the west.[5] By May, 1165, the army and its equipment was ready at Shrewsbury. With Henry at its head it marched northwestward to Rhuddlan, only to discover that the Welsh, under the command of Owen's son David, had retreated south from Rhuddlan down the valley of the river Clwyde, out of reach of the English from the north. Henry fortified the castle at Basingwerk and returned with his army to Shrewsbury to regroup his forces for an attack on the valley from the south. By August the army was once again ready to go. It marched past Oswestry and across the Ceiriog Valley to the base of the Berwyn range of the Cambrian Mountains. A steady rain which had been falling for a month made the mountain impassable and turned the normally dry roads into bogs. The English set up camp at the foot of the range to wait for the rain to stop but the weather failed to improve. Faced with a loss of provisions and disintegration of his supply lines, Henry had no choice but to retreat to Chester and rely on the outcome of the seaborne invasion. The ships that arrived from Ireland, however, were inadequate and the king called off the campaign and sent his soldiers home.[6] As with the Toulousian expedition, Henry failed to achieve his military objective. But also like the earlier campaign, he was later to gain through diplomacy what he had been denied through force of arms.

While Henry waited in the Welsh rain an event took place at the opposite end of his realm which was to be of greater consequence than his failure to subdue the Welsh. In Paris, near the end of August, the two-century-old Capetian luck in producing male heirs continued as the French queen gave birth to a son, named Philip. The prince's birth proved the wisdom of Henry's earlier move to marry his son to Margaret and thereby claim the Vexin, but at the same time it meant that Margaret now lost whatever chance she might have had to inherit the French kingdom. And even though Henry had physical possession of the Vexin, this male addition to the French royal family assured a future renewal of contention for that area. As it was to turn out, this infant was to mature into the most aggressive Capetian in over a century, and more than a match for Henry's own sons. In fact Philip, nicknamed Augustus, was to undo after Henry's death much of what the English king was working so hard to create.

All of France was jubilant over the blessed event. Throughout the night of Philip's birth Parisians celebrated with church bells, bonfires, and parades. The French had largely given up hope of a peaceful continuation of the Capetian line and had resigned themselves to the domestic and foreign disruption that was certain to accompany the passing of Louis. Now that was all changed. The birthday celebrations throughout the country were inspired not only by happiness for the royal couple, but also by a newfound confidence that the French monarchy could carry on its feud with its ubiquitous vassal, Henry Plantagenet.[7] The introduction of a new life into the royal family also brought new life to Louis. The French king's fortunes had decidedly taken a turn for the better during the year of 1165. Becket's presence in the kingdom gave Louis leverage both with the pope and with his English adversary. Louis had already shown, by his refusal the previous January to accede to Henry's demand to turn Thomas over to him, that he was ready to wring any advantage he could from the situation. The birth of a son in August gave him added incentive and a new reason to pull out all the stops in his battle to undermine Henry's position on the Continent.

Henry grasped the changed situation immediately, and this may have figured in his decision to abandon the Welsh expedition and concentrate on his eastern policy. Compared to the mounting continental storm, his attempt to bring the Welsh to heel suddenly lost much of its significance. He made the wise, if painful, decision to avoid military involvement on two widely separated fronts and made no further attempts during his reign to attack the Welsh, but rather focused his diplomatic and military efforts on the eastern edge of his realm. Here he had already begun, the previous spring, to build a diplomatic alliance as a counterweight to the French king's new stature and against the possibility of a male heir. To Rouen in April had come Rainald, the archbishop of Cologne and chancellor to Emperor Frederick Barbarossa, to put the finishing touches on an anti-French alliance with Henry which was sealed with a pledge of marriage between the emperor's cousin, Henry the Lion, duke of Bavaria and Saxony, and Henry Plantagenet's oldest daughter, Matilda.[8] The implication of this alliance was ominous not only for Louis, but for Becket and the pope as well, by its suggestion of a rapprochement between the Plantagenet king and the pope's archenemy. The birth of Philip four months later gave Louis a breathing spell and the opportunity to recast his anti-Angevin plans on a longer-range basis.

Before he left for the Continent, foreseeing another long sojourn there, Henry early in 1166 took a further step for the orderly prosecution of justice in England while he was away. Whenever he was in England, the king personally supervised the activities of his court as it moved about the island checking up on the local county and township courts. But when he was away this supervision was left to others. The last time he had been absent from England (1158–63) he had relied on the honesty of the sheriffs to see that justice was done in these local courts, but his trust had been misplaced. Determined to prevent a recurrence of abuses, Henry decided, at a sitting of the royal court (an assize) at Clarendon in February, to tighten up judicial practices throughout the counties by having members of the central government make periodic visits and inspections of the sheriffs' courts. This idea of traveling justices making a circuit (eyre) through the country was not new and its roots can be traced back at least to the *Missi Dominici* whom Charlemagne had dispatched from his court to unify his empire. Henry's Norman predecessors too had, on occasion, employed itinerant judges. However, as with the use of the jury, Henry II was reviving and regularizing a dormant and occasional institution and making it a permanent feature of the English judicial scene.

At the Assize of Clarendon the royal councillors drew up a list (also called an assize) of instructions for dealing with criminal cases which was to serve as a charter for the circuit lawyers in their first eyre scheduled for later that year, after Henry's departure. Unfortunately this original list no longer survives but we do have a similar document[9] dated ten years later which is probably a synthesis of the 1166 instructions and those practices which had crept into these judicial eyres in the intervening decade.[10] Even though we cannot be certain that all the historic measures of the later document existed in 1166, they had certainly become part of the judicial landscape by 1176 and clearly reveal the thrust of Henry's thinking before he departed England.

The Assize instructed the royal agents to have twelve men from each hundred and four from each township appear before them and reveal, to the best of their memory, the names of all the men in the area who had committed murder, robbery, or larceny, or who had harbored a criminal, coined money, or committed arson since the beginning of Henry's reign.[11] Besides creating a valuable list of offenders in the kingdom, the Assize gave new weight and added prestige to the institution of the accusing jury by applying it, for the first time, to criminal cases. Those accused were to be tried in the traditional manner of the ordeal by water[12] for, even though juries were being introduced into criminal cases to present indictments, judgment was still left to nature as it had been since the days before the Germans had accepted Christianity. Germanic religion worshiped nature as its god and the ordeal by water was used as one way of ascertaining the divine will. This method of judgment could be performed in one of two ways. The first, and more common in England, was the ordeal of cold water in which the accused, bound hand and foot, was thrown into a stream. If he sank to the bottom nature was signaling his innocence by accepting him. If, on the other hand, he floated on the stream's surface, nature was rejecting him as a guilty man. In the ordeal of hot water the accused was made to pick a heated metal bar from a boiling cauldron and carry it a specified distance. The amount of damage done to the accused's hand determined his degree of guilt or innocence. Although Christianity had not succeeded in excising this remnant of pagan justice from Europe, the ordeal had already begun to lose much of its credibility by 1166. Skepticism as to the efficacy of the ordeal was clearly behind the provision in the Assizes of 1166 and 1176 which decreed that even in the case where a man who was accused of more serious crimes came successfully through the ordeal, if he had a reputation as a criminal he was to be declared an outlaw and forced to leave the kingdom within eight days.[13] This was an important watershed in Anglo-Norman jurisprudence for it provided that a man's past record carried at least as much weight as a particular act of proof.[14] Within fifty years the ordeal would be gone, virtually killed by a papal decree at the Fourth Lateran Council against clerical participation in the ancient custom. Thanks to Henry's innovations, the jury would be available to replace the banned ordeal as the instrument for deciding guilt or innocence.

Although it would be stretching the evidence to maintain that Henry's sole, or even principal, aim in the Assize of Clarendon was to squeeze more money out of his feudal judicial rights, there is no doubt that financial considerations did play a part, as they did in most of the king's legislation. At the Clarendon meeting (or possibly a short time later) Henry took a second major step in spreading royal justice by making his court available to a greater slice of the feudality. The first step had been taken two years before, also at Clarendon, when the Assize Utrum opened the doors of the king's court slightly by granting admittance, for a fee, to anyone who wanted a decision as to the spiritual or secular nature of his fee. Now, in 1166, Henry opened the doors wider by extending the same procedure to another class of cases—that concerning violent seizure of land. The twelfth century still retained some of the violence of earlier times and in the minds of many physical might still provided a better solution than legal palliatives. Frequently a man would seize another's property, leaving the original possessor in poverty until long and complex litigation in the feudal courts could decide who had the legal right to the property. This widespread situation caused a great amount of tension and discontent in the kingdom and complicated Henry's task of ruling. In 1166 he ordered his itinerant justices to provide, on their eyres, an immediate remedy for those who had been deprived of their land in this way. By this commission (later called the Assize of Novel Disseisin) anyone who had been violently dispossessed of his free tenement could have it restored immediately by purchasing a writ from the king, while the court argued the question of rightful ownership. By this new and bold action Henry provided an effective safety valve to syphon off much of the pressure that had kept the kingdom unsettled, while at the same time he drew out of the feudal baronial courts, and into his own, questions of possession of free tenements. By charging for the writs, the Assize improved the royal financial situation. In addition, it furthered the spread of the use of the jury since determination as to who first possessed the land was up to twelve neighboring freemen. By applying this Assize to all parts of the kingdom through his itinerant judges, the king strengthened his own position vis-à-vis the barons by permitting more of his countrymen to use his court, which up till then had been the exclusive preserve of the tenants-in-chief. At the same time he took a major step toward commonizing English legal practices.

The justices were given other items to inspect. They were to make sure that each county had a jail for the detention of prisoners and, where one did not exist, they were to see that one was built. Sheriffs were authorized to enter counties other than their own to pursue and arrest criminals. The Assize also gave instructions for handling heretics who, by the middle of the twelfth century, were beginning to become a problem in Europe. Whether all of these items were included in the Assize of 1166, or whether some were added during the next decade, is relatively unimportant. In 1176, at Northampton, these instructions were reissued with additions which show that Henry II was coming to grips with the problem of domestic violence. As a by-product of his attempts to solve the problem of law and order, the Plantagenet king was creating the foundation of English common law.

As soon as these arrangements were completed Henry crossed to Normandy (March, 1166) for what was to turn into another four-year stay on the Continent. It is hard to avoid the conclusion that the monarch breathed more freely on his native soil and felt more comfortable amidst the rough and tumble of continental politics and diplomacy than he did in England. The center of gravity of Henry's realm in 1166 was on the mainland where were clustered the principal actors who were to engage his thoughts for the remainder of his life. Pope, emperor, French king, and archbishop —all were crammed into a relatively small continental area which at times threatened to become too small to hold them. Before long these expanding and plotting personalities were to be joined by Henry's own sons who, under the tutelage of their mother, were already forming ideas about their future which Henry did not share.

But Henry Plantagenet operated best under such challenging conditions, as the next four years were to prove. His first order of business on the Continent was to iron out with Louis the details of a joint fund-raising scheme to assist the Christian crusaders in Palestine. The French king proposed a revenue-matching plan whereby he would send each year to Jerusalem five shillings out of each pound of revenue that came into his treasury. Henry, not to be outdone, pledged double that amount the first year, and a sum equal to Louis's gift each year thereafter. The two monarchs decided that the money that was collected should be stored on neutral ground at Tours, a city shared by both kings. But the kings' agreement on the question of supporting the crusade in no way modified their enmity on matters closer to home. Henry's principal reason for having come to the Continent was to put down several revolts which were being supported (at least tacitly) by the French king. While the two monarchs discussed the financing of the crusade Henry received word of trouble in Maine and Brittany. Eight years had passed since Henry had pacified the county of Brittany and received the homage of Conan IV. During the intervening years Conan had proved a fragile instrument of Henry's policy and many of the Breton barons had allied with their neighbors in Maine to form a movement for independence from Plantagenet rule. While he was in England Henry had entrusted control of his continental lands to Eleanor but the queen, ruling from distant Poitiers, had had little success in preventing the defection. The natural ally of this liberation movement was Louis who made a pact with the rebels in which he agreed to support them and promised never to conclude a separate peace treaty with the English king.

Henry, as usual, met the crisis squarely. At the head of a large mercenary army hired from his continental domains he marched to the Maine-Breton border and besieged the castle of Fougères whose lord, Ralph, was at the head of the movement to overthrow

Conan and replace him with Eudo of Porhoët.[15] The castle surrendered after two weeks and Henry pressed on to Rennes in Brittany where he ravaged the land of Eudo and drove the hapless count and his supporters from the duchy. To military pressure the king now added diplomacy by betrothing his eight-year-old son Geoffrey to Constance, the four-year-old daughter of Conan, and forcing the unpopular prince to hand over the duchy to him.[16] The Breton barons seemed pleased with this solution and many of them traveled voluntarily to Thouars, in Poitou, to do homage to Henry.[17]

But this repacification of Brittany failed to have any impact on the English king's troubles elsewhere on the mainland. By autumn Henry was back in Normandy which was being threatened by Louis and his allies. Normandy's neighbors, Philip of Flanders, Matthew of Boulogne, and Theobald of Blois, had become incensed at Henry who had deprived them of some of their land and rights, and had been gradually edging toward an alliance with the French king. In a series of meetings with these important princes Henry was able to stop their drift toward Louis, for the moment at least, by granting them annual pensions in return for allegiance and the provision of soldiers.

Henry's diplomatic advances toward these princes had had as their target Becket as much as they did the French king. Now that Henry was on the Continent a showdown with the archbishop was inevitable and the king wanted to neutralize as many of the church leaders as he could. The coming struggle was rapidly taking shape as attitudes on both sides were hardening. During the two years since Becket had fled from England he had been living quietly at the Cistercian abbey of Pontigny, not far from Sens, and from this penitential retreat had become the silent center of frenetic diplomatic activity between Henry, Louis, the pope, and many other princes of Europe. The attitudes of the two kings toward the exile had now become polarized: Henry's initial patience with Becket, which had been surprisingly long-lived in the first place, had by now completely evaporated and he was determined to force the archbishop to return to the kingdom on his terms; Louis, on the other hand, supported Thomas unswervingly, as much out of a desire to embarrass the Angevin as from a belief in the correctness of Thomas's position. Caught in the middle was Pope Alexander who agreed with the archbishop in principle but, needing Henry's support against the imperial anti-pope, could not risk overt assistance to the prelate.

Since early in 1165 Henry's campaign against the distant Becket had taken the form of harassment against those members of the archbishop's party who remained in England. Succumbing to the advice of Becket's enemies, who were now advising him, the king had driven from the island, in the dead of winter, hundreds of the archbishop's relatives and supporters. The exiles made their way to Thomas's retreat at Pontigny, but facilities there were inadequate and Louis had relocated many of the refugees in other parts of his kingdom. Henry's action had backfired, however, for although it created temporary hardships for many of Thomas's followers, it reunited the archbishop with his staff of skilled administrators and advisers. They now proved valuable indeed to the prelate in his diplomatic contest with the king.

In the fall of 1166, after returning to Normandy from the Breton campaign, Henry took a further step to harass the archbishop. Becket's hosts at Pontigny, the Cistercians, were rapidly becoming the most powerful religious order in England. The king threatened to banish the entire order from the island if they did not stop harboring "his enemy." The threat was too much for the Cistercian General Chapter and Becket was forced to leave the abbey. Louis, anxious to keep the archbishop within his country, arranged another refuge for him, this time at the Benedictine abbey of Saint Columban, also near Sens. For almost four years Becket was to remain there studying, praying, and preparing appeals to the pope for a settlement between himself and the English king.

Between 1166 and 1170 Henry Plantagenet performed one of the most dazzling balancing acts of medieval times, alternating between warfare and diplomacy to combat the French king and to ward off the embarrassment caused by Becket's shadow across the Continent. During the fighting season each year (roughly from Easter to Michaelmas, celebrated on September 29) the monarch's mercenaries were occupied in putting down revolts in the king's possessions to the south of Normandy and fighting the French king in the duchy itself. During the times of military inaction Henry pressed his diplomatic campaign to discredit the archbishop and force him to return to England. In 1167 Henry's paid fighters earned their salaries by defeating the king's enemies in

Poitou during March, in Auvergne in May, and in Brittany once again in the autumn. Louis VII, frustrated by geography and the feudal oath, was prevented from taking an overt part in these rebellions. But in one area during this year the French king did get the opportunity to renew his warfare with his troublesome vassal. In March Raymond of Toulouse, who had become increasingly disenchanted with Louis since the Angevin attack on him in 1159, placed himself under Henry's protection by doing homage for his county to the English king. This was a major victory for Henry; he thus achieved through diplomacy what he had failed, seven years before, to gain through military pressure—a doorway into the Mediterranean. But the price Henry had to pay was the renewed enmity of Louis who struck into the Vexin in June and burned a number of villages near the French-Norman border. Henry retaliated by sacking the French arsenal at Chaumont-en-Vexin and a state of war once again flared up between the two monarchs. Desultory raids by both sides throughout the summer accomplished little and the fighting was halted by a cease-fire late in August, intended to last until the following spring. In the opening months of 1168 Henry again sent his forces into Poitou and Brittany to quell rebellions; concurrently, a series of conferences with the French king stretching throughout the year failed to bring them any closer together.

The diplomatic deadlock was finally broken early in 1169 when Henry and Louis agreed, at Montmirail near the Maine border, on the terms of peace between them. The two kings reviewed the entire continental situation, and the conditions of their agreement went far beyond settling the immediate conflict. It attempted to fix the future status of all the continental lands which Henry held from Louis. The feudal oath was still the most binding contract that could be made in treaties of this sort, and Henry did homage to Louis for all his mainland possessions. Then arrangements were made for the disposition of Henry's lands after his death. The English king's three oldest sons, who were present at the conference,[18] did homage for their shares of the fiefs. Prince Henry, then fourteen, was invested with Maine, Anjou, and Brittany. Richard, not quite twelve, became the duke of Aquitaine. Ten-year-old Geoffrey did homage to his oldest brother for Brittany.[19] In light of Henry's celebrated acquisitiveness and hesitancy to delegate authority it is surprising that the king agreed to this

division of his hard-earned fiefs. It was probably a condition imposed on him by Louis who saw in the partition an opportunity
to weaken the Angevin king by driving a wedge between him and
his sons. At any rate, Henry lacked any intention of backing up
these grants to his sons with the bestowal of any real authority.
The Treaty of Montmirail was sealed with a promise of marriage
between Richard and Alice, the eldest daughter of the French
king. The princess's dowry was to be Berry, the southern French
duchy which was almost as piercing a thorn in Henry's side as had
been the Vexin. Henry's later attempts to modify and wiggle out
of these commitments concerning his sons' inheritances and Richard's marriage were to cause him most of his troubles during the
two remaining decades of his life.

The Montmirail conference was also notable for the presence
there of Thomas Becket—the first meeting between king and
archbishop in almost five years. Thomas's attendance was the result of the actions of the papal legates who had invited him in
hopes of reconciling him with Henry. In their eyes a settlement of
the disagreement would be to everyone's advantage, with the possible exception of Louis. The controversy had dragged on far too
long for the good of either England or the papacy. One of the
archbishop's first acts after leaving England had been to excommunicate many of the leading English barons, including those
who had participated in writing the Constitutions of Clarendon
and those who had seized the property of Canterbury after he was
gone. His anathema had barely stopped short of Henry himself.
Although Henry had managed to have the censures removed, the
imminent possibility of their return kept the king and his barons
in a tenuous and nervous state. It also seems that Henry sorely
missed Thomas in the kingdom, no longer for personal reasons
but for his need of the prelate's exceptional administrative and
conciliar abilities. The effectiveness of English diplomacy and, to
a lesser degree, of Henry's domestic reforms, had gone into a noticeable decline since Becket's departure,[20] and the king still nur-
tured the hope that Thomas could be persuaded to return and
take up his former secular duties. Also in Henry's mind was his
desire to have his eldest son crowned and associated with him on
the throne. To Henry II the coronation of his son would be the
culmination of his life's work for it would assure the continuation
of his possessions within his family and minimize the risk of an-

other debilitating struggle for the crown, such as Henry had experienced in his youth. But English kings were anointed by the
archbishop of Canterbury and, even though exceptions had been
made in the past when the Canterbury incumbent was in exile,
Henry's obsession with legality and order would permit him to
leave no loophole in his son's position—he wanted Thomas back
to perform the ceremony.

Pope Alexander was no less unsettled by the dispute between
Henry and Thomas. He could ill afford to come down hard on
either side of the controversy, and as long as it continued his necessary vacillation weakened the image of the papacy throughout
Europe. Settlement of the rift was essential for Alexander's success against the imperially appointed pontiff. Two years earlier
the pope had sent commissioners to Henry, who was in France at
the time, but they had failed to budge the king. Now at Montmirail a second pair of legates tried their hand. At first their min-
istrations appeared to meet with success as Thomas, obviously
tired of exile and forced retirement, and anxious to resume his
episcopal duties, agreed to throw himself on the king's mercy.
Henry was delighted at the prospect of an end to the struggle.
But when the archbishop concluded his statement of capitulation
with the familiar phrase "saving God's honor," the king flew into
a rage and further negotiation became impossible.[21] By injecting
this clause into the agreement the archbishop indicated that his
position had not changed in five years—the battle lines remained
drawn as tightly as ever.

Shortly after the meeting at Montmirail the military season
opened and in March, 1169, Henry, free at last from French pressure in the north, marched south to Aquitaine and then to Gascony to discourage revolts and restore order. On Palm Sunday,
while the king was still in the south, Becket delivered a dramatic
sermon at Clairvaux in which he once again excommunicated
those English barons who had been instrumental in his downfall:
Richard of Luci, the justiciar; Gilbert Foliot, the bishop of London and special enemy to Thomas; Jocelyn, the bishop of Salisbury; Hugh Bigod, earl of Norfolk; Richard of Hastings, the
head of the English Knights Templars; Geoffrey Ridel, the archdeacon of Canterbury; and a number of others.[22] The archbishop
refrained from excommunicating Henry but was toying with the
idea of placing the English kingdom under an interdict, which

would legally excuse the English subjects from obedience to the king and barons. But this move required papal sanction and Becket had as yet been unable to persuade Alexander of the necessity of pronouncing it. Henry, hurt, bewildered, and furious, cut short his campaign and returned to Normandy; in September he issued orders aimed at averting the interdict by isolating England from the archbishop and the pope.

Alexander was more upset than Thomas by Henry's action and doubled his efforts to resolve his own dilemma by getting the antagonists together. In November his legates succeeded in bringing the king and archbishop to the conference table again, this time at Montmartre. Wanting to be rid of the troublesome clerical problem and ever fearful of the interdict, Henry toned down his antiecclesiastical decrees by withdrawing the offending customs and guaranteeing almost complete freedom to the Church. This was an amazing concession and Becket reciprocated by dropping his demand for inclusion of the "saving" clause and promising to return to England. Reconciliation between Henry and Thomas was all but complete when the archbishop asked the king to give him the kiss of peace as a token of his sincerity. The English monarch, apparently more fearful of this spiritual guarantee, which implied permanence, than he would have been of a man-made promise, refused and negotiations broke off once again with the two parties as far apart as ever. Plantagenet patience with the archbishop had run out. Important decisions concerning the future of England could no longer be postponed while waiting for the archbishop to return to the fold. In high dudgeon, the king returned to England in March, 1170, in answer to disquieting news that had reached him about internal affairs in the kingdom.

CHAPTER VIII

Peace with the Pope

(1170–1172)

HENRY II'S VISIT TO ENGLAND IN THE SPRING OF 1170 WAS A SHORT
one, lasting only three months. He came to arrange two specific
matters, both of which he quickly settled. The first matter of
business concerned abuses in local administration. In the course
of their eyres, which had criss-crossed the country while the king
was away, Henry's agents had uncovered a shocking amount of
corruption among the sheriffs. In the eight years since Becket had
resigned from the chancellorship Henry had found no lieutenant
of equal competence to replace him; the result was that the sheriffs, left largely to their own devices, had bit deeply into the
king's rights in the counties. As soon as he reached England he
held a council at Windsor where he ordered an investigation into
the sheriffs' activities,[1] and suspended all the sheriffs from their
duties until the inquiry was complete. The commissioners appointed to carry out the inquisition were instructed to make a
sweeping examination of the manner in which the sheriffs and
other local officials had carried out the king's instructions since
1166. They were given a list of specific abuses to look for. Complaints had multiplied about the size of the aid which these
county agents had collected in 1168 for Princess Matilda's marriage to Henry the Lion, and Henry wanted to find out if the
sheriffs or local lords had, on their own initiative, increased the
amount of the tax and kept the extra revenue for themselves. In
addition, the inspectors were told to make a full inquiry into the
value of all the property of convicted felons which, according to
the Assize of Clarendon, should have been confiscated and turned
over to the royal Treasury. The cash and property returns from
this source had been suspiciously low and Henry suspected that a
generous portion of these had found its way into the sheriffs'
pockets. There were also hints that the sheriffs had accepted
bribes from the guilty in return for clemency, and once it had

become known that the king would soon return to England, they had paid bribes to silence complaints against themselves. Inquiry into the truth of these rumors also formed part of the inquisitors' mandate.

Answers to these questions were reported to Henry in London in mid-June and they formed a severe indictment of the incumbent reeves. Fifteen of the 23 officers were replaced immediately,[2] with a different type of man. The new sheriffs were not, like their ousted predecessors, natives of the counties they administered, but were rather members of the central Exchequer being sent into the local areas, and for that reason they could be expected to look first to the interests of the crown instead of to their own advantage. This clever move by the king was another instance, akin to the introduction of the jury, in which Henry imported a continental custom into England. By tying the local agents more closely to his central court Henry hoped to check the spreading tendency of the sheriffs to look upon their position as hereditary. By the same stroke he took a further step in the direction of reintroducing sovereignty.

The second matter requiring Henry's immediate attention was the coronation of the young Henry. Becket's contumacy had split the English Church and had created a growing discontent on the island which made it less likely with each passing year that, when the king died, succession to the throne would be peaceful. The immediate crowning of his son, Henry decided, even if it could not be done by the archbishop of Canterbury, was preferable to leaving the choice of his successor to a bitter and divided Church. Conveniently interpreting a papal letter as permission for the coronation, he arranged for the archbishop of York to crown his son. The ceremony took place at Westminster Abbey on the 14th of June, but over the pomp and pageantry of the occasion hung a cloud of uneasiness made darker by the absence of two main actors who, under more normal circumstances, would have been present. Thomas Becket, who only the previous day had forbidden the ceremony to take place,[3] was still on the Continent as the holy oils were poured by his rival. Thus insult was added to injury as Thomas's most bitter opponent performed the quasi-sacramental rite which belonged by law and custom to the archbishop of Canterbury. Even more surprising was the absence of young Henry's wife, Margaret. Although the reasons for her absence are not at all clear, it is probable that Henry withheld the crown from Louis's daughter in hopes of dangling the prospect of her future coronation before the eyes of both Becket and Louis. To the former he could promise, in return for his capitulation, the honor of repeating the coronation of young Henry along with his bride, while to the latter he could hold out the bait of seeing a French princess on the throne of England.[4]

But if this were Henry's intent, it backfired, for the coronation spurred both Becket and Louis into action and placed the English king on the defensive. The archbishop began at once to prepare legal action against the prelates who had taken part in the ceremony, while Louis saw in the ceremony a gratuitous insult to himself and to his kingdom. The peace so recently arranged between the two monarchs quickly dissolved. Within a fortnight of the coronation Henry Plantagenet was hurrying back to the Continent to face the problems spawned by the crowning. He left the new kinglet behind in England to cut his teeth in his new role. But the Angevin's normally firm diplomatic hand was weakened and his usual aggressive confidence was shaken by the turn of events. He still felt the pressure of the impending interdict on his kingdom,[5] to which had now been added the prospect of still another war with Louis. Further limiting his options was his stubborn desire to have Becket take over the education of his newly crowned son. The youngster had been brought up in the archbishop's household and Henry still felt that Thomas was the best man to guide his son in the responsibilities of governing. Realizing the weakness of his position and wishing to settle the matter with Becket, he was ready to make concessions to the ecclesiastical party. A meeting with Thomas was arranged near Fréteval in Maine for July. Although in their verbal sparring at the conclave neither king nor prelate yielded an inch in principle, they both refrained from repeating the grating demands which had scuttled their earlier attempt to compromise at Montmartre. Becket no longer insisted on the kiss of peace, accepting instead a cryptic promise from the king that he would give it at a later date. Henry agreed (or at least so Thomas interpreted his words) to let the archbishop censure the prelates who had taken part in the coronation of young Henry.[6] The king further promised to see that all the lands of Canterbury were restored to the status they had enjoyed just prior to Becket's departure from the island six years earlier.[7] In his need for peace with the archbishop Henry felt that any accord, even one that fell short of dissolving all disagreements, was preferable to allowing the present situation to continue. But the accord reached at Fréteval was an uneasy truce, at best, and the tenuousness of the reconciliation was evident in the reaction of the followers of both camps. Over the years attitudes on both sides had hardened to the point where neither side trusted the other. Henry's partisans were disappointed with a settlement which implied a return of Becket to the king's confidence and a consequent loss of their own influence with the monarch. Becket's advisers were equally dissatisfied, realizing that nothing had been settled and that the safety of their leader had been jeopardized, despite the guarantees of the king.

Before Henry could make a public announcement of the reconciliation and issue the necessary writs to carry it out, however, he fell gravely ill and seemed on the point of death. Medieval chroniclers, normally content to limit their description of illnesses to a result of divine displeasure, provide us with precious little diagnosis of what was ailing the king. Henry had been kicked by a horse several years earlier and this apparently had created a chronic ailment which grew worse with increasing age. Whatever his complaint, he deemed it serious enough to draw up a will in which he divided his possessions and lands among his sons. Young Henry was to receive England, Normandy, Maine, and Anjou, and from among this inheritance was to provide for his infant brother, John. Richard, already duke of Aquitaine, was to inherit his mother's land when she died, and Geoffrey was to hold Brittany from the French king. Although the provisions of this testament did little more than reinforce existing arrangements, they show that Henry was more genuinely concerned with providing for his sons' future than with keeping intact the huge realm that he had created. He had learned from experience that the task of governing such a vast expanse of land was too much for one man and that the dynastic interest would best be served by a just distribution of the kingdom and duchies among his faithful sons. By so doing he staked the future of the Angevin lands on the loyalty and devotedness of his sons. Seldom has such trust been so misplaced, for the very terms of the will were to become the occasion, if not the direct cause, of the disloyalty which they were meant to prevent.

Royal health returned in August and the grateful king traveled south to the popular shrine of Rocamadour in Poitou to thank God for his favor. Four years earlier a new church had been erected on the rocky slopes of this Quercy village and had been dedicated to St. Amadour, a hermit who many centuries before had lived in this quiet retreat. By the middle of October the king was refreshed in body and spirit and ready to resume negotiations with Becket. The two met again, this time in Touraine, where the final terms of the reconciliation were hammered out. A public declaration of the reunion was made and Henry sent a message to the young Henry in England instructing him to guarantee Becket's safety and to see that all the possessions of Canterbury were restored to their 1164 condition. It had by now become standard practice to employ a jury of recognition in cases concerning the restoration of land, and the king's writ to his son stated that a sworn inquest should be held to determine what land Canterbury had held before Thomas's exile.[8] Thomas, for his part, remained silent on the question of the kiss of peace although he did try to trick the king into giving it to him by sitting next to the monarch at mass where the kiss was normally given. Thomas declined Henry's request to assume secular duties back in England and the king did not press the point. At the conclusion of the conference the two ex-foes agreed to meet in Rouen on the first of November and proceed together to England.

Henry, however, was drawn south by a French attack on Berry and was unable to keep his November appointment with Becket. In his place he sent one of his own clerical advisers, John of Oxford, with a message instructing the archbishop to cross to England in the company of John. This choice of a traveling companion for the archbishop did little to assuage Becket's suspicion of a plot against him, coming as it did hard upon the news from his advance party in England that the promised restitution of property had not been made nor were there indications that it ever would. Hesitant to ascribe perfidy to the king and choosing rather to blame his own enemies whose influence was strong with Henry, Thomas sailed for England on the first of December, confident that an interview with his former pupil, the young King Henry, would set all aright.

The fighting season in 1170 lasted longer than usual and kept Henry in the south until the middle of December. By Christmas he was back in Normandy and held his court at Bures. The king was in fine fettle as he reviewed the successes of the past year and reveled in the unchallenged position he enjoyed atop a peaceful realm. His eldest son had been crowned, his other boys provided for, and the recent reforms in English administration promised less grumbling and more revenue from the island. Things were quiet on the Continent, where the groundwork had been laid for peaceful expansion by the marriage that year of Henry's daughter Eleanor to the twelve-year-old ruler of Castile, Alfonso VIII. Most satisfying of all, Becket's six-year exile was over; being back within the king's jurisdiction, the archbishop could be watched and kept under control.

This royal euphoria evaporated, however, on the day after Christmas with the arrival at Bures of Archbishop Roger of York accompanied by Bishops Gilbert Foliot of London and Jocelyn of Salisbury, bringing news of Thomas's actions on the island. His first step upon reaching England, complained Roger, had been to reimpose the suspension of himself and the excommunication of the other prelates who had been involved in the recent coronation. Surrounded by the sympathetic ears of the king's court, the trio poured out an embellished tale of Becket's activities against the king and clergy over the past several weeks. From the mouth of Roger emerged a picture of Becket invading the island at the head of an army, refusing to meet with the young king, seizing land and striking with ecclesiastical censure anyone who stood in his path. As the archbishop's account unfolded court tempers flared until finally the king himself became convinced of Becket's treachery. His fury showed in his countenance which grew red and in his gestures which became wildly animated.[9] "I have nourished and promoted in my realm," he shrieked, "idle and wretched knaves, faithless to their lord, whom they allow to be mocked thus shamefully by a low-born clerk." [10] Four knights who had been standing on the edge of the crowd, seeing in the king's outburst an opportunity to improve their standing at court and at the same time to settle their own personal vendetta with the archbishop, detached themselves from the court and crossed to England intent on doing away with the prelate. It was not until after they had left that Henry learned of their departure and sent several barons to arrest the archbishop.

The scenes that followed are among the more familiar in Western history. The knights' journey to England, their conference with Becket's enemies, and their confrontation and murder of the prelate in his cathedral—all have been retold with exacting detail and speculation in works of history and literature, as well as in plays and motion pictures. Well-known, too, is Henry's reaction when he heard of the murder:

At the first words of the messenger the king burst into loud lamentation and exchanged his royal robes for sackcloth and ashes, acting more like a friend than the sovereign of the deceased. At times he fell into a stupor, after which he would again utter groans and cries louder and more bitter than before. For three whole days he remained shut up in his chamber, and would neither take food nor admit any to comfort him, till it seemed from his excessive grief that he had obstinately made up his mind to contrive his own death.[11]

General agreement as to what happened, however, has not masked the contrariety of opinion as to why it happened. On the surface the archbishop's murder appears to have resulted from a clash of personalities made worse by a string of unfortunate misunderstandings. More deeply, though, it should be seen as the effect of the confrontation between Henry's nascent concept of sovereignty and the Church's more universal image of all human beings as part of the same divine political unit. But the principal question that is asked, and has never been satisfactorily answered, is that concerning Henry's role in the death of his former companion. Did he order the murder or was it carried out unknown and unwanted by him? There is no dearth of evidence to support either contention. Henry's periodic fulminations against Becket, the unspoken judgment at Northampton, Henry's consistent refusal to seal the reconciliation with the kiss of peace, his laxity in providing Thomas's security and possessions once the prelate was back in England, the king's readiness to give credence to the exaggerations of Roger, and his final outburst at Bures which set the knights off on their murderous mission—all suggest a clever royal plan for Becket's removal with a minimum of blame to fall on the king. On the other hand, Henry's often expressed love for the archbishop, his trans-human patience in negotiating with Becket, the anticipated enmity of Louis and Alexander which the murder of Thomas was certain to evoke, Henry's apparently sincere proposal that the archbishop resume secular duties in England, and his public repentance over the murder, support Becket's own feeling that the king was led astray by counsellors who were bent on improving their own relations at court.

There is much to suggest that Henry was not entirely blameless in the affair. For him to have planned, or at least encouraged, some drastic action against Becket would have been consistent with the character of the king who, at the beginning of his reign, did not hesitate to remove former friends and allies who stood between him and his plan for autocratic control of England. Furthermore, for the assassination to have taken place without Henry's knowledge or encouragement suggests a laxity of royal control not evident elsewhere in the king's dealings with his nobility. The warning signals that preceded the murder were too frequent and too apparent to have been misread and gone unacted upon by a king as shrewd and powerful as Henry Plantagenet unless he wished to ignore them. Becket sensed what was in store for him and surely Henry, who was no less perceptive and far more conversant with the thoughts and plans of Thomas's enemies, could have known no less. And yet he allowed the prelate to walk unsupported into the lion's den. Henry's consistent refusal to seal his bargain with Becket was virtually an admission that he had no intention of abiding by the agreement.

That Henry was the cause, either directly or indirectly, of the archbishop's death was the immediate and universal judgment of Europe. The French king sent ambassadors to the pope urging him to bring the full force of the Church to bear on Henry by excommunicating him and pronouncing an interdict on his lands. Henry countered by dispatching to the papal court a delegation of his own bishops which succeeded in averting the excommunication. The pope, however, took the question of the interdict under advisement. While the matter was being considered the Angevin king embarked on a diplomatic and military program designed to influence papal deliberations. In the spring of 1171 he concluded an alliance with the count of Savoy, Humbert of Maurienne, one of the strongest pillars of the papal party and a dedicated anti-imperialist. By betrothing his son John to the count's daughter, Alice, Henry tried to gain a champion at the papal curia while at the same time spreading his influence across the Alpine passes into Italy and along the Mediterranean coast.

Although nothing was to come of these marriage plans, it is likely that Humbert's influence with the pope helped to avert the interdict.

More ambitious was the next step Henry took to appease Alexander. Affairs in Ireland had developed to the point where the time was ripe for the English king to undertake the long-postponed expedition to the island. In the first place, Henry's presence in Ireland would place him out of reach of the papal legates and their fearsome censure, should the pope decide to pronounce it. Secondly, a union of the Irish and English churches had long had the pope's blessing. Fifteen years earlier Alexander's predecessor had bestowed on Henry the hereditary possession of Ireland, and Henry's success in the venture at this time would help to diminish pontifical ire over the Becket affair. The church in Ireland had grown up in quite a different manner than it had in the remainder of Europe. Reflecting the general political anarchy of the country, the Irish church lacked effective central organization or direction. Bishops were for the most part unattached to specific ecclesiastical sees and recognized no superior among themselves. Christianity had developed on the island as a group of independent brotherhoods, each following the lead of a monastic bishop. Lacking a unifying hand, Christian morality retained a large amount of earlier paganism. Perched as it was on the western flank of European civilization and politically isolated from the rest of Christendom, the lone island had escaped the papal reforms which had brought a strong measure of unity to the rest of the Church in the preceding century.

Political and military conditions, as well, were favorable for Henry's move. For one thing, the looks of discontent that had crossed the faces of his three eldest sons when he had disclosed that they must provide for young John out of their inheritances, were not lost on the king. A conquered Ireland, reasoned Henry, would provide an ideal inheritance for his favorite youngest son and avoid future acrimony between the other boys. For another, Ireland, like Wales, had for over a millennium been the scene of decentralized anarchy and infighting between a large number of princes, each of whom was sovereign in his small territory. Although these rulers gave lip service to the primacy of one of their number, whom they styled the High King, this only added to the intrigue without stabilizing the country. In 1166, while Henry was quashing revolts on the Continent, one of these princes, Dermot MacMurrough, was exiled by the others for stealing the High King's wife and went to the Continent to seek Henry Plantagenet's assistance in reinstating him. Henry was too occupied at the time to give personal attention to the plea and detailed one of his lords from the Welsh marches, Richard earl of Clare (called Strongbow), to support the Irish prince. Little came of the venture at the time, but three years later another of Henry's barons, Robert fitz Stephen, landed in Ireland at the head of a small army and captured Wexford. The following year Strongbow, spurred to action by Robert's success, sailed to Ireland and together with Dermot unseated the High King and took Dublin and Waterford. A union of the adventurous Norman colonists took place in May, 1171, when Dermot died and Strongbow, on the strength of his marriage to Dermot's daughter, inherited his kingship and his lands.

Thus the situation that confronted Henry Plantagenet in the summer of 1171 was a familiar one—the tendency of Anglo-Norman colonists to create an independent principality within what he considered his own sphere of influence. Fortunately, developments on the island provided Henry with an opportunity to step in and appear as the protector of the Irish. Strongbow's assumption of the kingship in May was strongly opposed by many of the Irish chiefs to whom the elective principle of kingship was almost sacred. Several of them banded together and besieged the Norman knights in Dublin. In August Henry crossed from Normandy to England where he remained only long enough to visit the deathbed of the venerable Henry of Blois at Winchester. Leaving his son in nominal charge of the kingdom, he passed through England and into southern Wales where in September he began preparations for an expedition to Ireland. His first step was to conclude an agreement with his erstwhile enemy, Prince Rhys. In return for men and supplies which Henry could use against the Irish, the Welsh chief was granted custody of extensive lands in South Wales, including the much disputed castle of Cardigan and its environs.

By the end of September the royal forces, consisting of Welsh mercenaries and feudal knights, were assembled at Pembroke and ready to cross to Ireland. Richard of Clare, anxious to avoid incurring his monarch's wrath, came to the camp and surrendered to the king the chief Norman holdings on the island. Strongbow was permitted to retain the rest. Early in October Henry led his army of 4000 men to Waterford where he received the submission of the Irish kings of Cork and Limerick. In mid-November he reached Dublin where the remaining kings of southern Ireland accepted his suzerainty. As he had hoped, the Irish saw Henry as a liberator who was freeing them from the depredations of the ambitious Norman princes. Not wishing to tarnish this image by military action against the Irish, Henry refrained from marching into northern Ireland, whose chiefs remained hostile and unplacated. With three fourths of the island effectively under his control, the king could afford to be magnanimous.

Aware that pontifical eyes were following his every move, and that the strongest force for unity in his new possession was the Church, the king held an ecclesiastical council at Cashel which, under the leadership of his own chaplain, handed down a mass of decrees aimed at bringing the Irish church in line with that of England. At the council the king also arranged for the future governance of the island by distributing his land among a number of English barons who were to hold it from and administer it for the monarch. Strongbow was made governor of the country and granted some land in Leinster. In effect Henry created a clever balance of power between the Norman princes, the Irish chiefs, and himself. Without striking a single blow he destroyed the separatist movement, increased his own power and prestige, and gave the pope all the ammunition he needed to absolve him from guilt in the murder of Becket. Henry II's introduction of English authority into southern Ireland was to last exactly 750 years. Eight centuries later the native Irish in the north were still discontent with the nature of English rule.

The king remained in Ireland until April, 1172, making sure that his political and ecclesiastical provisions for the island got off to a good start. He celebrated Christmas at Dublin in a new palace built for him outside the walls of the city. In March he moved to Wexford where he received the most disquieting news that trouble was again brewing on the Continent. His mainland enemies had taken advantage of his absence to unite against him. But this time a new factor had entered the picture: Henry's own sons—Richard in Aquitaine and Geoffrey in Brittany—egged on by their mother, had succumbed to the blandishments of the

other disaffected continental princes and were close to joining a
new alliance against the English king. As the challenges piled up,
Henry realized at once that it was now more imperative than ever
that he settle the affair of Becket's murder so that he could give
his attention to these new developments. Consequently he left
Ireland in May, sped through Wales and England, and crossed to
Normandy so quickly that Louis was prompted to comment that
"the English king seems rather to come on wings than by horse or
boat." [12]

Although Henry Plantagenet was ready, within reason, to submit to whatever penance the pope proposed by way of retribution
for the murder of Becket, he was not prepared for the severity of
the suggestions which the legates placed before him when he arrived at Savigny in May. At first he refused to consider the papal
proposals and threatened to go back to Ireland. But several days
of thought convinced him that he had no choice but to agree to
the terms with the hope of having them modified later on. At
Avranches, on the 19th of May, he agreed to do public penance
for his part in the prelate's death and promised to support 200
soldiers on a crusade in the Holy Land for one year, to withdraw
the Constitutions of Clarendon and rescind any new customs he
had introduced into the kingdom, to return all of Canterbury's
possessions, and to fight the Saracens in Spain if the pope requested it.[13] The king was then escorted outside the church where,
in public view and on his knees, he was publicly absolved by the
legates for his part in the murder.

In Henry's eyes this was a small price to pay for the removal of
the nagging suspicion, shared by all of Europe, over his part in
the Becket murder—a suspicion that had tied his hands and kept
him from dealing openly with more immediate matters. Now he
could turn to the storm that was gathering on the Continent,
unhampered, he thought, by the division within the Church
and the nobility of England. During the summer of 1172 he tried
to defuse the situation created by his sons' discontent by mollifying them. In June he formally installed Richard as the duke of
Aquitaine and two months later, at Winchester, young Henry
was crowned again, this time with Margaret at his side. An indication of the lengths to which the king was prepared to go to
satisfy Louis and disarm the French monarch's attempts to turn
his sons against him is seen in the fact that the coronation was

performed not by Roger of York, who was totally unacceptable to the French king, but by Rotrou, the Norman bishop of Rouen. Yet these tokens of pacification were superficial. Henry continued to refuse his sons the only thing they really wanted—true authority to match their titles.

By September the king's emissaries had concluded their negotiations with the papal legates concerning Henry's penances. The final terms of the settlement, which were sealed at a synod held at Michaelmas, show that Henry was not going to give away much in that area either. The promise to supply 200 soldiers was commuted to a pledge to found three religious houses. Not surprisingly, the king and his counsellors had been unable to find any new customs to repeal among the constitutions. Henry did agree to lift the ban on clerical appeals to Rome, and he did back down and allow the continuation of clerical immunity from secular courts. On the whole, the terms of Henry's final concord with the Church represented a compromise in which the king gave way on several points which were important, but not critical, to his claim to sovereignty. Probably the most important effect of the Becket affair was to slow down the monarch's hitherto headlong plunge toward absolutism and provide ammunition to his enemies, both old and new, in their gathering campaign to curb his expansive tendencies.

By the end of 1172 Henry Plantagenet appeared to be at the height of his power. His persistence had paid off and he seemed, for the first time in his reign, to have total control of the intricate situations both at home and abroad. The most troublesome factor in both areas, Becket's defiance, had been removed and Henry had escaped from the threat in relatively good shape. The archbishop was gone and the king had managed to convince both the Church and the laity of his innocence in the affair. His drive for direct control of the administrative reins both in England and on the Continent was gaining momentum and he could look back with justifiable satisfaction on the judicial and political reforms which his court had inspired during the past eight years. He had managed, it appeared, to smooth the ruffled feathers of his domestic and foreign foes without yielding one tittle of his power. Upon his sons he had bestowed the titles to his lands and upon the French king a crown for his daughter. He had quieted the English baronage, and through a series of administrative appointments he had stifled the incipient murmurings among the nobility of his continental lands. He had brought Brittany into his realm and installed his son Geoffrey there as his viceroy. He had muted the dissatisfaction among the Aquitainians, always restless at the threat of foreign control, by appointing one of their own race, Richard the son of their duchess, to rule them. In addition, his tentacles were spreading, through the medium of the marriage alliance, into new areas: Spain, northern Italy, and Sicily. By 1172 negotiations were well under way for the marriage of Henry's third daughter, Joanna, to the Norman king of Sicily, William. As the beginning of his old age (40) approached, Henry II had every right to expect a satisfying twilight period in which the struggles of the past against the nobility, the Church, and the French king, would bear the fruits of peace and compliance with his indomitable will.

CHAPTER IX

A Family Mutiny
(1173–1174)

HENRY PLANTAGENET'S DREAM OF AN OLD AGE GRACED WITH PEACE and order was shattered by the effects of that very strain of his character which had given rise to the dream in the first place—his strong authoritarian temperament. Henry was the type of ruler who brought to every problem a preconceived solution designed to increase his own power. Most of his time and energy was then devoted to devising ways of forcing others to adopt his point of view. While he set the goals he relied on his counsellors and advisers to come up with the methods for reaching them. This technique had worked well in his relations with the barons and the clergy, to whom feudalism provided scant recourse and whom Henry was able to compensate in other areas. In his drive to install himself at the center of political life he seldom deprived a lord of his possessions without compensating him in some way, usually by giving him a fief for which the baron became his vassal. With the notable exception of Becket, the king had also been able to keep the clergy relatively calm by providing ecclesiastical rewards for compliance.

But the king's pride stopped neither at the door of his bedchamber nor at those of his sons. Queen Eleanor, who two decades earlier had turned to Henry in revulsion against the monkish qualities of her first husband, must often in the intervening years have wished for a miraculous infusion into her second spouse of at least a jot of Louis's monastic humility and gentleness. But Henry's personality was different from that of the French king. To him, as to most princes of the Middle Ages, marriage was primarily a divinely ordained method for the production of heirs and the cementing of alliances. No doubt the queen, whose romantic proclivities have been distorted and exaggerated by some of her biographers, to some degree shared her husband's view of herself as a vehicle for the building of the royal family. At

this enterprise she had been eminently successful, having produced eight children in the first fifteen years of their union. But
this point marked the outer boundary of agreement between king
and queen. Henry, rapacious as monarch, husband, and father,
was determined that his family should fall into line behind his
political ambitions. To what extent his inability to trust his family was politically motivated, and how much it was an expression
of his temperament, is impossible to determine. But Henry's
treatment of his sons bears all the earmarks of an overprotective
parent who continued to look upon his three eldest teen-age boys
as the helpless dependent waifs they had been a decade earlier.
Such an attitude can result in domestic strife in the humblest of
families, but when raised to the royal level, where weightier matters intrude, it could—and did—threaten the stability of an entire kingdom. It is not difficult to understand the dilemma created in the minds of the young Henry, now eighteen, Richard
who was fifteen, and the fourteen-year-old Geoffrey, by the con-
flicting pictures they held, on the one hand, of a world crammed
with exciting opportunities and, on the other, of a father who
appeared bent on keeping them from having a share of this
world.

The gravity of the situation was deepened by the fact that the
frustrations and deep inner resentments of the three boys were
supported, albeit for different reasons, by Eleanor, Louis, and
many of the nobles. The queen's bases for dissatisfaction were
several. In the arena of extramarital sexual activity Henry
seemed, as he had in other areas, to be returning to the practices
of his grandfather, although hardly on the grand scale of Beauclerc. Of recent years the king's affections had strayed from Eleanor in the direction of Rosamund, the daughter of a Shropshire
knight, Walter Clifford. During her younger days the queen had
not been entirely blameless in this regard, but now as her fiftieth
birthday approached she interpreted her husband's antics in a
different light. To her impatience with Henry's infidelities was
added a liberal maternal philosophy toward her sons. Herein lay
the basic differences between her and Henry. For all his clever
manipulations and undeniably great political acumen, Henry II
remained a large egg in a small basket. The arena of his travels
and first-hand knowledge was bounded by Ireland and Paris,
Scotland and the Pyrenees. Of the macrocosm outside these con-

fines the king seemed to have had little knowledge and less interest. Although he promised to go on a crusade, he never seriously
intended to make the effort. All his negotiations with princes east
of Paris were done by embassy or within his own lands. For all his
nervous peregrinations within his realm, he never left its boundaries except for an occasional trip to Paris or Flanders. This is
surprising since many of his ancestors had been at home in the
larger world which lay outside England and France. His mother
had been empress of the Germans before burying herself in Anglo-
Norman affairs. His Angevin grandfather, two of his uncles, and
his cousin had all been kings of Jerusalem.[1] But Henry, emulat-
ing his father, had restricted his talents to his homeland, the result being that he developed a rather circumscribed view of the
world and of the people that inhabited it. Eleanor's background
was quite different. She had grown up in a duchy where ideas
were oriented toward the Mediterranean and were in many ways
antithetical to those of northern European society. While she was
still married to Louis she had traveled to the Holy Land where
the apposition of her views to those of the northern French had
led her into difficulty with and ultimate separation from her husband. Her outlook was more cosmopolitan and her approach
more intuitive, more experienced and, in general, more liberal
than that of either of her matrimonial partners. It was from this
perspective that she viewed the future of her sons. The queen
realized, as the king apparently never did, that peace both within
the family and the realm would more surely be guaranteed by
investing her sons with both power and responsibility than by
Henry's policy of granting symbolic, but empty, titles. Not that
the boys were blameless. Like their father they too were grasping
and yearned for real power and authority and were extremely
jealous, not only of the king but of one another as well. The only
solution, in Eleanor's eyes, was a gradual, systematic recognition
of their rightful claims. When it became evident that Henry was
unwilling to make these concessions, the queen sided with her
sons.

Louis VII's support of Henry's three sons had a different motive. All the Angevins, including Henry himself, except in his role
as king of England, were his vassals and it remained his right and
responsibility to adjudicate grievances between them. Despite the
repeated treaties of peace and amity between the two kings, the

reduction of Henry to a position approximating true vassalage remained the unswerving goal of French policy. In addition, Louis was still unconvinced of Henry's innocence in the murder of Becket and not at all pleased to see the English king emerge from the affair as strong as ever. The opportunity which the Plantagenet children presented him was too great to let pass. Also rumbling in the background were the submerged complaints of many of Henry's English and continental barons who, disgruntled by the king's gradual erosion of their perquisites and chafing under much the same type of tutelage as the king's sons, were ready to join any movement which would provide a vehicle to deliver them from their discontent.

All of these festering frustrations coalesced around young Henry in March, 1173. A month before the young king had accompanied his father into Auvergne on a diplomatic mission aimed at strengthening the Plantagenet hand in the northern Mediterranean. At a conference at Montferrand Henry II had acted as a mediator between Raymond of Toulouse and the king of Aragon, who had been fighting over Provence. As a result of the prestige Henry gained through his successful arbitration between the two princes, the count of Toulouse did homage to the English king for his county. At the same conference, completed at Limoges a month later, Henry and the count of Maurienne put the finishing touches on their earlier arrangement for the marriage of young John to Humbert's daughter. The Angevin king, anxious to outflank Louis geographically by pushing his influence into Italy, acceded to Humbert's request for a dowry to accompany the marriage. Since nothing remained of his possessions after their distribution between his three eldest sons three years earlier, the king was forced to reclaim part of young Henry's inheritance. He promised Humbert that John's marriage portion would consist of the castles of Chinon, Loudun, and Mirabeau, traditionally the appanage of the youngest Angevin offspring. The three castles formed a strategic triangle in the heart of the Angevin lands and whoever held them occupied the key to communications between the far-flung sections of Henry's continental domains.

The young king was visibly upset by the agreement and refused to agree to it. All he could see was that he was being dispossessed by his six-year-old brother who was quickly becoming his father's favorite. On the return journey to Normandy, while the royal

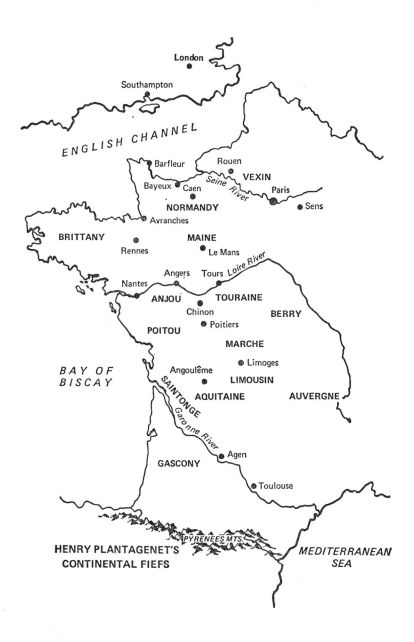

London

Southampton

ENGLISH CHANNEL

Barfleur

Rouen

VEXIN

Seine River

Bayeux Caen

Paris

Sens

NORMANDY

Avranches

BRITTANY

MAINE

Rennes

Le Mans

Angers Tours Loire River

Nantes

ANJOU

TOURAINE

BERRY

Chinon

POITOU

Poitiers

MARCHE

BAY OF
BISCAY

Angoulême

Limoges

LIMOUSIN

SAINTONGE

AQUITAINE

AUVERGNE

Garonne River

GASCONY

Agen

Toulouse

PYRENEES MTS.

HENRY PLANTAGENET'S
CONTINENTAL FIEFS

MEDITERRANEAN
SEA

party was resting at Chinon for the king's fortieth birthday (May 5), young Henry stole out of the camp at night and three days later joined his father-in-law at Chartres. The youngster took a circuitous route, riding first north through Alençon and Argentan before turning southeast toward Chartres. His purpose in going first into Normandy and then to France can only be surmised. Rather than being the result of indecision, the long trip was probably undertaken by Henry to alert his supporters in Maine and Normandy and inform them that he had thrown down the gauntlet and challenged his father. It would seem that the young king's flight to Chartres had been prepared in advance, with fresh horses posted along the 250-mile route. Eleanor, as miffed as her son by her husband's disregard, encouraged the flight. Henry took out after his son but was unable to catch him and turned back to fortify his castles along the French border. Louis welcomed the young refugee warmly and the two monarchs went together to Paris where they were joined, a few days later, by Richard and Geoffrey, also acting at their mother's prompting.

Five weeks passed before hostilities began. The great amount of diplomatic and military preparation that the young Henry had completed by the middle of June suggests that the groundwork for the revolt had already been laid before the fateful promises at Limoges, and that young Henry's desertion was the signal for the rising of the malcontents. At Paris, Louis treated young Henry as the only legitimate king of England and refused to receive an embassy sent by his father. The youth, enjoying at last the exercise of real authority so long denied him by his father, played the role to the hilt. At a grand meeting of Henry Plantagenet's enemies the young king forged an alliance with his father's insular and continental foes by promising them land after the English king's defeat. Before the eyes of the Scots king, William, he dangled the suzerainty of all the lands north of the river Tyne, and he tempted the monarch's brother David with the counties of Huntingdon and Cambridge. Hugh Bigod was guaranteed an increase of his lands in Norfolk. Philip, the count of Flanders, was weaned from his allegiance to Henry Plantagenet by the assurance of the county of Kent, while his brother Matthew, the count of Boulogne, was promised Mortain in return for his support of the insurrection. Theobald of Blois joined the rebels after he was guaranteed Amboise as his portion of the spoils. Three score of the lesser barons, drawn to Paris by their grudges against the English king, were persuaded that the father's days were numbered and that the future lay with the son. Missing from the cabal was the chief instigator of the affair, Eleanor. Shortly after her sons' successful escape the queen, dressed in men's clothing, set out after them but was seized by the agents of her husband and her period of freedom came to an end.[2]

Henry Plantagenet was now faced with a war on two fronts, a situation that he had scrupulously avoided up till then. With uncharacteristic calmness, he set up his headquarters at Rouen.[3] He considered that city the key to the continental phase of the coming conflict, and entrusted the defense of England to Richard of Luci and those barons whom he could trust. Of the two theaters, the situation on the Continent was the graver, for there the allies enjoyed an overwhelming superiority in men and supplies. Lacking time to call up his cumbersome feudal array—which in any case would have failed to provide him with a sufficient length of service for what promised to be a long campaign—Henry fell back on the practice which by then had become standard. He used his well-stocked Treasury to hire soldiers from the northern European duchies of the emperor.[4] The king planned his continental strategy to take the best advantage of the one asset he did have, that of interior lines. He built a "Maginot Line" along the eastern borders of Normandy by strengthening the string of fortresses that dotted the boundary, and his Brabantine mercenaries, stationed in the heart of the duchy, were to act as a mobile striking force which he could move to any point on the perimeter which his enemies chose to pierce. In England the contest was more evenly matched for, although powerful forces were arrayed against Henry, including the Scots king, Hugh Bigod, and the earls of Leicester and Chester, the majority of the nobles and clerics remained at the king's side.

The rebels' strategy on the Continent called for a two-pronged drive aimed at capturing the Norman capital. A southward attack from Flanders was to be coordinated with a northward push from the Paris-Chartres region of France. This pincer movement began at the end of June. After crossing into Normandy at Aumale, Philip of Flanders and his brother Matthew headed north for the seacoast and captured Neufchâtel after a two-week siege. The Flemings then advanced on Arques, near the coast, which they took after a hard battle. Henry's defensive perimeter had been punctured in the north, and as the allied drive there gained momentum it threatened to cut his realm in two by severing communications between England and its king. But then Henry had his first stroke of good luck. During the battle for Arques, Matthew of Boulogne was struck in the knee by an arrow and several days later succumbed to the wound. Philip, distraught by his brother's death, interpreted it as divine retribution for his desertion of the English king, called a halt to the invasion, and marched his army back to Flanders.[5] Relieved of pressure in the north, Henry was able to give his full attention to the southeastern front where the second arm of the pincer, led by the French king, had reached Verneuil and set up a siege around the town. The Angevin's army, swollen by the recent addition of a large contingent of mercenaries from Ireland under Strongbow,[6] marched south from Rouen. Upon reaching the beleaguered city Henry laid down an ultimatum to the French king, telling him either to stand up and fight or to withdraw from Verneuil. Louis chose the latter course and retreated to France, leaving behind an enormous store of military supplies and provisions. Both arms of the pincer had been withdrawn and the future of young Henry's rebellion looked bleak.

Displaying a suicidal lack of coordination, the rebels next staged an uprising in Brittany. Less than two weeks after Louis left Verneuil Henry's perennial opponent, Ralph of Fougères, aided this time by the earl of Chester, seized most of the duchy. Henry reacted swiftly by dispatching his Brabantines to the town of Dol on the Norman-Breton border and the mercenaries took the town along with the two rebel leaders and a score of important Breton knights.[7] Henry's exploitation of interior lines, greatly abetted by luck and the almost unbelievable ineptitude of his foes, put him in a commanding position on the Continent by the time the curtain fell on the fighting season in November.

Henry Plantagenet's success in Normandy during the summer and autumn of 1173 was duplicated in England. While Louis was besieging Verneuil in June, the royalist forces in England took the offensive against the stronghold of the island's traitors. These pockets of resistance were concentrated in three areas: in the north where Hugh, bishop of Durham, with the weight of the Scots behind him became the center of opposition from his numerous castles; in the eastern county of Norfolk, whose earl, Hugh Bigod, had joined the French alliance at Paris; and in the midlands around Leicester, whose Earl Robert, the son of Henry's late justiciar, was at the time on the Continent buying an army for use in England. In June the king's forces under Richard of Luci struck at Leicester, hoping to take advantage of the earl's absence to capture the city and castle and thereby drive a wedge between the northern and eastern enclaves of rebellion. Although the town of Leicester fell quickly to the king's army, the castle put up a stubborn resistance. Richard was forced to lift the siege at the end of July, when King William invaded from Scotland and threatened the entire north. Richard raced northward to meet the invaders and drove them back towards their border. Then the conflict flared up in the east. At the end of August Robert of Leicester landed on the East Anglian coast with his Flemish mercenaries[8] and, after conferring with Hugh Bigod at Framlingham, headed westward in an attempt to link his own midland strongholds with those of the Norfolk lord. Richard had to abandon his pursuit of the Scots. He concluded a truce with their king and hurried south to cut off Leicester's westward march. The two armies clashed north of Cambridge on the 17th of October. The Flemings were destroyed in a bloody battle and the earl of Leicester, along with his leading lieutenants, was taken prisoner. When the fighting season ended the royal forces were in an excellent position, having prevented a linkup of the scattered rebel areas and having seized one of the chief leaders of the revolt.

Henry Plantagenet had managed to frustrate the rebels' plans because neither in England nor on the Continent did he have to face serious concerted attacks on his positions from more than one quarter at a time. The rebels in England, realizing their error, changed their strategy the following year and coordinated their drives. In April, William of Scotland resumed his invasion from the north while Hugh Bigod set out on a campaign of harassing royal castles throughout eastern England. At the same time, young Henry and Philip of Flanders, recovered from the shock of his brother's death, were gathering a large force at Boulogne for an invasion of England. These concerted attacks proved more successful than the isolated uprisings of the previous summer. The Scots ruler, strongly supported by the northern barons, reached the Tyne before Richard could check his advance. But the pressure proved too stubborn for the English justiciar and in July he appealed to Henry to come to England from the Continent to assist him. Henry, who had been campaigning against the rebels in Maine and Anjou, rushed to England with his mercenaries on the 8th of July and in less than a month had cleaned out the eastern rebels. William the Lion was captured at Alnwick[9] and the submission of the northern barons followed in rapid succession. By the 8th of August the revolt was over in England and Henry Plantagenet was on his way back across the Channel with his Brabantines and 1000 Welsh infantrymen and archers whom he had added to his army.

Henry's quick departure from England was motivated by the disquieting news that Louis had again taken the offensive on the Continent. As soon as Henry had left for England the French king had once again invaded Normandy and reached its capital which he proceeded to besiege. Henry's destruction of the rebels in England had ruined the hopes of Philip's invasion, and the mass of arms and men that had been collected at Boulogne was diverted to Rouen to strengthen the siege. While Henry was en route to the Norman city the French tried to take the city by ruse. The 10th of August was the feast of Saint Lawrence, a martyr revered by both sides. Louis and the citizens of Rouen agreed to a 24-hour truce so that the holy day could be celebrated. Philip of Flanders persuaded the king to attack the city while its inhabitants were singing and dancing in honor of the saint. But a cleric in a wall turret noticed the French preparations and sounded the alarm. The French attack was beaten back with heavy casualties[10] but the dishonor incurred by the rebels in breaking their promise was more debilitating than the material losses. Henry and his mercenaries reached the city the following day and entered it by the back door on the Seine which had been kept open. He found among the inhabitants a revived sense of confidence and immediately sent his Welsh mercenaries, whose guerrilla tactics had been perfected against Henry's troops in Wales, into the woods around the capital to strangle the enemy supply lines coming from Paris. From their hidden concealments among the trees the Welsh kept up a steady attack on the French supply trains and after two days the loss of food and supplies began to have its effect on the besiegers. Louis, already shattered by the failure of his earlier attack, ordered the siege to be lifted and his army to return to France. With Louis's retreat from Rouen the continental phase of the revolt, like its English counterpart earlier in the month, came to an end. Independent rebel campaigns in the Angevin lands quickly ended. Richard, who had been campaigning in the south, raced to his father and pleaded for forgiveness when he saw the failure of his brothers and Louis to take Rouen. The most serious challenge to his rule that Henry was to experience throughout his reign was over.

Henry Plantagenet's conduct of operations in the two-year rebellion belies several common conceptions concerning the nature of medieval warfare. It has long been a tenet that medieval military activity lacked strategic thinking and planning, and was characterized by impetuous and uncontrolled charges of one opponent against another.[11] Henry's campaign against his sons is one instance among many which shows this conception to be ill founded. The English king's strategic and tactical moves against his rivals were of the highest caliber. He lacked no funds to prosecute the war and he did not hesitate to use them wisely to procure men and equipment. He recognized the strength of his interior position and took full advantage of it by siting his headquarters and a flexible fighting force in the heart of Normandy. Henry also possessed a well-organized and efficient (for the time) communication system; this resulted in a rapid flow of news and provided him with the intelligence necessary to plan his moves successfully. Even more impressive was his transportation system which facilitated the king's speedy movement from the Continent to England and back again on two occasions—the second with an army and a shipload of prisoners—to coordinate the two phases of the conflict.

The second cliché often heard is that the Middle Ages were marked by "supremacy of the mail-clad horseman," [12]—the feudal knight. Yet in the suppression of the rebellion of 1173–74, both in England and on the Continent, it was the king's mercenaries who supplied the most important victories for the king. In England the hired soldiers did in three weeks what the feudal forces had been unable to accomplish in two years, while at Rouen the defeat of the French once again illustrated that the mounted feudal knight, out of his area of expertise in siege warfare, was vulnerable to the artistry of guerrilla foot soldiers.[13] Nor was this conflict an isolated example of the growing importance of both strategic planning and the use of hired soldiers in warfare. As the twelfth century progressed the instances of sound strategic thinking and successful substitution of mercenaries for knights were multiplied to the point where this century can be considered a watershed in the reintroduction of these two important facets of military procedure.

But although Henry won the war against the rebels, the terms of peace he offered the vanquished show that the Angevin monarch had not changed his attitude toward his sons. The conditions of peace, agreed upon near Tours at the end of September, suggest that the monarch still wanted to have his cake and eat it. He could still not act decisively against his sons and with notable clemency he granted them a general amnesty demanding as security only that they again do homage to him. Even though his victory had been complete and had placed him in a position to dictate the settlement, he tried to mollify his sons with grants which, under the circumstances, were quite liberal. Young Henry was given two castles in Normandy which he was to treat as his own and an annual allowance of £4000. Richard received a pair of castles in Poitou and half the annual income from that duchy. Geoffrey received more land in Brittany. But John, whose inheritance had provided the spark that touched off the revolt, came out best of all. Besides the honors of Nottingham and Marlborough in England, he received estates and castles in Normandy and Anjou which placed him on a par with his older brothers. It was a curious compromise in which Henry tried to bring together the irreconcilable. For any strengthening of John, who was already in line for the Italian lands of Humbert of Maurienne, was bound to increase his brothers' envy.[14]

The monarch's leniency, however, was missing from his treatment of the other conspirators. Eleanor, whom the king had brought to England during his hurried trip there in July, 1174, was sent to the castle at Salisbury where she was to remain a prisoner for the next decade. The English lords who had defied the king were treated in the usual fashion by having the walls of their castles pulled down. But the harshest treatment was reserved for the Scots. Henry used King William's disloyalty as a pretext to bring the entire northern kingdom directly under English rule. The Scots king, his brother David, and all the barons and lords of

Scotland were made to do homage to Henry and to his eldest son. Through this measure the lords of Scotland were bound by oath to support Henry against their own king should William make any future move against the English monarch. The church in Scotland was placed directly under the English church, with English clerics given carte blanche to reform it and bring it into line with its southern neighbor. William was also forced to hand over to Henry the most important castles in his country; the English king could use them "at his pleasure." As surety that the castles would be surrendered, Henry took hostages from among the leading men of the realm.[15] As an outcome of the rebellion, Henry Plantagenet grafted the fourth (including Brittany) and final Celtic limb on the English body.

But the terms of reconciliation between father and sons were far from satisfactory to either side. This became clear in the spring of 1175 when young Henry, suspicious of his father's intentions and persuaded by Louis that the same fate awaited him in England as had befallen his mother, refused to return to the island with the king. Finally, after much argument and a tearful reconciliation with his father, the young king, armed with assurances against incarceration, joined the old in May and they crossed to England together. The monarch was faced with a tremendous task of reconstructing English institutions which during the two-year conflict had started to slide back towards a state of laxity. Once again he had to set about to rebuild or patch up the instruments of his authority. He was to remain in England for 27 months, his longest stay on the island during his reign, convening councils and keeping his oldest son at his side where he would have no opportunity to rekindle the revolt. He kept Richard and Geoffrey occupied on the Continent doing what they knew best—mopping up pockets of resistance in Aquitaine and Brittany.

CHAPTER X

Death of the Young King

(1175–1183)

PERHAPS THE MOST PERVASIVE EFFECT, IN THE LONG RUN, OF THE young Plantagenets' revolt against their father was the change it brought about in the character of the aging king. "After the grievous injuries inflicted upon him by his sons," reports Gerald, "he became an open violator of the marriage bond." [1] With Eleanor tucked safely away at Salisbury and Rosamund clothed in the habit of religion at Godstow (where she died in 1176) the king's attention now focused on Alice, the blossoming French princess who had been betrothed to Richard in 1169.[2] Like her sister Margaret years before, Alice had been taken to Normandy to be reared in the Angevin household. During the revolt, in 1174, when she was thirteen, the princess was moved aboard the same vessel that bore Queen Eleanor to her confinement, to England where, if Gerald is to be believed, she became Henry's mistress.[3] The king's incontinence, far from being a personal matter, touched directly upon his relations with France and was to become a major irritant in the diplomatic moves between the two countries for the rest of Henry's life. Alice remained at the English court right up till the king's last days and for fifteen years the combined efforts of kings, bishops, and popes failed to dislodge her. Her name came up in all the conferences between Henry and the French monarchs, first Louis and then Philip, who tried to force the Angevin either to marry her to Richard or to allow her to return to her homeland. But Henry Plantagenet found the young girl too profitable both personally and diplomatically to let her go.

Another of Henry's latent character weaknesses that became accentuated by the revolt was an exaggerated suspicion of the motives of those who surrounded him. The disloyalties of Becket, Eleanor, and his sons, coming as they did one hard upon another, coalesced to turn the monarch into an overcautious ruler who, after 1175, withdrew more and more from the affairs of state and became "dilatory in maintaining law and justice." [4] Seemingly gripped by a persecution complex, he "did not permit himself to be seen as good men desired but, shutting himself up within doors, he was accessible only to those who seemed unworthy of such approach." [5] What was perhaps more damaging, he became a practiced dissimulator whose promises and oaths became increasingly less worthy of trust. The forthrightness with which he had met difficulties during the first twenty years of his reign was noticeably missing during the final fifteen. This was an almost complete metamorphosis of personality—from one of easy access, wit, and charity,[6] to one of suspicion, unreliability, and aloofness —brought on by a combination of discouragement at the disloyalty of those closest to him and increasing old age and illness.

The results of this change that came over Henry after 1175 were most evident in the legislation of his court during the second half of his reign. This legislation consisted for the most part of modifications of existing assizes and decrees; indeed, we can search in vain through the 1170s and 1180s for legislation that bore the stamp of imagination and originality that had characterized his earlier decrees. Fortunately, the major enactments of his reign were already on the books and the institutions for keeping the state in good working order were already operating smoothly. This was evident during the revolt when the king had had no trouble finding money to finance the war, and the absence of a scutage for the campaigns shows that his system for collecting revenues had been refined to the point where the ordinary income from the kingdom was adequate to support a prolonged military effort. Still the drain on the Treasury had been great. Mercenaries' salaries alone had taken about one fourth of the recorded revenues of the kingdom and, even though Henry had other income whose total is unknown to us, he also had other expenditures for the war. Soon after his return to England in the spring of 1175, therefore, he set about to put the squeeze on existing institutions in order to force them to yield more money.

His eyes fell first on the royal forests. Like his predecessors Henry was extremely jealous of his royal rights in the English woodlands that had been set aside by the Conqueror as parts of the royal domain. These hunting preserves, "the sanctuaries of kings and

their chief delight," comprised extensive forested areas throughout England in which monarchs

repair to hunt, their cares laid aside the while, in order to refresh themselves by a short respite. There, renouncing the arduous, but natural,
turmoil of the court, they breathe the pure air of freedom for a little
space.[7]

Since they were parts of the royal domain, the forests remained
outside the normal jurisdiction of the sheriffs and were administered instead by royal foresters who were answerable directly to
the king. Stringent, but largely scatter-shot decrees, aimed at preventing destruction of these areas, had long been in effect regulat-
ing such things as habitation, the cutting down of trees, or the
hunting of animals within the forests. Henry had suspended the
Laws of the Forest on behalf of his partisans during the revolt but
now, in 1175, he ordered an investigation of all offenses that had
taken place in the past two years. All crimes that were discovered
by sworn inquests were to be reported to him. Even the pleas of
his justiciar Richard, who produced in his defense the king's writ
suspending the rules, fell on deaf ears, and when the inquest was
complete heavy fines were imposed on nobility and clergy alike.
Although these amercements by themselves were hardly sufficient
to replenish the Treasury, the king had found another way to
squeeze money out of his feudal rights. Within a decade these
lucrative regulations were to be put in an organized written form
and extended to all the subjects of his realm.

Economic recovery was rapid during the relatively peaceful
years that followed the rebellion, due largely to the stability of
the Exchequer which Henry had inherited from his grandfather
but which, during the early part of his reign, he had had to rebuild and reorganize. Before the decade of the 1170s had ended
Henry's treasurer, Richard fitz Nigel, wrote a handbook in which
he discussed in great detail the workings of that fiscal and judicial
organization. The production at this time of the *Dialogue of the
Exchequer,* which a later historian would characterize as "one of
the most wonderful things of Henry's wonderful reign," [8] further
suggests that Henry's innovative days were over, for only after an
institution has settled down and begun to harden is it considered

worthwhile to commit such a detailed description of it to writing. The essay, which forms an island of certainty in a sea of conjecture about the Exchequer, provides a lengthy exposé of the sources of Henry's revenue, of how it was handled at the Exchequer, and what were the duties of the officers responsible for the fiscal affairs of the realm. The author was a faithful servant of the king, being the third successive member of his family to serve the English monarchs in a fiscal capacity. His great-uncle, Roger of Salisbury, had organized, and probably founded, the Exchequer under Henry I, and Richard's father, Nigel, had been Henry II's first Treasurer. It should come as no surprise, therefore, to find Richard stoutly defending the practice of Henry and his predecessors of devising money-making schemes "from the hidden desires of their own hearts, or even on occasion from their own arbitrary acts." [9] The Treasurer's minute description of the jobs performed by the chancellor, president, treasurers, scribes, clerks, chamberlains, tellers, and the host of minor officials paints a picture of an institution that is infinitely more mature than that of Henry I.[10] For one thing, by the 1170s the fiscal instrument had competely divorced itself from the king's household and was functioning independently with its own set of officials whose duties were confined to collecting and passing judgment on the kingdom's funds. Also, as a result of this separation from the household, functions within the fiscal body had become, during Henry's reign, highly specialized and consequently more sophisticated. Whereas during Beauclerc's reign, for example, the Treasury was still the center for all financial transactions, by the time Richard wrote it had taken a back seat in the less sophisticated half of the Exchequer, known as the Lower Exchequer, and had become nothing more than a warehouse where the money which flowed in from the counties was weighed, sacked, and stored. It was in the more noble, Upper Exchequer that the financial policy-making decisions and judgments were reached concerning the rightness or wrongness of the accounts. This bureaucratic complexity was undoubtedly the result of Henry Plantagenet's policies and constant quest for funds. Gone were the days when money poured in and out of the royal coffers in haphazard fashion. Henry's regularization of scutages, fines, sales of writs, etc., and his unprecedented need for money for mercenaries, bribes, annuities, castle construction, and diplomacy had created a need for a learned body of economists and jurists to pass reasoned and often intricate judgments on the activities of the king's money collectors, the sheriffs. The Treasury had been pushed into the shadows because, in the words of fitz Nigel "it is easy enough . . . to discover by subtraction whether a debt has been paid or if anything remains. But when one begins to make a detailed investigation of the moneys which come into the Treasury in various ways, and are due for different accounts and are not collected by the sheriffs in the same manner, to be able to discover if the latter have acted in any wise other than they should, this is in many ways a serious business, and for this reason the science of the (Upper) Exchequer is said to be superior." [11]

To a large degree this first major impersonal institution in modern times grew up tangentially as a by-product of the Angevin monarch's attempts to cope with the return of a money economy which was taking place in twelfth-century Europe. Many of the goods and services which a century before had been provided through oaths or in exchange for similar goods and services were, by Henry's time, more conveniently acquired by cash. Henry Plantagenet found this increasingly true whenever he set out to supply himself with an army. The geometric increase in trade during the twelfth century, partly an effect of the Crusades and partly due to the reawakening of industry and the birth of European trade guilds, quickened the pace with which money came to replace the feudal oath as the wherewithal for obtaining the necessities of life. Henry himself probably played only a small direct role in the day-to-day development of the Exchequer. He was equipped neither by temperament nor intellectual bent to dream up the many imaginative and often tedious details that made the institution function as it did. He never remained still long enough to attain the continuity of thought required to work out such a system. The details he left to others—to those barons who, precisely because they were less peripatetic than the king, had the physical and mental stability to build such an institution.

But if Henry did not personally design his Exchequer, there is little doubt that through his experiments and his almost imperious demands for money to finance them he created the atmosphere in which the more mentally gifted could build this economic landmark. The king needed money for everything he did, in times of peace as well as during periods of conflict. The variety of activities for which cash was expended can be seen in the Pipe Rolls. No program seems to have required as constant and as large an outlay of cash as did Henry's castle building. These medieval fortifications, aptly called the "bones of the kingdom," [12] served in peacetime as residences for sheriffs and kings, as administrative centers and local treasuries, and as prisons. When war broke out they became military garrisons from which the king controlled the surrounding countryside. During the early part of his reign Henry had concentrated his castles on the eastern and western fringes, and in the interior, of his realm to discourage invasions from the Continent on the one hand and from the Welsh on the other. After the revolt of 1173–74, as his suspicions mounted, he doubled his efforts to protect the northern and eastern edges of the realm. At Newcastle on the river Tyne, and at Nottingham,[13] construction was completed of mighty fortresses which guarded the strategic approaches from Scotland. On the east coast Henry undertook what was perhaps his most ambitious military project: the enclosure of the keep at Dover Castle ("the gateway to the kingdom") with concentric curtain walls.[14] The cost of this latter fortification alone approached £7000[15] and gives some idea of the scale of the Angevin monarch's expenditure for security. During the 1170s Henry's engineers experimented with architectural variations, particularly in their design of the main building of a castle, the tower keep. Stone keeps both in England and on the Continent had been rectangular, like that of the White Tower in London. Even the large keep at Dover, which was still abuilding in the early 1180s, was square. But it was to be the last major one with that shape. It was slowly becoming apparent in the 1170s that the corners of these square keeps were vulnerable to the picks and bores of an attacker who could work on them undetected and uninterrupted from above. Although it was not until the following century that keep design became cylindrical to solve this problem, Henry after the revolt built some castles with polygonal towers, such as those at Orford on the east coast, Chilham in Kent, and Tickhill in Yorkshire, which pointed the way to the coming changes.[16]

Another modification of existing institutions took place early in 1176 when Henry convened his council at Northampton to consider the success of his itinerant justices. The experiment made a decade earlier of sending traveling judges out from the central court into the counties to spread the king's word, pronounce his judgments, and inspect his revenues, had proved promising, and the king now decided to make this an annual feature of his government. At this meeting the country was divided into six regions for the purpose of these visitations, and eighteen permanent inspectors were chosen to conduct the annual audit.[17] The list of instructions given to the justices at Northampton[18] differed from those of Clarendon in 1166 only in that they were more specific. With the disruption caused by the recent revolt still clearly before his eyes, Henry ordered that everyone in the kingdom, "even villeins," was to take an oath of homage to the king, and that anyone who refused to do so would be arrested as a traitor. In the course of their travels the justices were to make a list of all those who had fled the realm, and those who refused to return were to be branded as outlaws; moreover, their names were to be inscribed at the Exchequer and reported personally to the king. As a guarantee against another revolt the commissioners were instructed to see that those castles which had been marked for destruction at the rebellion's conclusion had indeed been razed. In addition, they were to prepare detailed rosters of all those who owed the king service by guarding his castles. Henry II was giving potential rebels no chance to build up their strength against him.

Henry was equally anxious to see what effect his earlier reformation of the sheriffs had had on the administration of justice and finance in the counties. He tasked his traveling justices to examine closely the books of the sheriffs to see if they had been playing the feudal game according to the rules and making the proper decisions regarding the king's rights in the counties. He wanted them to look closely into the success of the writ of Novel Disseisin, now ten years old, and to investigate all cases where the writ had been disobeyed. To this earlier writ he now added a new one (called Mort d'Ancestor) which opened the doors of the king's court to any heir of a dead man who had been refused his inheritance by the lord of the fief. As in the case of the earlier writs, judgment was to be made by a sworn inquest of twelve lawful men from the neighborhood who were to investigate what the deceased had possessed on the day of his death. By this writ the king again struck at one of the pillars of baronial strength, the feudal court, by taking away from the lords their jurisdiction over inheritance and drawing such cases to himself. At the same time, by making the judicial circuits annual affairs, Henry Plantagenet insured that Englishmen would come to look upon the king's brand of justice as more regular, and thus superior, to that of the lords. The spread of this brand of justice into every corner of the island guaranteed that it would become standard, or common, everywhere. Step by step Henry was creating common law.

The Assize of Northampton was modified in the succeeding years. The number of justices was changed and before long they came to be permanently located at the royal court. Apparently Henry did not feel at all happy with the reports he received from these justices of the way his castellans were guarding and administering the royal fortresses, for within a few years he replaced all of them with new men. Yet the Assize of Northampton remains a landmark in England's judicial, political, and economic progress. It regularized the institution of itinerant judges, which up till then had been occasional; it extended royal justice, at the expense of baronial, by widening access to the king's court; it provided a further enshrinement of the jury; and it tightened up even farther the revenue-producing instruments of the king.

Nor did Henry fail to take advantage of the potentially fertile field of revenue that existed across the Channel. In the same year as the Northampton meeting he dispatched one of the barons of the Exchequer, Richard of Ilchester, to the Continent to overhaul the Norman Exchequer and bring it into line with its insular counterpart. The results of Richard's fiscal organization in the duchy are reflected in the two remaining fragments of Norman Pipe Rolls for the following decade. These accounts suggest that by the 1180s the Norman fiscal structure was patterned on the English model, with one important exception. Whereas by 1180, the time of the first surviving Norman Pipe Roll, the system of itinerant justices was firmly established in England, there is no indication of a similar institution in the duchy. There the sheriffs (viscounts and bailiffs) continued to hold the center of the economic stage in the local areas, as they had on the island before 1170.

While Henry tinkered with the reins of government in England, the jealousies of his sons created a new crisis on the Continent. At the end of their revolt the Angevin king had decided to let them wear off some of their energy by subduing the many discontented lords who continued to cause trouble on the mainland. The main task fell to Richard, whose duchy of Aquitaine proved the most stubborn. In May, 1176, when he was still only eighteen years old, the Lion Heart led his mercenary troops against two of the most persistent troublemakers in his lands, Vulgrin of Angoulême and Aimar of Limoges, and defeated them, taking Limoges in the process. In the following month his brother Henry joined him and assisted (or at least was present) at the capture of Châteauneuf-sur-Charente. But young Henry, never a serious warrior and envious of Richard's developing martial abilities, deserted his brother for the pleasant life of tournaments and courtly dalliance in Italy. Richard continued to press the Angevin war against the rebels, and late in the summer seized the castle of Moulineuf with all the remaining rebel leaders. With the northern part of his duchy at peace by the end of 1176, the young warrior marched his forces into the south the following spring and captured castles all the way to the base of the Pyrenees where he forced the Basques and Navarrese to recognize his authority.[19] Richard was rapidly gaining a reputation as the most gifted practitioner of the military art in Western Europe, a reputation which he was later to enhance by his exploits on the Continent and in the Holy Land.

But Richard's success was more than young Henry could tolerate. The young king felt his position become even more meaningless in 1177 when Henry II crowned John, his favorite, as king of Ireland and sent the earl of Chester to the island to prepare the way for John's rule there.[20] Young Henry convinced himself that while he bore the title of king, his brothers were accumulating the meaningful lands and rights of their father's realm. Every attempt that Henry II had made to appease his eldest son had backfired. The situation was complicated at the turn of the decade when Louis suffered a stroke and his son, Philip, was crowned late in 1179 to reign along with his father. In September of the following year Louis died and Philip became the main Angevin rival on the Continent. This was a serious blow to the English monarch. From twenty-five years as his neighbor and rival Henry had come to know Louis well and to appreciate what he could expect from the Capetian ruler. Over the decades the Angevin king had become comfortable and confident in his relations with

Louis, allowing him to base his continental policy on a known factor—how far Louis would let him go and what the Capetian's reaction would be to any given move of Henry's. In Philip Augustus, however, Henry would now have to deal with a relatively unknown and, as it turned out, entirely different personality, one more akin to his own sons.

Furious at their father's repeated refusal to loosen his tight grip on the reins of government, Henry, Richard, and Geoffrey saw in the new French king an ally who could help them to apply pressure on the English king. Philip quickly saw the advantages to be gained for France from the situation and hit it off well with Henry's sons, who returned with him to Paris after the coronation ceremony. For the next two years the Angevin heirs appeared to pay more honor to their overlord Philip than to their immediate lord and father, Henry. In 1182 the three youths helped Philip put down a revolt by Philip of Flanders. Richard's relations with the young French monarch seem to have been particularly close and to have extended, according to the innuendos of several chroniclers, well beyond military and diplomatic cooperation.

Henry II was fast losing control of the situation and remained helpless in the face of young Henry's persistent demands for some territory he could call his own. The old king tried everything, short of granting him his wish, to appease his son. Early in 1182 the elder Henry came to the Continent where he promised the young king a generous annual pension.[21] The youth accepted, but before the year was out his dissatisfaction, fanned by the promptings of Philip Augustus, led him to make further demands for land. The king was truly faced with a dilemma, for any attempt he made to satisfy one of his sons immediately brought down upon him the renewed hostility of the others. At the Christmas court at Caen he tried a new approach. Summoning his sons, he insisted that both Geoffrey and Richard do homage to their older brother for the lands they had won.[22] Richard stoutly refused and informed his father that if his brother wanted land he should go out and fight for it as he himself had done. He then stormed out of the court and returned to Poitou where he put his castles on alert against the improbable event that his brother would take his advice. The king displayed his famous rage and transferred his anger from young Henry to Richard who up till then had still remained within the bounds of loyalty. Henry Plantagenet, per-

haps subconsciously agreeing with Richard that young Henry
should prove himself in battle, directed his oldest son to take off
after the Aquitainian duke and bring him back to court. Young
Henry, with Geoffrey at his side, departed from Caen but instead
of going to Richard he rode into Poitou and joined the rebels
whom his brother had been fighting for years.

The rivalry between Henry's sons had jumped family bounds
and escalated into a Continent-wide fray when Philip Augustus,
the duke of Burgundy, and the count of Toulouse, joined the
alliance against Richard. This was more than Henry had envisioned and he was quick to see that unless Richard were bailed
out of the situation his lands were in danger of being partitioned
among the allies. In February, 1183, he sent messengers to England ordering the immediate seizure and imprisonment of all
those who had sided with young Henry in his earlier revolt.
He then hurried south to Limoges to negotiate with his eldest son but was greeted at the city by a hail of stones and arrows.
Henry set up a full-scale siege of the city[23] while Richard chased
the young Henry's mercenaries out of Angoumois and Saintonge
and into Brittany. But matters worsened for the Angevin king
during the summer. Henry's position was in many ways more precarious than it had been ten years before, since the rebels and
foreign enemies of the king were now more united and more capable of concerted action than they had been in 1173-74. In addition, Philip lacked his father's gentleness and was much more determined than Louis had been to put an end to the Angevin
presence on the Continent. Only one bright spot illuminated the
otherwise gloomy landscape for the English king. This time he
had on his side the most capable military leader of the time, his
son Richard. But he had been maneuvered into the very position
he had dreaded throughout his reign—one from which no
amount of diplomacy could extricate him.

Deliverance came from a most unexpected quarter. In June,
while the king still sat before Limoges, young Henry, who had
left the city and was fighting elsewhere, was seized with an attack
of dysentery and died at the castle of Martel.[24] Henry at first refused to believe the report of his son's death, suspecting another
of the young king's tricks. When the news was confirmed the
king's reaction was ambivalent. As a father who had loved his son
and worked so hard for his coronation the old king was saddened

and saw to it that the youth was buried, in accordance with his last wishes, at Rouen. But as an autocrat whose lifework had been repeatedly threatened by his obstinate offspring, he breathed a sigh of relief, secretly happy that the millstone had been removed from around his neck.

With its focus gone, the alliance against Richard quickly evaporated. Limoges capitulated two days after young Henry's interment and before the week was out Geoffrey had made peace with his father and brother, turning over to Henry the castles of Brittany. It seemed that Henry Plantagenet was at last about to enjoy that peace which had so long eluded him. The way was now clear for a redistribution of the inheritance among his three surviving sons. The family gathered at Angers in September for the solemn announcement of the new arrangements. When he died Henry's possessions would devolve upon his sons according to the time-honored feudal tradition. Richard, now the oldest, would step into the inheritance of his deceased brother: king of England, duke of Normandy, count of Anjou, and suzerain of Brittany, Aquitaine, Scotland, Wales, and Ireland. The second son, Geoffrey, would hold Brittany from Richard, to whom he was to do homage. By the same feudal arrangement, John would hold Aquitaine under Richard's lordship. Determined to avoid a repetition of the troubles he had had with young Henry, the king decided against associating Richard with him on the throne, but instead thought it best to make him wait until his death to receive that honor.

Except for the elevation of John, there was nothing in these provisions that was either startling or revolutionary and Henry had every reason to believe that they were fair and legal. But he underestimated the deep attachment that Richard had developed toward Aquitaine over the years he had spent fighting for the duchy. The Lion Heart was in every sense the son of his mother from whom he had inherited a free spirit and a love of the southern regions of France where he felt more at home than in the north. During his ten years as duke of Aquitaine he had sunk solid roots in the area and had come to look upon it as his home. In his eyes he was now being told that he must trade his secure position in the south for the vacuous titles formerly held by his older brother. Probably the most telling blow of all was that his beloved Aquitaine was to be handed over to John who had done nothing to deserve it and who, as the king's favorite, was rapidly becoming the object of his brothers' hatred. Richard could not agree to this proposal and was supported in his defiance by Eleanor.[25] In open insult to his father, he left the court and hastened back once again to Poitou. Henry Plantagenet had traded one obstinate heir for another, more powerful, one.

Nor did young Henry's death bring improved relations with the French king. Philip had designed his anti-Plantagenet policy around the prospect of young Henry inheriting England. With his sister Margaret as queen and young Henry as his vassal, he would then have tremendous leverage against the bothersome Angevins. These Capetian dreams disintegrated with his brother-in-law's premature death. In trying to salvage what he could from the wreckage, Philip demanded of Henry that his sister's dowry, the all-important Vexin with its strategic castles which Henry had occupied 23 years before, be returned to him. Thus the Angevin king's troubles, rather than receding with his son's death, simply changed their shape. In one way the new shape was more to Henry's liking, for it gave him a wider scope for diplomatic maneuvers. In the autumn of 1183, after sidestepping the issue of Richard's intransigence by permitting the duke to continue to administer his southern duchy for the time being, he turned his attention to the problem of the Vexin. The weeks before Christmas were filled with conferences with the French king; Henry finally convinced him that he should be allowed to retain the Vexin and its castles, in return for which Henry was to provide Margaret with an annual pension of £2700 in Angevin money. But Philip's acceptance of these terms merely postponed the problem and did not prevent him from using the question of the Vexin as an excuse for attacks on Henry II in the years to come.

CHAPTER XI

"Let All Things Go as They May"
(1184–1189)

By postponing the showdown with Philip Augustus and Richard over their continental differences, Henry had bought time to get his house in order and to modify his policy to meet the new situation on the mainland. In the summer of 1184 he returned once again to England to take stock of his assets and insure that he had a strong insular base against the storm that was gathering on the other side of the Channel. The kingdom that Richard was now first in line to inherit was by 1184 a well-oiled state whose parts were highly responsive to the monarch's touch. With the Scots, Welsh, and Irish in a relatively pacified condition, Henry had become truly the ruler of the British Isles. By combining military and administrative instruments he had reduced the baronage to a position from which they could no longer mount a threat to him. Economically and judicially the kingdom was also in good shape as the historic legislation of the earlier years was beginning to bear fruit. To the earlier assizes (Utrum, Novel Disseisin, and Mort d'Ancestor) had been added, probably in 1179, the Grand Assize which went farther than its predecessors by adding to the list of cases which could be decided in the king's court those concerning the actual legal right to land. By the provisions of this assize, any tenant who wanted a decision as to his right to land was offered the choice of having the question judged either by a jury of knights or by the customary ordeal.[1] The cumulative effect of Henry's legislation had been to weaken the local and county courts and strengthen the king's tribunal, while at the same time amplifying the royal revenues. This development was even more welcome in light of the unsettled conditions in the continental part of the realm.

There remained little to be done in the legislative area, the result being that the ordinances of these later years were modifications of earlier decisions rather than new departures. Such was the case, for example, with the Assize of the Forest which was promulgated at Woodstock in 1184.[2] Essentially this law pulled together in one place the multitude of decrees that had been in effect for some time. Its importance lay more in the fact that the Forest Laws were written down and presented the first clear picture of how these areas were administered, than in any innovations they introduced. Since not all of the royal forests were located within the royal domain, there were many homes, and even some villages, situated inside the forests. The main threat to the conservation of the king's hunting areas came from these inhabitants and most of the Forest Laws were directed at them. Everyone over the age of eleven, for instance, who lived within the confines of the forest, had to take an oath that he would obey the king's instructions. No one was permitted to own bows, arrows, or hunting dogs without special permission. Forest dwellers were allowed to gather wood for their fireplaces, but only if one of the king's foresters was standing by to make sure that they were not "wasting." The crime of wasting was interpreted very strictly. Since trees were considered precious as shelter for the wild animals, it was decreed that no tree could be felled in any site where the lumberjack could see the stumps of at least five other trees that had been previously cut down. Unlike many of the other Forest Laws, this one allowed of no exceptions for rank or position, and heavy fines for wasting were levied on barons and villeins alike.[3] Knights who lived in the forest had, like the king, their own foresters who were to see that the laws were obeyed. Anyone who had livestock had to wait until the royal herds were fed before he could pasture his own cattle. Tanners and bleachers of hides could reside within the boundaries of the forests only if they stayed in the towns. In those areas of the preserves where wild animals normally had their lairs, all dogs were to have their claws clipped so they could not be used for hunting. Night hunting and the setting of traps were strictly prohibited.

Since these laws were the king's own, and not part of the common law of the realm, the monarch had a separate set of foresters and warders to administer them, as well as a host of knights to tend to the cattle, wild animals, fish, pigs, and clearings. Every third year members from the king's court inspected the forest and reported all transgressions to the monarch. For this purpose a detailed list of the forest clearings, encroachments, and wastings was

to be made. At Woodstock Henry announced that any leniency
he had shown in the past could not be counted on in the future
and that all offenders would receive "full justice as was done in
the time of King Henry, his grandfather." "Full justice" meant
that if any part of the royal domain was destroyed, the forester
responsible for that area would be seized and dealt with directly
by the king. Significantly, the clergy were to receive the same
treatment as others. Any encroaching cleric was to be haled before the king's court for judgment and not to be permitted to
claim the "benefit of clergy." These Forest Laws were among the
harshest of the king's decrees and the repeal of many of their
more stringent provisions would form an impressive segment of
the Magna Carta three decades later.

In the years that had passed since Becket's murder and his sons'
revolt, Henry had maneuvered new key personnel into his government. He had learned from the disappointments he had
suffered at the hands of his earlier appointees and now, by the
mid-1180s, was surrounded by advisers who, although undoubtedly competent enough, were hardly of a mind to cause the king
any trouble. Gradually the composition of the royal court had
come to resemble an impersonal bureaucracy whose members
were chosen more for their willingness to discharge with loyalty
the dictates of the king than for their capacity for independent
thought. In the early part of his reign Henry's court had contained a strong humanist strain represented by John of Salisbury
who, while aware of the secular and autocratic bent of Henry's
policies, continued to believe that the king's pragmatic view of
government could be integrated with the older, more idealistic
notions of political power. John's attempt to combine opposites,
which is reflected in his *Policraticus,* was no less valiant than
Aquinas's stab a century later at blending the seemingly irreconcilable ideas of Plato and Aristotle nor the attempts in our own
day to accommodate older comfortable values to more liberal
ones which challenge them. But Becket's murder spelled John's
failure and he left England in 1170 to become bishop of Chartres,
a post he retained until his death in 1180. The promotion that
same year of Ranulf de Glanville to the position of justiciar in
Henry's England clearly reflects the changed atmosphere of the
royal court. Since 1163 Ranulf had been sheriff of Yorkshire and
had come to the king's attention at the height of the revolt in

1174 by his important role in the capture of King William of Scotland. Two years later he moved up the bureaucratic ladder as an itinerant justice, and the elevation to the justiciarship in 1180 of Glanville, who was "an active, versatile man, ready at short notice to lead an army, negotiate a peace, hold a council, debate a cause and, above all, faithful to his master," marks the victory of the activist, and the defeat of the humanist, influence at Henry's court.

Ranulf was to remain as justiciar during the nine remaining years of Henry's reign faithfully discharging the military and judicial tasks of the office. In 1183 he led an army into Wales and an embassy to Norway. Three years later he was again in Wales on a peace mission and in France representing the king. Wherever Henry's army marched Glanville was with it. Yet his name is linked principally not with these military and diplomatic exploits but with the legal treatise *Concerning the Laws and Customs of the Kingdom of England* which describes the methods of trial in both civil and criminal cases and evaluates Henry's legal innovations—the sworn inquest, the possessory and Grand assizes, and the system of writs. This work did for the legal branch of Henry's household what fitz Nigel's *Dialogue* did for the Exchequer by solidifying and bringing together in one place the mass of legislation and decrees which, taken collectively, represent Henry Plantagenet's contribution to the development of English common law. What role Glanville played in this compilation, or even in the construction of English law as a whole, will probably forever remain a mystery. Whether this tract is the product of his pen or of those of his assistants is still very much debated.[4] Surely as sheriff, itinerant justice and, finally, justiciar, he learned the intricacies of local justice and the implications of Henry's reforms. He was precisely the type of man the king wanted in his new court—loyal, knowledgeable, and blindly obedient.

Ecclesiastical counsellors at the post-Becket royal court were equally pliable. Henry had kept the see of Canterbury vacant for four years after Thomas's murder, as much for its revenues as out of fear of more trouble with the Church. This practice of postponing as long as possible the appointment of a successor to a deceased prelate or baron was not one which Henry II invented, but he seems to have resorted to it on a much grander scale than

any of his predecessors. According to Gerald of Wales, he learned
this trick from his mother who "taught him to protract all men's
business, to hold fast for a long period whatever possessions fell
into his hands and so enjoy the fruits of them, and to keep in
suspense those who coveted them." [5] Henry followed her advice
completely. It was not until April, 1174, that Richard of Dover, a
spineless prelate and the antithesis of Becket, was installed in the
see of Canterbury, and although the king lost a major source of
revenue by the appointment he was undoubtedly consoled by the
presence of an archbishop who carried out his will and did not
arouse the Church by reminding it of its responsibilities. Richard's successor a decade later, Baldwin of Worcester, was equally
vacuous when it came to standing up to the king, and in him
Henry found the perfect vehicle for enforcing the Constitutions
of Clarendon. In 1187, for example, Baldwin suspended the
monks of Canterbury who, in turn, appealed to the pope. The
archbishop reacted by informing the king who was then on the
Continent of the monks' illegal appeal. Henry, acting through
Glanville, forbade the monks to proceed with the appeal until,
as outlined in the Constitutions, they conferred with him and
received his permisson.[6] Henry took advantage of this absence of
a strong clerical voice to keep, on the average, eight episcopal sees
vacant during the remainder of his reign.[7] The most important
of these was the other English archbishopric of York which, after
the death of Roger in 1181, continued pastorless until the king's
own death eight years later.[8]

But if England was under control, Henry's continental possessions, on which he had lavished so much care and where he had
spent most of his time,[9] showed no such unity. The forces which
twenty years later were to roll back the Angevins from most of the
mainland were already in place. Philip Augustus, still only
twenty years old in 1185, was proving to be every bit as adept as
the aging English king in manipulating the subtleties of diplomacy and arranging the strategies of war. His policy was aided
immeasurably, although perhaps not decisively, by the antics of
Henry's three remaining sons. During these last five years of his
life Henry Plantagenet fell back increasingly on diplomatic attempts to solve his expanding problems and for a while, in hopes
of creating an image of himself as a wise and powerful ruler, he
even took the diplomatic offensive. His initiatives were weak-

ened, however, by the lowered caliber of his court officials, his own failing health and, above all, by his sons' apparent dedication to obstructing his plans. In 1184 he tried to mediate between the two Philips, of France and Flanders, who were arguing over the Vermandois. The tenuous position of the Flemish count in this disagreement underscores the almost total absence of sovereignty in the twelfth century. Although a vassal of the French king, he was also a vassal of the emperor for other of his possessions, while at the same time he owed service to Henry Plantagenet in return for his annual pension. Such entanglements, which were more the rule than the exception in feudal Europe, made diplomatic solution the only rational way to settle disputes, since a resort to arms could place the holder of such split allegiance in a difficult legal position. Henry's effort at mediation failed to settle the basis of the dispute but it did bring about a one-year truce between the king and the count.[10]

A further attempt by Henry at negotiation on a yet wider front a month later met with even less success. In July the Archbishop of Cologne came to England on a pilgrimage to the shrine of St. Thomas Becket, who had been canonized in 1173. The king tried to take advantage of the chancellor's presence in his country to bring about a reconciliation between Emperor Frederick and his nephew Henry, the duke of Saxony and Bavaria. Duke Henry had married Henry Plantagenet's daughter Matilda in 1168 but twelve years later was shorn of his titles and banished from the empire for anti-imperial activities. Since 1180 he had resided with his wife at the English court and had taken an active part in the royal household. Henry II's bad luck with archbishops continued as the German chancellor refused to hear his plea for a settlement of the argument.[11] The breach was healed by Rome a year later but apparently without Henry's services.

Early in 1185 England played host to an even more impressive visitor, Heraclius, the Patriarch of Jerusalem. One reason that Anjou had remained internally peaceful during Henry's reign was that an entire branch of the king's family had left the duchy and gone to the Holy Land during the First Crusade ninety years before. These Angevins continued as kings of Jerusalem throughout the twelfth century. The present monarch, Baldwin IV, a first cousin to Henry Plantagenet, was dying of leprosy and the kingdom was in the hands of a regent. For several reasons the position of the Christian kingdom in the Middle East was precarious. Bickering between the several Christian princes and among the members of the regency in Jerusalem had seriously weakened the monarchy. In addition, the initial fervor of the First Crusade had long since worn itself out and the needed assistance from Europe was constantly dwindling. Within the past two decades Islam had overcome that fateful disunity which had allowed the Christians to gain a foothold along the eastern coast of the Mediterranean and was rallying behind the banner of a new leader. Saladin, an Armenian Kurd, had for twenty years been working to conquer and unite the lands which girdled the Christian kingdoms. In turn he had conquered Egypt in the south, Syria in the north, and Mesopotamia in the east. By 1185 the thin Christian coastal strip was surrounded entirely by a revivified Islam which threatened to push the Crusaders into the sea. Heraclius's purpose in coming to England was to offer the throne of Jerusalem to Henry as head of the Angevin family or, failing that, to one of his sons. The king discussed the matter with his council, and it advised him to decline the offer and remain at home to finish the work he had begun there. Henry also refused to allow his sons to take the cross, preferring to keep them under his watchful eye. This was a bitter pill for Richard whose natural martial instincts had led him to harbor visions of military triumphs against the Saracens and of combining the crowns of England and Jerusalem in himself.

Several weeks after Heraclius departed empty-handed from England Henry's revised plans for his sons began to unfold. On the 31st of March he knighted John and had him prepared to be sent off to Ireland as governor. Richard, who a year earlier had refused to yield Aquitaine to Henry, was acting up on the Continent by fortifying the castles of Poitou and attacking his brother Geoffrey's duchy of Brittany. Henry took immediate action. He insisted that Richard hand over Aquitaine to him, and told him that continued refusal would bring an army, led by Eleanor, to reclaim her land. Henry freed the queen, who had been virtually a prisoner in England since the revolt, and sent her to Poitou to receive her native land from her son. This move was well calculated, for the Poitevins liked their duchess and despised Richard who had treated them brutally and cruelly. The queen was the only one who could rouse the barons against Richard. At the same time Henry could win over the gratitude of his wife whose sole desire was to return to the familiar surroundings of her duchy. Realizing that further resistance was fruitless, the prince surrendered the duchy to his mother and returned to England, smoldering with resentment at the outcome of events which saw his brother John's position vastly improved and his own seriously weakened.

Henry II's refusal to help his desperate relatives in the Holy Land was inspired partly by his distrust of the French king. One diplomatic matter above all had created a running sore with Philip. As far back as 1169, at Montmirail, Henry and Louis, in trying to arrange a sweeping and permanent settlement of their differences, had agreed that Richard would marry Louis's daughter Alice. The young princess had since been living in Henry's household in England and rumors persisted, and even found their way into the chronicles,[12] that Henry's roving eye had settled on Alice who had become his mistress. There were even suggestions that Henry, physically and politically weary of Eleanor, planned to set her aside and marry the French princess. These reports apparently had reached Louis, for in 1177 the French king had requested the pope to straighten out the matter. Pope Alexander, through his legates, tried to force the English monarch either to let Richard marry the princess or return her to France. Henry temporized by agreeing to the marriage but omitting to mention a date. When Philip succeeded his father, Alice was still living at the English court. Besides personal concern for his sister, the new French king saw in Alice's position an opportunity to put Henry on the defensive. The two kings met at Gisors early in 1186[13] and once again Henry agreed to let the marriage take place, although still no date was set. Philip's diplomatic hand was further strengthened in August when Geoffrey, Henry's second son, died while participating in a tournament in Paris, leaving the duchy of Brittany in the hands of his infant daughter, Eleanor. Since Brittany was a fief of the French crown and now held by a minor, Eleanor's guardianship fell, by feudal law, to Philip. In October the French king demanded of Henry the wardship of Geoffrey's daughter and threatened to take Normandy if it were not granted.[14] Once again the English king delayed and the usual winter truce was agreed upon to last until the following spring.

The Plantagenet king's delaying tactics were caused by events elsewhere in his lands. John's military mission to Ireland the year before had ended in a fiasco, the young prince having shown himself militarily and politically inept. Henry had been forced to recall his son to England in December, 1185,[15] and replace him with one of his barons. This development delighted Richard who was suspicious of the favoritism his father had shown toward his brother. It was during John's stint in Ireland that Henry had relieved Richard of Aquitaine and given it to Eleanor. But this dispossession seems to have been aimed more at putting Richard in his place than at destroying him; this is indicated by the fact that when the king left for England shortly thereafter he bought and equipped an army which Richard took south to attack the count of Toulouse. This latest threat to one of his vassals provided another verse in Philip's litany of complaints against Henry.

Although a decision on the matters between the two kings had been delayed until early the following year, the smell of war was in the air late in 1186. Shortly after Philip's demand for Eleanor's wardship, the English king, in November, 1186, sent justiciar Glanville to Wales to recruit an army of Welsh mercenaries for the anticipated troubles with France. The Pipe Rolls of the year come alive with payments for these soldiers from the royal revenues of the marcher shires. Over £16 were spent by the sheriff of Shropshire for the delivery of 250 foot soldiers, and more than £7 for mounted mercenaries. More than £17 were taken from the returns of Herefordshire and spent for another 250 soldiers.[16] From these documents we learn the cost of transporting these mercenaries to the Continent, as well as the amount of money paid to transfer the treasury aboard the king's galley to Normandy. Henry went to the Continent in February, and in April, at a meeting with Philip, he made one last attempt to avoid bloodshed. At Gue St. Remy the by now familiar demands and refusals were reiterated and both sides left the conference agreeing only to postpone the beginning of hostilities until the 24th of June. Henry divided his forces into four armies and to each he assigned the defense of specific areas and castles. Two of these armies were led by Richard and John. The third was under the command of William of Mandeville, while the fourth was the responsibility of Geoffrey, one of Henry's illegitimate sons, who had been serving as chancellor of the realm during the past six years.[17]

Philip did not wait for the truce to expire but in May plunged into Berry where in quick order he captured the frontier castles of Issoudun and Fréteval without a fight. The French king then moved rapidly to Châteauroux which was strongly defended by Richard and John. Henry marched down from Normandy to raise the siege of Châteauroux and as his mercenaries drew within sight of the town the French forces pulled back and prepared for a pitched battle. The papal legates who accompanied the two armies threatened both kings with interdicts if they did not settle their grievances. The monarchs conferred and agreed to a two-year truce during which Philip would retain Fréteval and Issoudun if he withdrew from Châteauroux. Following this concord the two kings returned to their own lands but, to Henry's consternation, Richard rode off to Paris with Philip.

All of Richard's pent-up frustrations, fueled by his father's refusal to grant him the crown and Henry's favoritism of John, were behind this insult to Henry. When the English king sent messengers to Paris begging Richard to return, the prince took advantage of the offer to ride with a small party to Chinon where he stole the English war chest and carried it off to Poitou.

While this desultory game of chess was being acted out in Europe, more momentous events were taking place in the Holy Land. Early in May, while the English king was drawing up his forces in Normandy, the Master of the Hospitallers was slain in Jerusalem. While the disbanded armies were leaving Châteauroux after the July truce, Saladin was inflicting a disastrous defeat on the Christian armies at Tiberius. And while Richard was at work in October shoring up his Poitevin castles with the stolen treasure, Jerusalem fell to the Saracens after 88 years of Christian rule. News of the fall of the center of Christianity in the eastern Mediterranean swept through Europe like a cyclone, and produced a revival of that fervor which had not been seen since the Second Crusade forty years before. In January, 1188, Henry again met Philip at Gisors and, although the question of Alice's marriage again came up, it was principally the situation in the Holy Land that occupied the negotiators. Henry, Philip, and Richard, in response to the preaching of the archbishop of Tyre, took the cross, vowing to go on a crusade to relieve Jerusalem. Of the three probably only Richard had any serious intention of fulfilling his promise but even he balked at going unless his brother John accompanied him, or at least until his father solemnly proclaimed him his heir. His position was understandable: he feared that in his absence his father would install John in his inheritance and even possibly place on the head of his younger brother the crown of England. Henry's refusal to let John go heightened Richard's suspicion that the king had indeed washed his hands of his oldest son and was planning to disinherit him. The two kings promised to raise money for the crusade and Henry, back in England in February, arranged the details for the collection of the revenue throughout his possessions. Since the crusade was a holy matter, each parish in his lands was set up as a collection point for the Saladin Tithe, as the tax was called. Both income and property were taxed as each man was ordered to donate 10 percent of his revenues and the value of his movable property to finance the crusade. Each taxee was to come with his offering to the parish church the following February and present it to the local committee which was to consist of the parish priest, the rural dean, one Knight Templar, one Knight Hospitaller, a representative and a clerk of the king, a representative and a clerk of the local baron, and a clerk of the bishop. The penalty for tax evasion was excommunication. The familiar sworn inquest of neighbors was used to decide each man's liability. As with any income tax some exemptions were allowed. Knights and clerics were permitted to claim exemptions for the instruments of their trade: arms, horses, and clothing for the warriors; horses, books, garments, and vestments for the religious. Anyone going on the crusade was excused from all payment, and was to use the money owed by his vassals for his own expense on the armed pilgrimage.[18] The king had lists drawn up of the richest merchants in the country, along with estimates of their wealth, and threatened with imprisonment those who were lax in their payments. He also threatened those Jews who did not contribute to this holy cause with banishment and permanent exile.[19] The tithe was a heavy financial burden for Henry's subjects who did not hesitate to complain of its severity. All told, about £13,000 were collected in England alone, half of which came from the Jews.[20] This was an impressive sum for the time, representing approximately half of the normal annual revenue that the king received from the island.

While the details of the Saladin Tithe were being worked out in England, Richard kept his army in fighting trim in southern France. Soon after he left Le Mans in January, where he had taken the cross, the prince went to Poitou to continue his campaign against the rebellious count of Angoulême and the Lusignans. Once again these perennial malcontents were defeated by the Poitevin prince and the castle of Taillebourg was handed over to Richard. The Lion Heart then marched from Aquitaine into Toulouse and seized a number of castles. Much conjecture has surrounded Richard's motives in this expedition. It was hinted that Henry had prompted the Toulousian count to provoke his son, as he had prompted the Aquitainian rebels to do. Others saw in Richard's attack on Raymond the hidden hand of Philip Augustus seeking an opportunity to resume the war against the Plantagenet monarch by using Raymond's refusal to go on the crusade as a pretext. Still others attributed Richard's precipitate attack to Raymond's seizure and mutilation a short time before of some of Richard's men. Whatever the cause, Richard's attack on the city brought from Raymond a plea to his lord Philip for assistance. This resulted not in military succor but in a warning from the French king to the English monarch to restrain his son. Following a fruitless conference between the two kings in June, Henry gathered up his English knights and Welsh mercenaries and invaded France the following month. Richard, still ostensibly on his father's side, was sent to Berry to defend that county against the expected counterthrust of Philip. But the French attack never came. Philip encountered an alarming lack of enthusiasm for fighting among his nobles, many of whom left his army and returned home to prepare for the grape harvest which was near.[21] Philip called for yet another meeting with the English monarch but his demands at the conference in October were so unreasonable that his main lieutenants, the counts of Flanders and Blois, refused to help him any longer, claiming that they would not fight against a fellow crusader. Philip was so enraged by these developments that he had the huge elm tree, whose shade had traditionally sheltered the site for meetings between the French kings and Norman dukes, cut down and burned.[22]

But the absence of shade did not prevent further attempts at negotiation, and two more meetings were held during the winter. Later that same month Philip agreed to restore all the possessions he had taken from Henry since January. Just as Henry was about to agree, Philip added that he wanted the castle of Pacy-sur-Eure as a pledge of Henry's sincerity. Weak and ailing as he was, the Angevin king still had strength enough to fly into a rage and the negotiations were broken off. Philip repeated his promise of restitution the following month, but once again insisted that Richard and Alice be married immediately and that Henry make all his subjects swear an oath of allegiance to Richard. This idea had been worked out secretly between Philip and Richard, the latter of whom saw in the French king an instrument for obtaining his inheritance. When Henry indignantly refused to be coerced, Richard fell at Philip's knees and solemnly did homage to him for Normandy and all the continental possessions which were held of Philip. The Capetian accepted the oath of fealty and promised the young prince all the castles which he had recently taken in Berry.[23] This was, in effect, an alliance between Richard and Philip against Henry, and all that the English king could salvage from the meeting was a truce until the following January.

The year 1189 began, like so many of its predecessors, with the forces of the two European monarchs observing a cease-fire while preparing for the resumption of hostilities. As soon as the truce expired the Breton nobles again took up their revolt against Henry while the army of Richard and Philip invaded Maine from the east, probably hoping to link up with the Bretons and cut Henry's realm in two by isolating Normandy. The new pope, Clement III, alarmed and disgusted at the childish bickering between the crusading leaders, sent his legate, John of Anagni, to restore the peace. The cardinal worked quietly behind the scenes and persuaded both kings to extend the truce until after Easter (April 9) and then arranged for a full-scale conference between the royal courts. The site chosen for the peace talks was at La Ferté Bernard, a town on the Huisne River midway between Henry's headquarters at Le Mans and Philip's encampment at Nogent-le-Rotrou, farther up the river in French territory. Earls and barons of both sides were joined early in June by the archbishops of Canterbury, Rouen, Bourges, and Reims, and the bishops of Lincoln, Ely, Rochester, and Chester at the conclave presided over by the cardinal-legate. But Philip refused to budge an inch. To his former demands that Richard should marry Alice and receive the homage of all Henry's subjects he now added an insistence that John should accompany Richard on the crusade. This had been Richard's demand all along and was now taken up by his new ally and made part of the formal negotiations. When Henry refused and countered with the proposal that Alice marry John instead of Richard, a nasty scene ensued. The legate threatened to lay Philip's land under interdict if he did not soften his demands and lay the groundwork for an honorable peace between the crusaders. Richard then threatened the cardinal with physical violence and the conference broke up in an uproar.[24]

From the meeting Henry returned to Le Mans while Philip and Richard retreated to Nogent-le-Rotrou. There the allies collected their army and marched back down the Huisne toward Le Mans, seizing castles on both sides of the river and picking up allies as they went. The barons of eastern Maine, sensing that the ailing Henry had lost control and that Richard represented the future, deserted the father and threw in their lot with the son. Just as the allied army approached Le Mans, however, it veered south and headed toward Tours on the river Loire. Henry Plantagenet, holed up in Le Mans with 700 knights and a larger host of mercenaries, breathed a sigh of relief when he saw that the superior French forces were not going to attack his birthplace. But his relief was premature and turned to consternation the following day when, under a blanket of fog, the forces of Richard and Philip retraced their steps and appeared before Le Mans. In front of the city ran the river Huisne, and between the city walls and the river lay the new town, a jumble of wooden homes and shops built rather recently to accommodate the expanding town. While the French were fighting their way across the stone bridge leading to the city, one of Henry's lieutenants set fire to these suburbs hoping to deprive the advancing enemy of a shelter beneath the city walls. A wind shift, however, carried the flames back into the city and Henry had to flee. The only escape route out of the city was to the north, across the river Sarthe. But the stream was swollen and only the mounted knights could cross it. The king had to leave his mercenaries behind and they were slaughtered by the French as they captured the city.

Henry and his small band of knights, with his son Richard in

pursuit, reached Fresnay fifteen miles north of Le Mans near the
Norman border. Here he strengthened his forces with Norman
knights and sent Glanville to England to recruit a new mercenary
army. The king then headed south for Anjou, skirting to the west
of Le Mans, and reached Chinon at the end of June. But time
was running out for him. As soon as he reached Chinon he took
to his bed, stricken by a recurrence of the old wound which had
virtually paralyzed his leg. Philip advanced down from Maine
into Touraine, east of Anjou, and seized Tours, a scant twenty
miles from Henry's sickbed. The English king, incapacitated by
illness and deserted by his followers, was ready for peace, but
Philip, realizing that Henry had nothing left with which to bargain, would hear of no compromise. The kings met on the 5th of
July at Columbières, midway between Tours and Chinon: Henry
critically ill and scarcely able to remain in his saddle; Philip
haughty and confident of success. The English monarch had no
choice but to accede to his opponent's demands, which amounted
to a total capitulation, and hope for a better day. He agreed to do
homage to Philip for all his continental possessions, to surrender
Alice who was to marry Richard as soon as the Lion Heart returned from his crusade, to pay an indemnity of 20,000 marks and
turn over a number of castles as security, and to make his barons
swear fealty to Richard, allowing those who deserted to Richard
to remain with the prince. Worn out by the negotiations and disgusted with their outcome, the king was carried back to Chinon
to receive the list of those who had joined his son against him.

If Henry Plantagenet were not already dying during this conference with Philip, what followed would have insured his death.
Heading the list of rebels, which was read to him that evening,
was the name of his son John, on whose behalf he had risked so
much and for whose inheritance he had gambled and lost. Upon
hearing the name the king sank back on his bed and moaned,
"Now let all things go as they may. I care no longer for myself or
for anything else in this world." [25] On the following day, attended
only by several of his knights and his illegitimate son Geoffrey,
Henry Plantagenet died, bereft of his family and a large part of
his possessions.

Epilogue

OF THE TWO PILLARS OF HENRY PLANTAGENET'S MONUMENT, THE continental fiefs of the Angevin lands and an England that was assuming some of the early trappings of nationhood, the first did not survive the life span of his sons while the second continued on with varying fortunes to become a political unit that would occupy the center of world history and turmoil for seven centuries. The Angevin realm, like its creator, foundered on the ineptitude and pettiness of Henry's sons. For a decade following the first Plantagenet's death Richard reigned as an absentee monarch. In the succeeding sixteen years John presided over the dismantling of his father's continental structure. This second generation of Plantagenet rulers permitted this to happen by imitating the less desirable qualities and practices of their father. Richard treated England solely as a source of revenue for his continental and crusading adventures. John, also in imitation of his father, continued to turn the screws on the English nobility whose resentments, which had smoldered under Henry and become exacerbated by Richard, broke out into open blaze and overwhelmed the king. By 1204 the French monarch had dispossessed his Angevin vassal of Normandy and taken back most of his fiefs on the mainland. When John died in 1216 many of the English institutional and political gains that Henry had made were neutralized by the Magna Carta. Anyone judging Henry's work in that year would have pronounced it a failure.

But later developments came to his rescue. Whereas the continental empire was never reconstructed, despite several centuries of English yearning and campaigning, the edifice that Henry Plantagenet built in England was to emerge after many unsuccessful attacks on it as one of the foundations of the modern English nation. The problems that Henry inherited and the manner in which he set about to solve them give the lie to those who see

[177]

twentieth-century societal disruptions as unique and unprecedented, as well as to those who feel that any changes made to ameliorate these problems are a prelude to the Last Judgment. Henry Plantagenet, no less than any political leader in the second half of the present century, was confronted with such varied problems as law and order, a war weariness which brought about a military organizational revolution, economic inflation, the choice between isolation and "internationalism," sovereignty, and even, on a personal level, women's lib. To maintain that any of these tensions are new to the twentieth century is the highest form of self-adulation and to hold that nothing can be learned from their past appearances the height of historical near-sightedness.

Although the term "law and order" perhaps serves some useful purpose as a campaign slogan in our own society, it connotes nothing that has not come within the experience of political leaders since the dawn of mankind. It refers in general to the challenge which every ruler has faced of striking a happy balance between repression and license in order to insure the continuation of a relatively satisfied society. To say that different things have satisfied different societies at different times does not change the equation but rather begs the question. It was appreciated long before the twelfth century, principally by the Church, that a society cannot be run by physical force alone and that the more violent the society the less lasting is the success achieved through a violent cure. Henry Plantagenet inherited a relatively violent society—more violent than our own but less so than those of the seven centuries which preceded his reign. In his society, whose members still remained close to nature and the destiny of whose inhabitants was still largely determined by the unpredictable vicissitudes of that nature, physical might still had its rewards. In 1154 Henry came to rule a people who had not known the benefits of peace and a stable law for at least an entire generation and who were in danger of sliding back to the lawlessness of an earlier age. For three and a half decades he labored to bring stability to his lands by combining repression with the more subtle but, in the long run, more permanent antidote of providing personal security for his subjects. When violence was done to him, whether by his barons or by his own family, he responded in kind by taking immediate and effective steps to avoid prolonged and dangerous expressions of discontent. Revolts from the western marcher lords in 1155, from his brother Geoffrey the following year, from his own sons in 1173–74, and from many of his continental vassals throughout his reign were met with undelayed violence on the king's part. But this was only a small part of his efforts to restore law and order to the realm. To him, as to many since his time, order was synonymous with political centralization, and in effecting this centralization lies one of Henry Plantagenet's greatest accomplishments. By the time of his death all eyes looked to the king. Former political revolutionaries had been rendered quiescent with lands and titles and brought into the body politic. Lawful holders of land knew that their continued tenancy was insured by the mantle of the king's court. Plaintiffs at the royal tribunal (who still represented a single-numbered percentage of the population) were coming more and more to appreciate the benefits of the unified system of justice which Henry had created for them. Petty envies and cries of inequality from the courts became more muted as Henry's justices worked to make the law orderly and identical in all parts of the realm. Economic order also returned during the reign of the first Plantagenet. The tight control which the meddlesome king exerted over the currency and over his fiscal agents produced an economy that was headed in a single direction—that of the king—in contrast to the earlier one that was flying in several directions at once. Even ecclesiastical eyes were focused on the monarch during the final years of Henry's life. The inability of his sons to keep the balance between these forces which Henry had set up in no way detracts from his accomplishment. By 1189 he had achieved in England many of the elements, if not the name, of sovereignty. He had set in motion the movement to rid the country of those who would compete with him for the loyalty of the inhabitants—his own baronage, foreign princes, and the pope.

Another stone which Henry placed in his edifice and which would later become one of the building blocks of the modern state was the initial step he took toward depersonalizing the government. He made but a start in this direction and it remained for others to finish the process. Throughout his reign and those of his sons the departments of state were still essentially appendages to his personal household. Yet Henry's many absences from England (see Appendix) forced him to develop laws and practices which could be applied effectively whether or not he was present. Into the hands of justiciars, who were supported by a growing bureaucracy, fell the responsibility for many of the vital tasks which up until then often went begging when the monarch was not around. By the time of Henry's death the Exchequer had set up its own office outside the household and it is hard to imagine that the king, constantly on the move, had time to concern himself with the details of that historic institution. The standardization and almost mass production of writs that was a consequence of his legal reforms make it improbable that he stopped his pursuit of more immediate matters to become involved with the details of justice. However unintentional this development might have been, and however much he might have been forced into the situation by the pressures of time and his own wanderlust, Henry Plantagenet started England on the road toward an impersonal bureaucracy and administering a unified law and set of practices.

Antiwar sentiment in Henry's England brought about a major revision of the feudal military arrangements which had become hallowed since the time of the Conqueror. Henry Plantagenet, faced with complaints and foot-dragging service from a population that was bone-tired of war and anxious to share in the domestic opportunities which Henry's astute governance had opened to them, came more and more to rely on a volunteer army of paid mercenaries as an adjunct to the dutied knightly force. To accomplish this he had to fly in the face of tradition which looked upon a cash nexus as savoring of sin and somehow dishonorable. He succeeded in spite of the odds against him and was able to prove that mercenaries often displayed more military expertise in the current type of warfare than their knightly counterparts. Hired soldiers served the monarch with distinction in Wales, at Toulouse, in all his continental lands, and even in England on the one occasion, in 1174, when he had the temerity to lead them to the island. After Henry II the composition of the English army and its method of conducting warfare would never be the same. Mercenaries, whether Welsh, Flemish, or Gascon, came to occupy an accepted niche in the fighting forces of that country for many centuries to come.

The word inflation was, of course, unknown to Henry and his contemporaries in these days before the invention of a science of

economics. But the reality was vivid enough and the king's measures show that he understood basically what was happening. He
did a remarkable job of stabilizing the currency while seeing to it
that the profits from what inflation there was came to him and
did not end up in the pockets of his agents. By revising upwards
the knight quotas of his tenants-in-chief and the farms of his sheriffs he was, in a sense, contributing to the inflationary spiral but
it was certainly not on a scale to cause concern. The annual income of the crown, once it returned to the "normalcy" of the first
Henry during the first few years of the second, remained constant
throughout the remainder of the reign.

Many and heated must have been the debates at the royal court
over "foreign" policy. Matilda's veto of the Irish expedition early
in the reign, Henry's consistent refusal until near the end of his
days to undertake a crusade outside the borders of Europe, and
the fact that the Angevin monarch never invaded, or contem-
plated an invasion, of any country over which he felt he did not
have some legal claim, suggest a disposition toward isolationism
on the part of the first Plantagenet. The feudal rules of lordship
and vassalage, and the potentially disastrous effects of breaking
them, go far to explain the absence of world wars and "international" invasions in the Middle Ages. Henry was content to remain within his feudal boundaries which enclosed the British
isles and those western fiefs of France which were part of his inheritance.

At first glance it would seem that the only problem Henry
Plantagenet faced which his modern counterparts have been
spared was his altercation with the Church. But actually the contention behind that argument remains: only the actors have
changed. For what Henry was combatting within his empire was
a system of benefits and privileges clothed in clerical garb which
threatened to weaken his sovereignty. In most twentieth-century
democratic societies, the niche occupied by the Church in
Henry's time has been filled by industry and its claims to special
treatment, and it remains the leader's task, no less than it was
Henry's, to protect the claims of sovereignty (which he usually
exercises on behalf of the people) by finding a balance between
the weight of benefits and exemptions he can grant to industry to
insure a healthy economy and the amount he must withhold to
avoid being overwhelmed by industry. Henry's personality, in a

chemical reaction to that of Becket, intruded itself into the argument leaving a bitter taste and an unclear outcome. Although personalities have largely been removed from the modern impersonal state, the tensions of sovereignty remain.

The twelfth century was a good one for the ladies, and the two strongest females of the age played crucial roles in the life of Henry Plantagenet. His mother gave him not only an inheritance but the aggressive spirit and fortitude to grasp it and rule it with energy and imagination. Matilda's career was a remarkable one which suggests that a woman of ability could go far (although admittedly probably not all the way) to overcome the male domination of the times—a domination which makes our own time look totally egalitarian by comparison. Eleanor too showed that she had a mind of her own which came into play at every critical turn of Henry's kingly career. She ruled England during many of her husband's trips abroad and stood in his stead on the Continent when Henry was in England. She emerged from a decade of eclipse at Salisbury to regain her preeminent position in Aquitaine, governing with a sagacity lacking in the male rulers of the surrounding duchies. After Henry's death, during the reigns of her two sons, she assumed the role played earlier by Matilda and became an important force in determining the destinies of England and the Continent. The contributions of Matilda and Eleanor to the creation and continuation of the Angevin lands show that women who were willing to learn and play the game according to feudal rules could succeed in twelfth-century Europe.

In the final analysis it was the personalness of government that best explains both Henry's successes and failures. Surrounded by a household and court that still represented an infinitesimal percentage of his subjects, Henry could transform his will and plans into action with enviable haste. His restless and suspicious nature propelled him into every corner of his land where he was determined to play a personal role in the critical activities of his empire. On the whole his judgments were well suited to accomplish his purpose. On the debit side, the two failures of his reign, with Becket and with his sons, arose from his personal misjudgments of the men and their causes and point up one of the shortcomings of personal rule.

Henry Plantagenet raised up England from the dark days that followed the White Ship disaster and the subsequent feebleness of

Stephen's reign. Even though the final act of his life was the first step in the dismemberment of his continental empire, his work in England was done well and entitles him to be included in any list of the greatest rulers and statesmen of the world.

Appendix

TIME SPENT BY HENRY II IN ENGLAND AND ON THE CONTINENT

PERIODS IN ENGLAND (including Wales and Ireland)	NO. OF MONTHS	PERIODS ON THE CONTINENT	NO. OF MONTHS
Dec. 54–Jan. 56	13	Jan. 56–Apr. 57	15
Apr. 57–Aug. 58	16	Aug. 58–Jan. 63	53
Jan. 63–Feb. 65	25	Feb. 65–May 65	3
May 65–Mar. 66	10	Mar. 66–Mar. 70	48
Mar. 70–Jun. 70	3	Jun. 70–Aug. 71	14
Aug. 71–May 72	9	May 72–Jul. 74	26
Jul. 74–Aug. 74	1	Aug. 74–May 75	9
May 75–Aug. 77	27	Aug. 77–Jul. 78	11
Jul. 78–Apr. 80	21	Apr. 80–Jul. 81	15
Jul. 81–Mar. 82	8	Mar. 82–Jun. 84	27
Jun. 84–Apr. 85	10	Apr. 85–Apr. 86	12
Apr. 86–Feb. 87	10	Feb. 87–Jan. 88	12
Jan. 88–Jul. 88	6	Jul. 88–Jul. 89	12
	159 (13.2 yrs.)		257 (21.5 yrs.)

Of 13 visits to England: Only 6 lasted longer than one year and only 2 lasted longer than two years.

Of 13 visits to the Continent: Only 5 lasted less than one year, two of which were for eleven months.

Notes and References

PROLOGUE

1. Those of Henry's illegitimate children who have been identified with certainty are discussed in Geoffrey H. White (ed.), *The Complete Peerage* (London: 1949), Vol. 11, App. D; they are also listed in the form of a genealogical chart in Appendix II of David C. Douglas and George W. Greenaway, *English Historical Documents, Vol. II: 1042–1189.* (London: 1953). (Hereafter *EHD*).

2. Frank M. Stenton, *The First Century of English Feudalism 1066–1166*, 2 ed. (Oxford: 1961), pp. 36, 259–60.

3. John H. Round, *Feudal England,* reprint (London: 1964), pp. 182–245; see also note 1, Chapter 1 below.

4. William of Poitiers, *Gesta Willelmi ducis Normannorum et regis Anglorum* in *EHD*, 225.

5. William Stubbs, *Seventeen Lectures on the Study of Mediaeval and Modern History* (Oxford: 1886), p. 301.

6. William fitz Stephen, *Life of Becket* in *Materials for the History of Thomas Becket.* Ed. J. G. Robertson. 7 vols. Rolls Series (London: 1875–85), iii, 17; David Knowles, "Archbishop Thomas Becket—The Saint," *Canterbury Cathedral Chronicle,* No. 65 (1970), p. 9.

7. Richard of Devizes, *De Rebus Gestis Ricardi Primi.* Ed. R. Howlett. Rolls Series (London: 1886), p. 394.

8. William of Malmesbury, *Gesta Regum Anglorum.* Ed. W. Stubbs. Rolls Series. 2 vols. (London: 1887–89), ii, 469; also in *EHD*, 297.

9. For accounts of the White Ship disaster see: Florence of Worcester, *Chronicon ex Chronicis.* Ed. Thorpe (London: 1848–49); Henry of Huntingdon, *Historia Anglorum.* Ed. T. Arnold. Rolls Series (London: 1879); Ordericus Vitalis, *Historiae Ecclesiasticae.* Ed. Prevost. 5 vols. (Paris: 1838–55); William of Malmesbury, *Gesta,* ii, 469–70 and in *EHD*, 296–98.

10. Henry of Huntingdon, *Letter to Walter,* trans. T. Forester, in *Bohn's Antiquarian Library* (London: 1853), p. 307.

CHAPTER I

1. During the past two decades no problem has occupied medieval historians of England more than that of the degree of change introduced

into the country by the Norman Conquest. Even the most cursory bibliography concerning the question must include, on the side of those favoring innovation: Stenton, *The First Century;* David C. Douglas, *William the Conqueror* (Berkeley, 1963); Round, *Feudal England; English Historical Documents,* introduction; C. Warren Hollister, "The Norman Conquest and the Genesis of English Feudalism," *American Historical Review,* (Apr. '61); and among those more recent authors who stress continuity: H. G. Richardson and G. O. Sayles, *Governance of Mediaeval England from the Conquest to Magna Carta* (Edinburgh; 1963).

2. Douglas, *William the Conqueror.*

3. Osker Rössler, *Kaiserin Mathilde, Mutter Heinrichs von Anjou und das Zeitalter der Anarchie in England* (Berlin, 1897), pp. 417–20, argues that Matilda was William's twin sister; *The Handbook of British Chronology* places her birth in 1102, one year before that of William.

4. For eleventh and twelfth-century Anjou, see Josèphe Chartrou, *L'Anjou de 1109 à 1151* (Paris, 1928); Louis Halphen, *Le comté d'Anjou au XIᵉ siècle* (Paris, 1906); Robert Latouche, *Histoire du comté du Maine* (Paris, 1910); Jacques Boussard, *Le comté d'Anjou sous Henri Plantegenêt et ses fils* (Paris, 1928); Jacques Boussard, "Les institutions de l'empire Plantegenêt," in F. Lot and R. Fawtier (eds), *Histoire des institutions françaises au moyen âge,* I, 35–70; Jacques Boussard, *Le Gouvernement d'Henri Plantegenêt* (Paris, 1956), pp. 99–103, 178–92, 226–55 *passim,* 285–338 *passim,* 357–79. Robert Southern has written a sensitive chapter on Henry's Angevin ancestors in his *Making of the Middle Ages.*

5. John le Patourel, "The Plantagenet Dominions," *History,* Oct. 1965, p. 291.

6. Robert Fawtier, *The Capetian Kings of France,* trans. L. Butler and R. J. Adams (New York, 1966); Charles Petit-Dutaillis, *The Feudal Monarchy in France and England from the Tenth to the Thirteenth Century,* trans. E. D. Hunt (London, 1964), pp. 76–96.

7. John Horace Round, *Geoffrey de Mandeville* (London, 1892), App. Y, p. 405; Austin Lane Poole, "Henry Plantagenet's Early Visits to England," *English Historical Review,* xlvii (1932), pp. 447–49. (Hereafter *EHR*).

8. Gervase of Canterbury, *Chronicles of the Reigns of Stephen, Henry II and Richard,* Rolls Series, (London, 1879–80), I, 125, 131.

9. John Beeler, *Warfare in England 1066–1189* (Ithaca, N. Y., 1966), p. 131.

10. Round, *Feudal England,* pp. 182–245; C. Warren Hollister, "The Annual Term of Military Service in Medieval England," *Mediaevalia et Humanistica,* xiii, 40–47.

11. *Gesta Stephani,* ed. and trans. K. R. Potter (London, 1955), p. 73.
12. *Ibid.,* p. 113.
13. *Ibid.,* p. 106.
14. *Ibid.,* p. 99.
15. William of Malmesbury, *Historia Novella,* ed. W. Stubbs, Rolls Series, (London, 1887–89), ii, 528.
16. Stenton, *First Century,* pp. 250–56, 286–88.
17. *Ibid.,* p. 250; Round, *Geoffrey,* pp. 279–80.
18. Austin Lane Poole, *From Domesday to Magna Carta, 1087–1216* (Oxford, 1951), p. 133 n. 3.
19. Round, *Geoffrey.*
20. John Beeler, "XIIth Century Guerrilla Campaign," *Military Review,* xlii (Aug. 1962), 39–46; John Beeler, *Warfare in England,* pp. 136–42.

CHAPTER II

1. Poole, *EHR* (1932), 450–51, argues against the statement of Gervase of Canterbury (p. 131) that Henry's first visit lasted four years.
2. Boussard, *Le Gouvernement,* p. 4.
3. Henry of Huntingdon, *op. cit.,* trans. Forester, p. 287.
4. Gervase of Canterbury, *RS,* I, 140.
5. *Gesta Stephani,* pp. 143–48.
6. Z. N. and C. N. L. Brooke, "Henry II, Duke of Normandy and Aquitaine," *EHR* lxi (1946), 81–84; R. L. Poole, "Henry II, Duke of Normandy," *EHR,* xlii (1927), 569–72, argues that Henry was invested with the duchy of Normandy the year before while still in England. He uses charter evidence to support this claim.
7. Patourel, "The Plantagenet Dominions," p. 297.
8. Boussard, *Le Gouvernement,* p. 10.
9. William of Newburgh, *Historia Rerum Anglicarum* in *EHD,* p. 327.
10. Boussard, *Le Gouvernement,* p. 10.
11. Henry of Huntingdon, *op. cit.,* trans. Forester, pp. 289–90.
12. *Gesta Stephani,* p. 102.
13. *Ibid.,* pp. 152–53.
14. Richardson and Sayles (p. 251) doubt that Henry was given any part in the government.
15. The text of the "Treaty of Winchester" can be pieced together from the following: Henry of Huntingdon, *Historia* in *EHD,* p. 311, and in a charter of King Stephen printed in the same volume, pp. 404–407; L. Delisle and E. Berger, *Recueil des Actes d'Henri II,* 4 vols. (Paris, 1906–27), I, 61; Thomas Rymer (ed.) *Foedera, Conventiones, Litterae et Cuiuscunque Generis Acta Publica* (London, 1816–69), I,

18. An animated discussion of possible interpretations of this important diplomatic agreement can be followed in Richardson and Sayles, pp. 251–64, and Austin Lane Poole, *From Domesday Book to Magna Carta, 1087–1216* (Oxford, 1951), pp. 165–66.

CHAPTER III

1. William Stubbs (ed.), *Select Charters and Other Illustrations of English Constitutional History*, 9th ed. (Oxford, 1921), p. 158; *EHD*, 407.

2. Gervase of Canterbury, *RS*, i, 160.

3. *Dialogue of the Exchequer, EHD*, p. 526.

4. *Materials for the History of Thomas Becket, RS*, iv, p. 11.

5. Walter Map, *De Nugis Curialium, EHD*, p. 389.

6. Peter of Blois, quoted in Stubbs, *Seventeen Lectures*, p. 119.

7. Stubbs, *Seventeen Lectures*, pp. 115–55.

8. Henry of Huntingdon, *op. cit.* trans. T. Forester, pp. 288–89.

9. Robert of Torigni, *Chronicle*, ed. Howlett. Rolls Series (London, 1889), p. 184.

10. R. W. Eyton, *Court, Household and Itinerary of King Henry II,* (London, 1878), p. 10, places William's death in June of that same year, 1155, but most other authorities put it in the following year.

11. The New Forest is described by a modern native, Duncan Grinnell-Milne, in his *The Killing of William Rufus* (Devon, 1968), chapters 1 and 2. See especially pp. 66–67 for an account of the hunt as it was performed in the late eleventh century and, presumably, during the time of Henry II.

12. Papal Bull *Laudabiliter, EHD,* pp. 776–77.

13. John of Salisbury, *Metalogicon, EHD,* p. 796.

14. William of Newburgh, *EHD,* p. 327.

15. William Stubbs, *The Constitutional History of England* (Oxford, 1880), i, 491.

16. Examples of scutage in the reign of Henry I have been found in 1100, 1101, 1107, 1119, ca. 1120, 1127, and 1130. See, respectively, W. A. Morris, "A Mention of Scutage in the Year 1100," *EHR*, xxxvi (1921), 45–46; H. W. C. Davis (ed.), *Regesta Regum Anglo-Normannorum 1066–1154* (Oxford, 1956–70), ii, 285, no. 1882; *Calendar of Charter Rolls* (London, 1903), i, 257; Round, *Feudal England*, 268, 270; *Magnum Rotulum Scaccarii de Anno Tricesimo-Primo Regni Henrici Primi,* J. Hunter (ed.), London, 1833), pp. 44, 47, 49.

17. *Gesta Regis Henrici Secundi,* ed. W. Stubbs, Rolls Series (London, 1867), II, xciv; Kate Norgate, *England Under the Angevin Kings* (N.Y., 1887), i, 444, n.3.

18. Gerald of Wales, *Opera*, eds. J. S. Brewer, J. F. Dimock and G. F. Warner. 8 Vols. Rolls Series (London, 1861–91), v. 303; translated in *EHD,* p. 386.

19. Bryce D. Lyon, *From Fief to Indenture* (Cambridge, Mass., 1957).
20. F. M. Powicke, *Loss of Normandy, 1189–1204*, 2nd. ed. (Manchester, 1961), pp. 10, 13, 15.
21. Robert of Torigni, *RS*, 189–90.
22. *Ibid.*, 187.
23. See above, page 55.

CHAPTER IV

1. Robert of Torigni, *RS*, 193; Richardson and Sayles, *Governance*, 261.
2. John Beeler, "The Composition of Anglo-Norman Armies," *Speculum*, xl (1965), 408.
3. Robert of Torigni, *RS*, 192.
4. John Beeler, *Warfare in England*, p. 242, sees the campaign as merely a punitive expedition.
5. Eyton, *Itinerary*, pp. 29–41.
6. Robert of Torigni, *RS*, 196.
7. Quoted in Petit-Dutaillis, *The Feudal Monarchy*, p. 109.
8. Eyton, *Itinerary*, p. 41.
9. Robert of Torigni, *RS*, 197.
10. Peter of Blois, quoted in *The Times*, London, January 2, 1971.
11. Eyton, *Itinerary*, p. 42.
12. Robert of Torigni, *RS*, 202.
13. Frederick Pollock and F. W. Maitland, *The History of English Law*, 2 ed. reissued (Cambridge, England: 1968), i, 272, note.
14. Roger of Hoveden, *Chronicle*, ed. W. Stubbs. Rolls Series (London, 1868–71), i, 217.
15. Delisle and Berger, *Recueil*, i, 194–95; Eyton, pp. 49–50.

CHAPTER V

1. Doris M. Stenton, *English Justice, 1066–1215* (Philadelphia, 1964), p. 22.
2. Apparently Henry had chancellors while he was still duke of Normandy. Z. N. and C. N. L. Brooke, *EHR*, lxi, 89.
3. The unusual scarcity, even by medieval standards, of surviving records from the reign of Stephen has usually led to the conclusion that the administrative machinery of the state disappeared between 1135 and 1154. This has become a generalization for the entire realm based on tales of local devastation recounted by several chroniclers and has been the general tone of most of the modern accounts of the reign, such as: Round, *Geoffrey;* R. H. C. Davis, *King Stephen* (London, 1967); and John T. Appleby, *The Troubled Reign of King Stephen* (London, 1969). Something of a corrective has been applied recently by H. A. Cronne in his *The Reign of Stephen 1135–54: Anarchy in Eng-*

land (London, 1970), where the author examines in detail the administrative, financial, and judicial activities of the reign and shows that despite a disruption of these institutions they did continue to function, if only at half-speed.

4. Richardson and Sayles (Chs. XI–XII) maintain that the Exchequer did not arise out of the household. The entire question is still the subject of argument.

5. Stubbs, *Seventeen Lectures*, p. 303.

6. Pollock and Maitland, *English Law*, i, 158–59.

7. Richard Winston, *Thomas Becket* (N.Y., 1967), p. 142.

8. Boussard, *Gouvernement*, pp. 421–22; Haskins, *Norman Institutions*, pp. 170–71; Pollock and Maitland, *English Law*, i, 151n.

9. Richardson and Sayles, *Governance*, pp. 205–208.

10. This happened in 1215 when, at the Fourth Lateran Council, the Church prohibited further clerical participation in the ordeal. By that time the clergy had become so intertwined with feudalism that the Church's refusal to support the practice spelled the eventual end of the ancient Germanic method of proof. Since the jury was already in use for other purposes and ready at hand, it gradually became accepted as the new method for determining guilt or innocence.

11. Robert of Torigni, *RS*, p. 209.

12. *History of the King's Works*, ed. R. A. Brown (London, 1967), i, 73.

13. Eyton, *Itinerary*, pp. 54–55.

14. Pipe Rolls 1161–62: Southampton.

15. *Materials for the History of Thomas Becket, RS*, iv, 14; *EHD*, p. 709.

CHAPTER VI

1. John of Salisbury, *Materials for the History of Thomas Becket, RS*, ii, 305; *EHD*, 708, n. 3.

2. None of these writs have survived and it is not certain when they were issued to the sheriffs. Since the returns were compiled in 1166 and this famous document, the *Cartae Baronum*, bears that date, it is customary to ascribe the inquest to the early part of that same year. The archbishop of York's complaint that he "made as thorough an investigation as the short time permitted" (*EHD*, 906) would at first seem to support the 1166 date. This, however, flies in the face of contemporary chronicle evidence, such as Ralph of Diceto, *RS*, i, 311, and Roger of Wendover, *RS*, i, 538, which clearly places the inquest in 1163. Although it might strain the credulity of twentieth-century efficiency experts to equate Roger's "short time" with three years, it might very well have been so in the twelfth century.

3. *Red Book of the Exchequer,* ed. Hubert Hall, Rolls Series. 3 vols. (London, 1896), i, 186–445.

4. *EHD,* p. 908.

5. Boussard, *Le Gouvernement,* p. 447.

6. Edward Grim, in *Materials for the History of Thomas Becket,* ii, 373; Stubbs, *Select Charters,* p. 152.

7. *Materials for the History of Thomas Becket,* iii, 41.

8. *Ibid.*

9. *Ibid.,* ii, 28; iii, 281; iv, 39, 96, 202; Pollock and Maitland, *English Law,* i, 448.

10. *Ibid.,* iv, 299.

11. Although the use of such terms as "international" and "foreign" is anachronistic for the twelfth century and should be more properly reserved for the time of a later English Henry, six numbers removed from the Angevin monarch, it was in the twelfth century that the reality which these words were later to depict was coming into existence.

12. Gervase of Canterbury, *Chronicle, RS,* i, 178; Stubbs, *Select Charters,* pp. 163–67; *EHD,* pp. 718–22.

13. Pollock and Maitland, *English Law,* p. 449.

14. Gerald of Wales, *Expugnatio Hibernica, EHD,* p. 387.

15. Knowles, "Archbishop Thomas Becket," p. 9.

CHAPTER VII

1. Ralph of Diceto, *RS,* 537; *Materials for Becket, RS,* iii, 70.

2. James H. Ramsay, *The Angevin Empire,* (London, 1903), p. 74n; Round, *Feudal England,* p. 216; Michael Powicke, *Military Obligation in Medieval England* (Oxford, 1962), p. 50.

3. Pipe Rolls 11 Henry II, pp. 19, 31, 37, 74, 81, etc.

4. William of Newburgh, *Historia Rerum Anglicarum,* ed. R. Howlett. Rolls Series. 2 vols. (London, 1884), i, 145.

5. Poole, *From Domesday Book,* p. 293.

6. Beeler, *Warfare,* pp. 249–52.

7. Gerald of Wales, *De Principis Instructione,* in *Opera,* ed. Brewer, Dimock and Warner. Rolls Series. 8 vols. (London, 1861–91), viii, 290.

8. Robert of Torigni, *RS,* 124.

9. Stubbs, *Select Charters,* pp. 167–73.

10. Richardson and Sayles, *Governance,* pp. 438ff.

11. *Ibid.,* 198 n. 6, 441: Pollock and Maitland, *English Law,* i, 152; Stubbs, *Select Charters,* p. 170.

12. *EHD,* p. 408, Article 2.

13. *Ibid.,* 409–10, Art. 14; 411, Art. 1.

14. *Ibid.,* 477, n. 1.

15. *Materials for the History of Thomas Becket,* v, 421.

16. William of Newburgh, *RS*, i, 146.

17. Boussard, *Le Gouvernement*, p. 29; Eyton, *Itinerary*, p. 97.

18. John, who was only two years old, was absent.

19. Gervase of Canterbury, *RS*, i, 208.

20. Winston, *Becket*, pp. 326ff.

21. *Materials for the History of Thomas Becket, RS*, vi, 537–39.

22. *EHD*, p. 750, gives the list.

CHAPTER VIII

1. Gervase of Canterbury, *RS*, i, 219.

2. Boussard, *Le Gouvernement*, p. 52.

3. *Materials for the History of Thomas Becket, RS*, iii, 103.

4. Boussard, *Le Gouvernment*, p. 54.

5. Eyton, *Itinerary*, p. 140.

6. Herbert of Bosham, in *Materials for the History of Thomas Becket, RS*, iii, 465–67: *EHD*, p. 755.

7. Eyton, *Itinerary*, p. 146.

8. *Ibid., EHD*, p. 756.

9. *EHD*, p. 758.

10. Edward Grim, in *Materials for the History of Thomas Becket, RS*, ii, 429; Bosham in *ibid.*, iii, 487.

11. *EHD*, p. 770.

12. Ralph of Diceto, *RS*, i, 351.

13. *Materials for the History of Thomas Becket, RS*, vii, pp. 513–18; Charles Lebreton, *La pénitence d'Henri II Roi d'Angleterre et le concile d'Avranches en 1172* (Saint-Brieuc, 1884).

CHAPTER IX

1. Poole, *From Domesday Book*, p. 343 n.

2. Gervase of Canterbury, *RS*, i, 242.

3. Ralph of Diceto, *RS*, ii, 571.

4. William of Newburgh, *RS*, i, 172.

5. William of Newburgh, *EHD*, p. 344.

6. Ralph of Diceto, *RS*, ii, 375.

7. Boussard, *Le Gouvernement*, p. 481.

8. Roger of Hoveden, *RS*, ii, 64; Ralph of Diceto, *RS*. ii, 375; Gervase of Canterbury, *RS*, i, 246.

9. An eyewitness account of the English-Scots phase of the rebellion can be found in the French poem by Jordan Fantosme in his *Chronicle*, ed. and trans. by R. Howlett, Rolls Series (London, 1886).

10. William of Newburgh, *EHD*, pp. 354–55.

11. C. W. C. Oman, *The Art of War in the Middle Ages, A.D. 378–1515*. Ed. John Beeler (New York, 1953), p. 57.

12. *Ibid.*

13. John Schlight, *Monarchs and Mercenaries* (New York, 1968), p. 11.
14. William of Newburgh, *EHD*, pp. 355–56; *Gesta Regis Henrici Secundi*, i, 77; Roger of Hoveden, *RS*, ii, 67.
15. *EHD*, pp. 413–15; *Gesta Regis Henrici Secundi*, i, 96–98.

CHAPTER X

1. Gerald of Wales, *EHD*, p. 387.
2. See above, p. 120.
3. Gerald of Wales, *De Principis Instructione, RS*, viii, 232.
4. *EHD*, p. 387.
5. *Ibid.*, p. 400.
6. *Ibid.*, p. 386.
7. *Dialogue of the Exchequer, EHD*, p. 528.
8. Pollock and Maitland, *English Law*, i, 162.
9. *EHD*, p. 491.
10. *Constitutio Domis Regis, EHD*, pp. 422–27.
11. *EHD*, p. 499.
12. William of Newburgh, *RS*, i, 331.
13. Pipe Rolls 21 Henry II, p. 184; 30 Henry II, p. 95.
14. Pipe Roll 30 Henry II, p. 150.
15. William Anderson, *Castles of Europe* (New York, 1970), p. 116; *History of the King's Works*, ed. R. A. Brown. 3 vols. (London, 1967), i, 65, 66.
16. *Ibid.*, i, 77.
17. Pollock and Maitland, *English Law*, i, 155–56.
18. *The Assize of Northampton, EHD*, pp. 411–13.
19. *Gesta Regis Henrici Secundi*, i, 131–32.
20. Eyton, *Itinerary*, p. 214.
21. *Gesta Regis Henrici Secundi*, i, 290–91.
22. *Ibid.*, 291–92; Ralph of Diceto, *RS*, ii, 19; Roger of Wendover, *RS*, 129–30.
23. *Gesta Regis Henrici Secundi*, i, 293.
24. Eyton, *Itinerary*, p. 251.
25. *Ibid.*, p. 252.

CHAPTER XI

1. Doris Stenton, *English Justice*, p. 49.
2. Stubbs, *Select Charters*, pp. 185–88; *EHD*, pp. 417–20.
3. *Dialogue of the Exchequer, EHD*, p. 528.
4. Josiah Cox Russell, "Ranulf de Glanville," *Speculum*, Jan. 1970, pp. 69–79; Pollock and Maitland, *English Law*, i, ch. VI; G. E. Woodbine, *Tractatus de Legibus et Consuetudinibus Regni Angliae* (Yale, 1931); *EHD*, pp. 462–79; 937–43.

5. Walter Map, *EHD*, p. 390.

6. Eyton, *Itinerary*, p. 280.

7. *Ibid.*, p. 267.

8. Boussard, *Le Gouvernement*, p. 551.

9. See Appendix below.

10. Eyton, *Itinerary*, p. 252.

11. *Ibid.*, p. 257.

12. Gerald of Wales, *RS*, viii, 232.

13. Eyton, *Itinerary*, p. 267.

14. *Ibid.*, p. 264.

15. *Ibid.*, p. 266.

16. Pipe Roll 33 Henry II, Shropshire, Herefordshire.

17. *Gesta Regis Henrici Secundi, RS*, ii, 6.

18. *Saladin Tithe.* Stubbs, *Select Charters,* pp. 188–89: *EHD*, pp. 420–421.

19. Boussard, *Le Gouvernement*, p. 576.

20. Eyton, *Itinerary*, p. 285.

21. *Ibid.*, p. 290.

22. *Gesta Regis Henrici Secundi, RS*, ii, 47; Boussard, *Le Gouvernement*, p. 597.

23. *Gesta Regis Henrici Secundi, RS*, ii, 50.

24. Eyton, *Itinerary*, p. 295.

25. Gerald of Wales, *EHD*, p. 384.

Selected Bibliography

PRIMARY SOURCES

Narratives

From an abundance of contemporary narratives on the reign of Henry II several stand out for their excellence and overall trustworthiness. Since the most complete narrative sources come to us from England rather than from the Continent, Henry's story is invariably told with an English emphasis.

Gerald of Wales. *Giraldi Cambrensis Opera.* Eds. J. S. Brewer, J. F. Dimock, and G. F. Warner. 8 Vols. (Rolls Series) London, 1861–91. As a royal chaplain Gerald came to know well and dislike heartily Henry Plantagenet. The most valuable sections of these volumes are the *Expugnatio Hibernica* (Vol. 5) in which Gerald treats of Henry's conquest of Ireland, and the *De Principis Instructione* (Vol. 8) where he moralizes on the less attractive qualities of the Angevin monarch and his sons. Despite its anti-Henrician bent it is full of facts and details and provides a valuable corrective to the many more laudatory accounts of Henry II. A translation of the *De Principis* by Joseph Stevenson can be found in his *Church Historians of England* series (Hereafter *CHE*) Vol. 5, pt. 1, and also in *Bohn's Antiquarian Library* (Hereafter *BAL*), 1863.

Gesta Regis Henrici Secundi. Ed. William Stubbs. 2 Vols. (Rolls Series) London, 1867. This chronicle, mistakenly published under the title *Benedict of Peterborough,* is the most important individual narrative source for the reign of Henry II after 1170. The introduction by William Stubbs, which extends to both volumes, still remains one of the most incisive essays on the first Plantagenet king of England. There is no complete English translation.

Materials for the History of Thomas Becket. Ed. J. G. Robertson. 7 Vols. (Rolls Series) London, 1875–85. The first four volumes contain biographies of the saint written by those who shared his fortunes and misfortunes: William fitz Stephen, Edward Grim, Herbert of Bosham, Roger of Pontigny, John of Salisbury, Alan of Tewkesbury, William of Canterbury, and Benedict of Peterborough. In spite of their closeness to the martyr their work is surprisingly objective. The final three volumes bring together all the correspondence and official papers relating to Thomas Becket. Although not translated *in toto,* large sections in English may be found in J. A. Giles. *The Life and Letters of Thomas Becket.* London, 1846, and in W. H. Hutton. *Saint Thomas of Canterbury.* London, 1889.

Ralph of Diceto. *Opera Historica.* Ed. William Stubbs. 2 Vols. (Rolls Series) London, 1876. These two volumes, which contain the author's *Abbreviationes Chronicarum* and *Ymagines Historiarum* were written by Ralph after he became dean of Saint Paul's in 1180 and are invaluable for the details they give of events during the last years of Henry's life.

William of Newburgh. *Historia Rerum Anglicarum.* Ed. R. Howlett. 2 Vols. (Rolls Series) London, 1884. A most important account of Henry's reign. Although it continues its narrative on into the reign of Richard, it takes second place in value to the *Gesta Regis Henrici Secundi* for events after 1170. Its chief merits are its author's impartiality, remarkable judgment, and good sense in his treatment of men and events. A translation is contained in *CHE,* IV, ii.

Many other narratives explore either directly or tangentially the reign of Henry II or its immediate antecedents:

Florence of Worcester. *Chronicon ex Chronicis.* Ed. Benjamin Thorpe. London, 1848–49. Although the chronicle of Florence, who died in 1118, is mainly of importance for the reigns of William the Conqueror, Rufus, and the first half of the rule of Henry I, its two continuators, also monks of Worcester, supply many details up to the accession of Edward I in the thirteenth century. Translations have appeared in *CHE* (II,i) and *BAL,* London, 1854.

Gervase of Canterbury. *Chronicle.* Ed. William Stubbs. 2 vols. (Rolls Series) London, 1879–80. Gervase's history started when he became a monk at Christ Church, Canterbury, 1163, and continued into the first decade of the next century. Although deficient in imagination and accuracy, the works of Gervase are at times useful. Stevenson has a translation of the *History of the Archbishops of Canterbury* in *CHE,* V, i.

Gesta Stephani. Ed. and trans. K. R. Potter (Nelson Medieval Texts) London, 1955. This is the principal narrative source for Henry's activities in England during the reign of Stephen. The unidentified author was an assistant to Stephen's brother, Henry of Winchester. The chronicle's fulsome details offset its absence of dates and the partisanship of its author. Potter's edition has made obsolete all earlier versions (Duchesne, 1619; Sewell, 1846; Rolls Series, 1886) by the inclusion of long-missing chapters concerning the final days of Stephen's kinghood. Pre-Potter translations (Stevenson and Forester) suffer from the same lacuna as their Latin originals.

Henry of Huntingdon. *Historia Anglorum.* Ed. T. Arnold (Rolls Series) London, 1879. The archdeacon of Huntingdon's narrative comes down only as far as the accession of Henry II in 1154. Yet it provides valuable details of the background to Matilda's struggle against Stephen and of Henry's precoronation campaigns on the island. *BAL* has a translation by Forester (1853).

Jordan Fantosme. *Chronicle.* Ed. and trans. R. Howlett (Rolls Series) London, 1886. This French poem, by the chancellor of the diocese of Winchester, gives an eyewitness account of the English-Scots phase of the rebellion of 1173–74. The editor provides an English translation. It is also printed in French in the *Chronique des ducs de Normandie par Benoit,* Vol. III, and another translation has been made by Stevenson in *CHE, IV, i.*

Ordericus Vitalis. *Historiae Ecclesiasticae.* Ed. Prevost. 5 Vols. Paris, 1838–55. The author, an Englishman who spent most of his life at St. Evroul in Normandy, presents a brilliant picture of the reign of Henry I. A four-volume translation exists in *BAL,* London, 1853–56.

Richard of Devizes. *De Rebus Gestis Ricardi Primi.* Ed. R. Howlett (Rolls Series), London, 1886. Of principal interest for the period 1189–1192, this chronicle helps to illuminate by reflection the state of the realm at Henry's death. Stevenson has translated it in *CHE, V, i.*

Richard of Hexham. *Historia de Gestis Stephani et de Bello de Standardo, 1135–39.* Ed. R. Howlett (Rolls Series) London, 1886. Besides providing a valuable contemporary account of the Scots invasion of England in 1138, this work supplies important eyewitness testimony of the conditions in northern England during Stephen's reign—conditions which faced Henry II when he became king. It has been translated in *CHE, IV, i.*

Rigord. *Gesta Philippi Augusti (1179–1208).* Ed. H. F. Delaborde. Paris, 1882. This chronicle sheds some light on the relations between Philip and Henry II during the final decade of the Angevin's reign.

Robert of Torigni. *Chronicle.* Ed. R. Howlett (Rolls Series) London, 1889. Robert of the Mount, abbot of Mont St. Michel from 1154 until his death in 1186, was strategically situated in the path between England and Normandy during most of Henry's reign and has kept an important record of Henry's foreign policy and of the internal affairs of England in the mid-1150s when he visited the island. There is a translation in *CHE, IV, ii.*

Roger of Hoveden. *Chronicle.* Ed. Wm. Stubbs. 4 Vols. (Rolls Series) London, 1868–71. The author was a member of Henry's court in France in 1179 and served as an itinerant justice in England near the end of Henry's reign. Although the most original part of this work begins after Henry's death, Hoveden's coverage of the period 1169–1192 is spiced with important documents to which he had access. A two-volume translation by H. T. Riley appears in *BAL,* 1853.

Walter Map. *De Nugis Curialium.* Ed. T. Wright (Camden Society) London, 1850. Like that of Gerald of Wales, Walter Map's essay is a satirical commentary on the court of Henry II, of which he was a member from early manhood. As an eyewitness to Henry's travels both in England and on the Continent he has provided valuable insights into the operations of the household and has embellished his account with colorful anecdotes. A more recent Latin text can be found in M. R. James, *Anecdota Oxoniensis,* 1914, and a translation by the same author exists in the Cymmrodion Record Series, No. IX, 1923.

William of Malmesbury. *Gesta Regum et Historia Novella.* Ed. Wm. Stubbs. 2 Vols. (Rolls Series) London, 1887–89. The essential part of this chronicle is the contemporary account of the years 1100–1142. William was a partisan of Matilda and his account of the struggle for England during the early years of Stephen supplies a valuable counterweight to the *Gesta Stephani* (see above). An excellent later edition, with an English translation by K. R. Potter is found in *Nelson's Medieval Texts,* London: 1955. Earlier translations were made by J. A. Giles in *BAL,* 1847, and by Stevenson in *CHE,* III, i.

Records

In addition to the many documents buried in the above narratives the following are the main published record sources:

Delisle, L., and Berger, E. *Recueil des Actes d'Henri II concernant les provinces Françaises et les affaires de France.* 4 Vols. Paris, 1909–27. This collection of Henry's official pronouncements gives an appreciation of the too often overlooked fact that he was a continental prince as well as an English king.

Dialogue of the Exchequer. Eds. A. Hughes, C. G. Crump and C. Johnson. Oxford, 1902. One of the most important documents of Henry's reign, this essay by Richard fitz Nigel explains in fulsome detail how the sheriffs' accounts were treated when they reached the Exchequer and what happened to that money that did not get that far. Together with the Pipe Rolls it forms a complete exposé of

Henry's financial system. An excellent translation of the entire work appears in *EHD,* II, pp. 490–569.

Douglas, David C., and Greenaway, George W. *English Historical Documents. Vol. II, 1042–1189.* London, 1953. An indispensable volume which contains translations not only of the pertinent records of the period but also many of the narratives. The authors have included bibliographies and introductions which tie together the latest scholarship concerning the English sources of Henry's reign.

Foedera, Conventiones, Litterae et Cuiuscunque Generis Acta Publica. Ed. T. Rymer, London, 1816–69. This collection of documents contains a few that are helpful for the reign of Henry II.

Pipe Rolls:

Magnum Rotulus Scaccarii de Anno Tricesimo-Primo Regni Henrici Primi. Ed. Joseph Hunter. London, 1833. The only surviving Pipe Roll from the reign of Henry I allows us to make some comparisons between the financial arrangements in effect under the first and the second Henry.

Magnus Rotulus Pipae 1155–58. Ed. Joseph Hunter. London, 1844. The first three Pipe Rolls of Henry II have been published separately from the succeeding financial records.

The Great Roll of the Pipe for the Fifth to the 35th Year of the Reign of King Henry the Second, 1158–1189. London, 1884–1915. By far the most important economic documents of the reign, these annual accounts of the sheriffs go far to unravel the king's income and expenditures as well as shedding light on numerous details of county management.

The Great Roll of the Norman Exchequer under the English Kings. Ed. T. Stapleton. 2 Vols. London, 1840–44. These Pipe Rolls from Normandy, although fragmentary, indicate that the English system had taken root in the duchy by 1180.

Red Book of the Exchequer. Ed. Hubert Hall. 3 Vols. London, 1896. The most important section is the *Cartae Baronum* in Volume I, pp. 186–445, which contains the replies of the barons to Henry's inquest, made around 1163, into the status of enfeoffment of knights.

Regesta Regum Anglo-Normannorum, 1066–1154. Eds. H. S. Cronne, C. Johnson and R. H. C. Davis. 4 Vols. Oxford, 1913–70. The third volume of this important series, covering the reign of Stephen and edited by Cronne and Davis, includes the charters and writs of King Stephen, the Empress Matilda, and the dukes Geoffrey and Henry Plantagenet. Would that we had similar volumes for the succeeding reign. The fourth volume in the series presents facsimiles of many of the documents and a valuable treatise on paleography.

Stubbs, William. *Select Charters and Other Illustrations of English Constitutional History.* 9 ed. revised by H. W. C. Davis. Oxford,

1921. Contains the Latin texts, with introductions, of the most important records from Caesar to Edward I. Still useful for the reign of Henry II.

Tractatus de Legibus et Consuetudinibus Regni Angliae. Ed. G. E. Woodbine. Yale, 1931. The best edition of the legal tract, attributed to Glanville, which describes the judicial work of Henry II. Sections have been translated in *EHD*, pp. 462–79; 937–43.

SECONDARY SOURCES

Books

Anderson, William. *Castles of Europe.* New York, 1970. A large, beautifully illustrated volume whose text does justice to the story of the development of the castle in Europe from the time of Charlemagne until the Renaissance. The castle is discussed in its nonmilitary as well as its military aspects.

Appleby, John T. *Henry II, The Vanquished King.* New York, 1962. A good biography of the Angevin monarch which stresses the king's misfortunes.

———. *The Troubled Reign of King Stephen.* London, 1969. Tends to excuse Stephen and put most of the blame for his troubles on the evil counsel of his advisers. This book presents interesting characterizations of Geoffrey of Mandeville, Ranulf of Chester, and others of Stephen's men who later joined Duke Henry.

Baker, Timothy. *Medieval London.* London, 1970. A well written, accurate, and interesting street-by-street guide to the growth and the inhabitants of this city during the Middle Ages, and to the city's relations with the kingdom and the Church.

Barber, Richard. *Henry Plantagenet. A Biography.* London, 1964. A most dispassionate and complete story of Henry's life.

Barlow, Frank. *The Feudal Kingdom of England, 1042–1216.* London, 1955. This panoramic essay emphasizes the continuity of English institutions across the period of the coming of William the Conqueror and thus, by implication at least, minimizes the contributions of Henry Plantagenet.

Barrow, G. W. S. *Feudal Britain. The Completion of the Medieval Kingdoms, 1066–1314.* London, 1956. Political developments during this long historical period monopolize the pages of this work.

Beeler, John. *Warfare in England, 1066–1189.* Ithaca, 1966. A thoroughly researched and interesting work on the strategy, tactics, logistics, and composition of English armies from the Conqueror to Henry II and on how they were used in England, Wales, and

Ireland. The author's military background has allowed him to bring valuable insights to the records of the period.

Boussard, Jacques. *Le comté d'Anjou sous Henri Plantegenêt et ses fils (1151–1204)*. Paris, 1938. An almost exclusively institutional study of the development of the native county of Henry II. This early work of the author provides one of the building blocks for his later full-scale account of Henry's reign.

——. *Le gouvernement d'Henri II Plantegenêt*. Paris, 1956. By far the most thoroughly documented treatment of all aspects of the reign of Henry II. The author's French vantage point allows him to apply a needed corrective to all other accounts of the monarch which are strictly English.

——. *Les institutions de l'empire Plantegenêt* in Lot and Fawtier. *Histoire des institutions françaises au moyen âge*. 2 Vols. Paris, 1957–58. This chapter, which forms part of the first volume, is one of the better sections of what is a rather uneven collection of institutional studies of medieval France.

Chartrou, Josèphe. *L'Anjou de 1109 à 1151: Foulque de Jérusalem et Geoffroi Plantegenêt*. Paris, 1928. Chartrou's study of Henry Plantagenet's two immediate predecessors in Anjou considers Angevin-Norman relations, internal problems with the barons, Angevin and Norman institutions, and the Church in Anjou during the first half of the twelfth century. Chapter Five discusses Geoffrey's family. The acts of Geoffrey which are appended (pp. 284–316) reflect Henry's gradual assumption of Normandy before his father's death.

Chrimes, S. B. *An Introduction to the Administrative History of Medieval England*. New York, 1952. A dependable treatment in Chapter Three of the consolidation of the king's court under Henry II and his sons.

Clark, George T. *Mediaeval Military Architecture in England*. 2 Vols. London, 1884. Although much work has been done on individual castles since the publication of this work, the author's archaeological and historical examination of 102 castles of England and Wales remains the best compilation of military fortresses.

Complete Peerage of England, Scotland, Ireland, Great Britain and the United Kingdom. Ed. Geoffrey H. White. 13 Vols. London, 1910–1953. Of great value for particulars about families and individuals. The level of scholarship in these volumes is very high, and the work contains many important appendices.

Cronne, H. A. *The Reign of Stephen, 1135–54: Anarchy in England*. London, 1970. Nine separate essays, without an overall conclusion, on the machinery of government during Stephen's reign. The impression one derives from this book is that somehow the king did manage to keep the institutions of rule intact, even if barely so. The questions asked by the author form an important prelude to any consideration of Henry Plantagenet's institutional accomplishments.

Curtis, Edmund. *A History of Medieval Ireland, 1086–1513.* London, 1923. Rewritten 1938. Pertinent to this book are Chapters Three, Four, and Five which handle convincingly the Norman invasion, Henry's conquest, and John's "lordship" of the island.

Davis, H. W. C. *England Under the Normans and Angevins.* London, 1949. A standard, detailed narrative of the work of the Conqueror and his successors on the island.

Davis, R. H. C. *King Stephen.* London, 1967. The author minimizes the amount of disruption that came to England with Stephen and emphasizes that disloyalty was not as widespread as is generally thought.

Dictionary of National Biography. Eds. Leslie Stephen and Sidney Lee. Vol. XXVI. London, 1891. The opening article in this volume is a dazzling biography of Henry II by Kate Norgate which ties together in accurate and succinct form the conclusions of nineteenth-century scholarship on the subject.

Douglas, David C. *William the Conqueror.* Berkeley, 1963. It is Douglas's contention that William the Conqueror succeeded so well by taming and harnessing the energies of the secular and ecclesiastical aristocrats of pre-Conquest Normandy, and then using them to conquer and rule England.

Eyton, Robert W. *Court, Household and Itinerary of King Henry II.* London, 1878. An indispensable Baedeker for retracing the footsteps of the first Angevin monarch of England. Contains many charters and the references on the whole are quite accurate.

Fawtier, Robert. *The Capetian Kings of France.* Trans. L. Butler and R. J. Adams. New York, 1966. An outstanding survey of the rise of the Capetians from obscure beginnings until the early fourteenth century. The subject is treated both chronologically and topically.

Foreville, Raymond. *L'Eglise et la royauté en Angleterre sous Henri II Plantegenêt 1154–1189.* Paris, 1943. On the whole an unsympathetic view of Henry's difficulties with the Church.

Green, Mrs. J. R. *Henry the Second.* London, 1892. A Victorian treatment of the king wholly from the English patriotic vantage point.

Grinnell-Milne, Duncan. *The Killing of William Rufus.* Devon, 1968. A whodunit in which the author tries to heat up the clues which have been growing cold for almost nine centuries. The book contains an interesting description of parts of the New Forest as they must have looked during the reign of Rufus and, presumably, during that of Henry II.

Hall, Hubert. *Court Life under the Plantagenets.* London, 1890. Cast in a semi-novel form, this essay traces the impressions of one Richard of Anesti as he wends his way through manor, church, court, and the other institutions of twelfth-century England.

Halphen, Louis. *The comté d'Anjou au XIe siècle*. Paris, 1906. The doctoral thesis of Halphen, this work ends with the death of Fulk Rechin in 1109. The story is continued by Josèphe Chartrou (see above). This book provides valuable background material for the institutions of Anjou in the century before the coming of Henry II.

Harvey, John. *The Plantagenets*. New York, 1959. A cursory treatment of the whole dynasty.

Haskins, Charles Homer. *Norman Institutions*. Cambridge, 1918. Reprint, 1960. This pioneer work on the organizational structure of the duchy before and after the Conquest of England remains the most solid institutional study of Normandy during the time of Henry II. Haskins shows that much of the English institutional development was based on that of Normandy.

———. "Henry II as a Patron of Literature," in *Essays in Medieval History Presented to Thomas Frederick Tout*. Manchester, 1925. Like Stubbs, Haskins makes the point that Henry did collect around his court an impressive coterie of scholars and poets, but skirts the issue of Henry's own intellectual accomplishments.

Henderson, Philip. *Richard Coeur de Lion: A Biography*. London, 1957. This irregularly documented biography of Henry's son contains many inaccuracies in details but is useful for a general picture of the Lion Heart.

History of the King's Works. Ed. R. A. Brown. 3 Vols. 1 and 2: *The Middle Ages*. Vol. 3: *Plans*. By H. M. Colvin and A. J. Taylor. London, 1967. Volume I, Chapter Three, details the building programs of Henry and his sons and includes a discussion of both military and domestic construction. Volume II, Chapters 13 and 14, contain lists of royal castles and the king's houses. Written by R. A. Brown, much of it is a repeat of his two articles in the *EHR* (see below). A valuable list of expenditures for castles is appended to the second volume.

Hollister, C. Warren. *The Military Organization of Norman England*. Oxford, 1965. A military institutional study which stresses the importance of the national militia and of mercenaries as alternatives to the feudal array after 1066.

Hutton, William H. *Thomas Becket: Archbishop of Canterbury*. London, 1926. A sympathetic general account of the archbishop.

Kelly, Amy. *Eleanor of Aquitaine and the Four Kings*. London, 1952. Miss Kelly's volume remains one of the most exhaustive and delightful biographies of Henry's queen.

Knowles, Dom David. "Archbishop Thomas Becket—A Character Study."

In *The Historian and Character.* Oxford, 1963. An attempt to get at the enigmatic personality of Becket.

————. *The Episcopal Colleagues of Thomas Becket.* Cambridge, 1961. The author presents a valuable character analysis of Becket's confreres which helps to explain many of the pressures under which the archbishop operated.

Latouche, Robert. *Histoire du comté du Maine.* Paris, 1910. Still among the most authoritative treatments of this county which figured so prominently in the story of Henry Plantagenet.

Lebreton, Charles. *La pénitence d'Henri II Roi d'Angleterre et le concile d'Avranches en 1172.* Saint-Brieuc, 1884. Examines the details of the council and the maneuvering of Henry to shed the guilt for the murder of Becket.

Lloyd, J. E. *History of Wales from the Earliest Times to the Edwardian Conquest.* 2 Vols. 2nd ed. London, 1912. These volumes remain the definitive survey of the history of Wales. Although many particulars have received fuller treatment since its publication, the general picture is good and valuable for Henry's activities there.

Lot, Ferdinand et Fawtier, Robert. *Histoire des institutions françaises au moyen âge.* 2 Vols. Paris, 1957–58. The first volume of this uneven series is particularly useful for the development of institutions in the duchies and counties of France during the period of Henry II. The essays are written by different authors and are not all of the same quality. Boussard's chapter on the Angevin Empire and Fliche's on Toulouse are the best of the lot. The second volume, concerned with royal French institutions, is only peripherally of interest for Henry II.

Lot, Ferdinand. *L'Art militaire et les armées au moyen âge.* 2 Vols. Paris, 1946. Continental concentration makes this work of limited use for the accomplishments of Henry Plantagenet in England. Yet in its treatment of the general nature of medieval warfare it is a classic.

Lyon, Bryce. *From Fief to Indenture.* Cambridge, 1957. This pioneer work on the money fief sheds light on an important dimension of Henry Plantagenet's military and diplomatic policies and expenditures.

Lyttleton, Lord G. *History of the Life of King Henry II.* 4 Vols. London, 1767. A quaint and readable story of Henry II which contains all the strengths and weaknesses of mid-eighteenth-century historiography.

Michel, Francesque. *Deux années du regne d'Henri II Roi d'Angleterre. 1173–74.* Poitiers, 1841. Many details of the French phase of the revolt of Henry's sons. The author makes good use of his sources.

Mitchell, Sydney Knox. *Taxation in Medieval England.* Ed. S. Painter. London, 1951. A highly technical examination of the development of taxation before, during, and after the reign of Henry Plantagenet.

Norgate, Kate. *England Under the Angevin Kings.* 2 Vols. London, 1887. Despite its age this work is still one of the best surveys of Angevin lordship in England. It is exceptionally well documented and the author's insights remain one of the best starting points for a consideration of Henry.

Oman, C. W. C. *The Art of War in the Middle Ages* A.D. *378–1515.* Ed. John Beeler. New York, 1953. This revised edition of Oman's undergraduate essay of 1884 contains the essence, in generalized form, of his later and more famous volumes on medieval military history, including his questionable theories that the Middle Ages were cavalry-ridden and devoid of tactics and strategy.

Orpen, Goddard H. *Ireland Under the Normans, 1169–1216.* 4 Vols. Oxford, 1911–1923. The most important work for the details of Henry's conquest of Ireland. The author treats with fulsome detail the many controversies which have surrounded the Norman occupation of the island, such as the authenticity of the Bull *Laudabiliter* (Vol. I, Ch. 9), and the reasons for John's failure as governor and king (Vol. II, pp. 91–108). These volumes also contain insights into the personalities of those involved.

Painter, Sidney. *Studies in the History of the English Feudal Barony.* Baltimore, 1943. A topical study of the composition and problems of the English nobles during the reign of Henry II.

Petit-Dutaillis, Charles. *Feudal Monarchy in France and England from the Tenth to the Thirteenth Century.* Trans. E. D. Hunt. London, 1936. Reprinted 1964. Incisive comparison of the development of royal power in the two medieval kingdoms, despite its archaic and confusing system of documentation.

———. *Studies and Notes Supplementary to Stubbs' Constitutional History.* 3 Vols. Manchester, 1908. In these volumes the author has updated many points of Stubbs's indispensable tomes on English constitutional history (see below).

Pollock, Sir Frederick, and Maitland, Frederick W. *The History of English Law.* 2 Vols. 2nd ed. London, 1898. (Paperback edition: Cambridge, England, 1968). After seventy years these volumes are still the starting point for any discussion of the legal innovations of Henry Plantagenet. The majority of what the authors have discovered has yet to be superseded.

Poole, Austin Lane. *From Domesday Book to Magna Carta, 1087–1216.* Oxford, 1951. A useful survey of how the Conqueror's innovations fared in the twelfth century. The bibliography at the end of the volume is helpful for primary sources, and for secondary ones up till the time of publication.

Powicke, F. M. *Loss of Normandy, 1189–1204.* Manchester, 1913, 2nd ed. Reprint 1961. Although this is primarily the tale of the post-Henrician fate of his realm, the author's introductory remarks on the continental part of Henry's lands are very valuable. The book contains a good description of Henry's castle building in Normandy.

Powicke, Michael. *Military Obligation in Medieval England.* Oxford, 1962. Concentrates on obligatory military service, especially conscription and the fyrd. Some note is made in passing on the role of mercenaries in the twelfth century.

Ramsay, Sir James H. *The Angevin Empire in the Three Reigns of Henry II, Richard I, and John* (A.D. *1154–1216*). London, 1903. One of the most detailed accounts of twelfth-century England.

———. *Revenues of the Kings of England 1066–1399.* 2 Vols. Oxford, 1925. The first volume includes the period of Henry Plantagenet and gives a year-by-year financial account from the Pipe Rolls. It contains sections on scutages, tallages, etc. Annual revenues and the amount sheriffs paid for their farms are given in tabular form.

Richard, Alfred. *Histoire des comtes de Poitou 778–1204.* 2 Vols. Paris, 1903. The bulk of the second volume, from 1126–1204, is devoted to Eleanor of Aquitaine and contains sections, in chronological order, of her relations with the barons of the duchy, Louis, Henry, and her sons.

Richardson, H. G., and Sayles, G. O. *The Governance of Mediaeval England from the Conquest to the Magna Carta.* Edinburgh, 1963. A critical, sometimes cantankerous, attack on the nineteenth-century view of feudalism held by Bishop Stubbs and his followers. The authors' convoluted arguments largely defeat their purpose and their vituperations, unheard since Round, elicit sympathy for the person, if not the ideas, of the prelate.

Rössler, Osker. *Kaiserin Mathilde, Mutter Heinrichs von Anjou.* Berlin, 1897. Still among the best biographies of Henry's mother, this book treats the empress with more sympathy than is the wont of most of her biographers.

Round, John Horace. *Feudal England.* London, 1895. Reissued 1964. This collection of essays, particularly *The Introduction of Knight Service into England* (pp. 182–245), sparked the revision about the effects of William's conquest of England. To support his theory of cataclysm Round inspects, in this essay, the *Cartae Baronum*, the quotas for knight service, and the scutages, aids, and "gifts" of Henry II's reign.

———. *Geoffrey de Mandeville.* London, 1892. Until the recent revival of interest in Stephen (see Appleby, Cronne, and Davis) this was the most detailed work on the reign. It still forms the basis for the others.

Salzmann, L. F. *Henry II.* London, 1917. One of the first twentieth-century biographies of Henry Plantagenet, this volume is still useful for a general view of the reign.

Schlight, John. *Monarchs and Mercenaries.* (Studies in British History and Culture, Vol. I) New York, 1968. A description of how the Anglo-Norman and early Angevin kings of England gradually turned to hired soldiers when they found their feudal military resources either inadequate or uninterested.

Southern, Richard W. *Making of the Middle Ages.* New York, 1953. In ten pages of Chapter II the author pens an accurate, delightful, and valuable description of the rise of Anjou and the part it played in the scheme of twelfth-century Europe. The entire book is well worth the reading.

Stenton, Doris M. *English Justice, 1066–1215.* Philadelphia, 1964. An excellent survey of the development of the courts of justice in the twelfth century. Appended are documents in Latin and English that support the author's text.

Stenton, Frank. *The First Century of English Feudalism, 1066–1166.* 2nd ed. Oxford, 1961. A further explication of the Round thesis that the Normans introduced feudalism into England. These lectures, first given in 1929, present intriguing details of the inner diplomatic relations between knights, barons, and kings. Particularly useful are the documents reproduced in the Appendix.

Stubbs, William. *The Constitutional History of England.* 3 Vols. Oxford, 1880. Despite its age, this remains the best general work on the constitutional history of England from the Conquest to the death of Henry Plantagenet. It must be read in conjunction with Petit-Dutaillis's supplementary volumes mentioned above.

―――. *Seventeen Lectures on the Study of Mediaeval and Modern History.* Oxford, 1886. Chapters VI and VII, both entitled "Learning and Literature at the Court of Henry II," present an undocumented but nevertheless useful discussion of the learned men that surrounded the king. Little of substance has been added to the subject since the publication of this work.

Articles

Beeler, John, "The Composition of Anglo-Norman Armies," *Speculum,* xl, 1965. This article shows convincingly and within the context of the current debate on the subject that hired soldiers and militiamen played at least as important a role in medieval English warfare as did the feudal knights.

———. "XIIth Century Guerrilla Campaign," *Military Review,* xlii, 1962. Geoffrey of Mandeville's campaign against Stephen in the fens around Ely is seen in the more recently fashionable terms of a guerrilla war. This article is repeated with additions in Chapter 6 of the author's *Warfare in England.*

Boussard, Jacques. "Les mercenaires au XII siècle. Henri II Plantegenêt et les origines de l'armée de métier," *Bibliotheque de l'Ecole des Chartes* cvi, 1947. One of the first articles which emphasizes the importance of Henry II's innovation of using mercenaries.

Brooke, Z. N. and C. N. L. "Henry II, Duke of Normandy and Aquitaine," *EHR,* lxi, 1946. Emphasis on Henry as a continental prince.

Brown, R. Allen. "Royal Castle Building in England, 1154–1216," *EHR,* lxx, 1955, and "A List of Castles, 1154–1216," *EHR,* lxxiv, 1959. Both articles contain valuable tabular information relating to English castles in Angevin times. The same information was later incorporated by the author in his sections of *The History of the King's Works.*

Hollister, C. Warren. "The Annual Term of Military Service in Medieval England," *Mediaevalia et Humanistica,* xiii. Suggests that the annual term of knight service decreased from sixty to forty days around the middle of the twelfth century. This article adds another argument to the growing thesis of knightly military decline during the reign of Henry II.

———. "The Norman Conquest and the Genesis of English Feudalism," *AHR,* 1961. A review up until the time of publication of the debate as to the amount of feudalism the Normans introduced into England.

Knowles, Dom David, "Archbishop Thomas Becket—The Saint," *Canterbury Cathedral Chronicle.* No. 65, 1970. A reasoned attempt to separate Thomas the Saint from Thomas the Martyr. In a general way Dom David goes about as far as one can in delineating the character of the archbishop and the motives which inspired him.

Morris, W. A. "A Mention of Scutage in the Year 1100," *EHR,* xxxvi, 1921. This article introduced a new and important document into the field of medieval institutional history.

Patourel, John le. "The Plantagenet Dominions," *History,* Oct. 1965. Emphasizes Henry II as a continental prince who valued England mainly for its treasury.

Poole, Austin Lane. "Henry Plantagenet's Early Visits to England," *EHR,* xlvii, 1932. Poole argues that Henry's first visit to England lasted four years.

Poole, Reginald Lane. "Henry II, Duke of Normandy," *EHR,* xlii, 1927. By a manipulation of documents Poole is able to argue that Henry was invested with Normandy in 1149 while he was still in England, rather than the following year.

Prestwich, J. O. "War and Finance in the Anglo-Norman State," *Transactions of the Royal Historical Society,* 5th series, iv, 1954. A pioneer work in the relationship between the rising money economy and the use of mercenaries in the Anglo-Norman period.

Russell, Josiah Cox. "Ranulf de Glanville," *Speculum,* xlv, 1970. A good treatment of the career of Henry's last justiciar and the controversy surrounding his authorship of the legal tract which bears his name.

Index

Adela of Blois: marries King Louis VII (1160), 85
Adela of Louvain, wife of Henry I: 24
Adrian IV, Pope: 57; dies (1159), 84
advowson, 97
Agen, 75
Aimar of Limoges, 157
Alan, earl of Richmond, 32, 37
Alençon, 141
Alexander III, Pope: elected (1159), 84; recognized by English and French, 85; 100, 106, 109, 117, 121–122, 129–31, 169
Alfonso VIII of Castile, 128
Alice, daughter of Humbert of Maurienne, 130, 140
Alice, daughter of King Louis VII, 120, 149, 169, 171, 174–76
alms, 82
Alnwick, 145
Amboise, 141
Angers, capital of Anjou, 27, 31, 160
Anglesey, 67
Angoulême, 173
Angoumois, 62, 159
Anjou, *Prol 2*, 23, 58, 60, 61, 75, 76, 84, 87, 119, 126, 145, 147, 160, 167, 176
annulment, 82
Anselm, archbishop of Canterbury, *Prol 5*, 92, 106–7
Aquitaine, 29, 47, 60–61, 65, 72, 75, 87, 119, 121, 126, 132, 134, 148, 157, 160, 168, 170, 173
Aragon, king of, 140
architecture, castle, 154
Argentan, 141

Aristotle, 164
Arques, 142–43
Arundel, 87
Assize; Clarendon, 112–15; Forest, 163; Grand, 162, 165; *Mort d'Ancestor*, 162; Northampton (1176), 115; *Novel Disseisin*, 114–15, 162; possessory, 165; *Utrum*, 101–2, 114, 162
Aumale, 142
Auvergne, 62, 119, 140
Avranches: falls to Geoffrey Plantagenet (1143), 38; 70, 72, 134

bailiffs, 156
Baldwin IV, king of Jerusalem, 167
Baldwin of Redvers, earl of Devon, 32
Baldwin of Worcester, archbishop of Canterbury, 166
Bamborough Castle, 64
Barcelona, 75
Barfleur, *Prol 1*, 44
Basingwerk Castle, 66, 67, 110
Basques, 157
Bayeux, 38, 72, 88
Beaugency, Council of (1152), 41
Beauvais, 85
Bec, Abbey of, 92
Becket, Thomas: as a student in Paris (1137), 29; made chancellor (1155), 53; character, 53; death, 53; 56; against tax of 1156, 59; 68; embassy to Paris (1158), 70; at the siege of Toulouse, (1159), 75; first disagreement with Henry II, 76–77; 79, 86, 89; ordained and consecrated bishop, 90; archbishop, 90; resigns